SHAFTESBURY SCHOOL

LEARNING

SUPPORT CENTRE

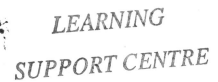

CHERRIES IN THE RED

CHERRIES IN THE RED

How one football fan saved his club and became chairman

Trevor Watkins

HEADLINE

First published in 1999
by HEADLINE BOOK PUBLISHING

10 9 8 7 6 5 4 3 2 1

British Library Cataloguing in Publication Data

Watkins, Trevor
   Cherries in the red: how one fan saved his club
   and became chairman
   1.Watkins, Trevor
   2.Bournemouth Football Club
   I.Title
   796.3'34'0942338

   ISBN 0 7472 2284 3

Typeset by Palimpsest Book Production Limited,
Polmont, Stirlingshire
Printed and bound in Great Britain by
Mackays of Chatham plc, Chatham, Kent

HEADLINE BOOK PUBLISHING
A division of Hodder Headline PLC
338 Euston Road
London NW1 3BH

To those who have kept my feet on the floor and become the very best of friends, and for one who gave all without ever asking, I owe you everything.

CONTENTS

Acknowledgements

For Mum and Dad, thanks for making sure there was always a clean shirt in the wardrobe; Andrew and Sally Kaye, thank you for your friendship, support and a wealth of bagels; Ken Dando and Andrew Noonan, you are the pillars of what we have built; Mel, patient to the last, and Jo, for all your understanding and friendship (my boots are still in the car!); Geoffrey Hayward, John Saunders, Kieran, Rod Taylor, Brian Bronsden and Phil Hordle for your support, encouragement and wisdom shared; Daws, Lisa, Jonathan and Elliot, you are a special part of our lives; Andy, Julie and Philip Smith, heaven is New England at Thanksgiving; Michael and Jackie Robin, you helped so much, we miss your company; Malcolm, Kevin and now Michael, Jeremy and all our team at Lester Aldridge for the success we are building and your excellence; Michael and Pat, you are an inspiration; Peter Aldersey and Tony Swaisland, for your excellence.

To Lorraine Jerram and Ian Marshall at Headline for their patience, faith and understanding on all those deadlines! And to Ivo Tennant for his support, dedication and commitment throughout the writing of this book.

And to Henry, Thomas and Sidney for the joy you have brought to my life and Mandy who has made me what I am today. To all the hundreds, thousands, who silently made this all come true, I thank you.

Prologue

Open this book and you will begin an adventure. A story of an ordinary person in an extraordinary situation, where a single decision changed his own life and the lives of thousands of people he has still not met. I write this as I saw it through my own eyes but it is not a tale of 'I', it's a tale of 'we'.

I am just a normal guy; a mortgage to pay and a job to earn the money to do so, with simple tastes and conventional expectations. Like any other kid I dreamt of being an astronaut, driving a steam train or playing football for my team. I actually became a lawyer ... Life has been kind. I have got used to falling on my feet with the help of a loving family and friends. And I have been privileged enough to be given the opportunity, the responsibility to give something back to the town where I grew up, to be able to tell a story like this.

I often wonder whether, when I am old, I will look back and see where I turned left one morning and ask where a turn to the right would have led me. Would I change anything even if I could? Mine is a life many would dream of leading, one that I feel honoured to have had the opportunity to experience. Much of it has come my way by chance; what at the time seemed random, unconnected choices, with hindsight seem more like fate.

Behind my words there are a thousand untold, behind those characters you will come to know a hundredfold more without whom this story would not end so happily. It is a triumph of ordinariness, of people over wealth, of belief over greed. A lesson in getting others to do what they might not want and like it, having the will to carry on. A tale of seizing opportunities, believing, not turning from a view, and having the courage of one's convictions.

By the end of this book, this journey, maybe you will agree that everything is possible, that each one of us has a strength and potential waiting to be unlocked. I know that. I have seen it happen in the thousands of people who have come with me along the way. I hope you will read and join that spirit, that adventure that can unlock the doors to open up the most amazing worlds.

CHAPTER 1

In the Beginning

A solitary light bulb lit the converted bar. Wedged in a creaking chair Roy Pack grinned, booted feet swung up on his desk. Blackcurrant faced, daffodil shirt now slightly crumpled, arms waving, Norman Hayward boomed: 'I'll have the lot of you! You've had it, you hear – it's taken my wife, my life and I ain't going to let you get in the way.' I reckoned it was time to leave.

Outside Knyveton Road was steaming in the summer rain as the six of us caught our breath. Ken Gardner, puffing on his trademark pipe, wheezed up behind us. 'This, gentlemen' – he pulled a piece of creased paper from his pocket – 'is the key to your survival.' As the last vestiges of the red-light traffic passed by the well-kept two-star hotel it was time to go home, away from where it had all begun six months earlier. Tomorrow would bring an end to this journey that had begun implausibly and turned my life on its head.

I had grown up in Bournemouth, a Victorian seaside resort popularly and incorrectly depicted as a town with old morals and an ageing population. Right down on the south coast of England it hardly ever snows and palm trees dot the gardens. A quiet place slowly building its way to becoming England's premier modern seaside holiday destination. Maybe I was naive but I had never considered that people might be anything other than basically good, honest and caring. In those last few months life had peeled back the cover to show the deep well of humility that exists in adversity but also the rank rottenness that may lurk beneath the surface of modern sport.

Nineteen ninety-seven was the defining year of my life, when the unexpected met the unbelievable. It was a year in which, at just thirty-one, I had planned to get that partnership at my law firm in the City, score a few more goals in my feeble attempt to keep my footballing 'career' going (Bournemouth Parks Saturday League, division four) and start giving the right attention to my home life. The future was bright. I was old enough to remember the first man on the moon and young enough to look up each night and wonder if I might ever get there. Going up and down to London each day, up at 5.30 a.m., home at 7.30 – it was tiring but the buzz of the City, walking up past all the historic buildings to the futuristic structure of the Lloyd's Building and dealing with challenging litigation work made it all worthwhile and the money was good. Coming home in every sense each day made it all the more bearable. Mandy and I had a small house, typically English with leaded windows and a garden full of roses set in a quiet location. Our two black and white cats Henry and Thomas would play out happily and contentedly surrounded by oaks, beech, cedar and holly, chasing the blue tits, woodpeckers, pigeons and owls as well as the occasional fox! It was a retreat, a place to relax by the roaring log fire and shut the world out. We had met on a train five years earlier. Gentle, kind, with a wonderful caring disposition, she never asked, never took, but would always give and understand. It was Mandy who had taught me how to appreciate taking time to sit in the garden drinking a hot cup of tea on a summer's evening, who brought life and happiness to our house, and introduced me to the joy of having cats. She was, is, and always will be my guardian angel.

Born in the year Winston Churchill died, I grew up in the warmth and security of a loving and caring home. All that you read, all that I have achieved owes much to the love that my parents gave me when they made me the foremost thing in their lives. I had a great

2

childhood, every weekend an adventure with my parents (and pretty soon my brother Adrian who arrived three years after me). Sunday afternoon games of cricket out in the New Forest with picnic – unless the ponies got to it first! We always used my dad's bat with Len Hutton's signature on it. I was proud of him. He had played for Kent once or twice on trial before the War, had a trophy for the best bowling performance by a schoolboy in the whole country and once bowled out two West Indian stars in the 1950s. He rarely talked about it, even though I would have been proud to know more.

Sport was something I loved to take part in, always managing to play to a level I could enjoy without feeling foolish. I would never be the one to pick a team but was never the last to be chosen either. I would give 100 per cent and get great enjoyment not only from taking part but from the great friends that I made. Athletics, cross-country running, basketball, hockey, rugby, tennis, swimming – I tried the lot – but it was football that I most enjoyed. Maybe it was because it was the easiest thing to play, requiring little more than two coats, a ball and a bit of land to get your own re-enactment of the 1966 World Cup final underway. When we were kids our next door neighbours were German. The whole thing was that bit more realistic as time and again we repeated the rivalry of those arch enemies. The 1970s was a great time to be growing up, so much happening in a changing world. While I can remember eating by candlelight when strikes stopped the power supply, my best memories are of the endless carefree days of summer spent tunnelling to Australia in the wet sand, then riding the waves of the ocean ignorant of what we now know is in the water!

I was very lucky that my teachers were dedicated, committed to ensuring that every pupil got the most from his education. None of the 'it's four o'clock and we're off home' routine but endless hours spent working for excellence. Even though I am a reasonable weight (although not as trim as I might have been but for lager and curry) you might still say I would have been better concentrating on achieving academic excellence than indulging in sports I would never be much good at. My school reports were a parent's joy but I was never going to make the sacrifice to be a 'straight A' student.

I was really very happy to do enough to get me where I wanted to go. Not that I didn't take pride in my work. I wanted to succeed. Learning, luckily, came easy, particularly for exams. I was doggedly determined and have invariably achieved my goals in life. Maybe it's down to luck or fate.

From being part of the drama society, leading the Christian fellowship, playing chess or just knocking a ball around – cricket or soccer – in my friend Mark's back garden while his mother made tea and brought out the bottomless biscuit box, my teenage years were full of energy and variety. I did get O levels, ten of them, A levels in Mathematics, English Literature and Philosophy/Ethics and a credible degree in Law but there's more to life than studying. I also enjoyed my various part-time jobs working in Boots on Saturdays, running a youth group, guiding American tourists round Europe or teaching English to foreign students.

I studied at Reading and embarked on a career in the City. My sporting achievement never advanced beyond playing football for St Catherine's primary school, Bournemouth School second eleven and the University of Reading third team. I could add to that my contribution to hall of residence soccer. Endless Sunday mornings spent kicking a ball on a muddy park pitch after the long night before probably seems like madness to the wider world. But every game had its meaning. Of all the thousands of games played each year we all remember our own. From beating the chemistry department in the inter-hall championship and scoring a goal in the Bradford Sunday league to seeing our substitute running the line and being sent off before he even got on – games to be remembered in my eternal quest for fitness yet now forgotten by the two men and a dog who watched.

I grew to love watching sport on television – virtually everything but Saturday afternoon wrestling. Yet I can pinpoint one day when my love affair with football really began. I can remember Dad coming home on a Friday evening in February 1974 to say that the next day we were going to watch a game. To tell the truth the only images of football I had at that time came from the stories he had told me about his days as a kid in London watching Charlton

Athletic playing in front of 70,000, being passed over the heads of men down to the pitchside so he could see. I did not quite understand what a crowd of 70,000 might look like (I assumed it would be all black-and-white just like the newsreels), nor did I realise that times had changed and maybe there wouldn't be quite so many at the game I would see – Bournemouth *v*. Walsall. When I went to sleep that night I was excited. I knew nothing, let alone who 'we' would be playing. Strange, this 'we', an immediate bond with a team that I had never seen, didn't know and who just happened to play in my home town. The main stand at Dean Court had been bought from the Wembley Exhibition of 1924. That did it for me. My favourite stamp from Dad's collection commemorated that event – it was a sign!

We didn't park near the ground that day. In fact in all the years since we have not. If I wasn't chairman now then I guess we would still be doing things the same way. Bournemouth's ground must be one of the most picturesque in the country. King's Park is an area dedicated by one of the founding families of the town for public use, ninety-five acres of open heathland, grass fringed with gorse and bracken. Neither flat nor hilly, not beautiful yet functional, never really cared for but maintained for the good people of the borough. It became a tradition to leave the car on the other side of the park and walk up the gully across the grass to the ground.

It was a typical February day. The year had turned but winter still had us in its grip. A bitter day, the wind cut through the warmth of our clothes (I like to think I have blocked out the memory of the balaclava my mother made me wear). The sky was blanketed by a hollow stretch of whitish cloud the nondescript pallor of ash, shutting out the blue.

I knew nothing about the team then but know now that the club had entered a period of instability and turmoil that reflected the situation in early 1997 when I became drawn in. After a couple of years of promotion near misses down in the third division, the Cherries had begun the 1973–74 season with high hopes. In Ted MacDougall there was a player who had been one of the most prolific goalscorers in the League – he had even scored nine goals in one game, a record for the FA Cup that still stands. In an 11–0 drubbing of Margate, Mel Machin (current Bournemouth boss) got one of the other goals. By November 1973 MacDougall had been sold and John Bond, the manager, resigned to take a job in the then first division with Norwich. On his doing so, many of the best players left, condemning the club to a long period of decline and insignificance.

Not the best circumstances to see a team play for the first time, but it didn't matter to me. I was as excited as any boy would be going to his first game with his dad. While 17,000 had watched the game against Brighton a week earlier, this Saturday only 9,000 turned out. Still it looked full to me – I could barely see over the fence! My dad decided that we would stand on the Brighton Beach End. It wasn't much like a beach or anywhere near Brighton and was actually the away end. In those days everyone could mix together. Behind us there was a board on which half-time scores were placed. An old gent used to rest a ladder on the wall, climb up in the buffeting wind and carefully affix numbers beside letters. By reading the programme you could identify the matches that each letter related to and decipher the scores. And the whole occasion cost under a pound for the two of us with a programme . . . and we won courtesy of a Phil Boyer goal. Bond bought him too a few weeks later.

I was hooked! Over the next twenty-five years come rain, snow or shine I have followed this team. Don't ask for rhyme or reason, there is no logic to it. For me, supporting my team carries the power to elate, to sadden, to change my day in a moment but, throughout, my belief is constant. Just as my father took me, I now take him and one day I will take my children.

My dad set me on the track but as time went by he came less often and I went with my school friends. We slowly worked our way around the ground from the cheapest open standing to being covered and then to a seat. There were years when only 2,000 would turn up. Still, my best friends and I would get there early to make sure of our favourite place. In 1980 I did a school project on my future career. Forget being a lawyer! I had no intention or ambition to be one. It just happened that way. No, I chose to do an essay on being a professional footballer. There was never any hope of that but still it got me access to *my* team, behind the hallowed doors. I will always remember how courteously they treated me, the physio 'Captain' John Kirk and the staff. One year the team came to play our first eleven at Bournemouth School. For one hour we graced the same turf as those we watched from afar each week; I didn't get to play but felt I was privileged to stand on the line within touching distance of those I watched each week in awe of their sublime skill. Not that I guess the followers of Premier League teams would agree but in among the no-hopers there were pearls to be found. Supporting a club like Bournemouth is like following the best team in the world, yet still plunges me in the deepest depression after a bad defeat. Every crumb of success nourishes you in the years of bleak and barren performance. One great win goes a long, long way. In 1984 Manchester United, the then cup holders, were at the peak of their form. Knocking them out of the FA Cup was bliss. Three years later we were promoted to the then second division for the first time in our history and remained there for three seasons. The last game of the 1989–90 season was at home to Leeds United. We lost 0–1, condemning us to relegation on goal difference. That weekend their 'fans' systematically ransacked our town and fought pitched battles in the park, leaving our players, management and fans in tears not only for the result.

Seven years on we were still paying the price for that solitary game. The club never bounced back. Burdened by the constraints of a lower division existence with the expense of player contracts made in a higher league, the club entered 1997 almost £5 million in debt. Six months later, as I stood on this balmy June evening, the rain having stopped, the night sky caught a shooting star. I was just an ordinary supporter who had been given the chance to decide the fate of his own club.

CHAPTER 2

And Then There Were Three

Chicago, Cleveland, Boston, New York. Seeing the Hohausers, Steve Petras, getting back to Jackson, New Hampshire, it had been a very successful trip to North America at the end of November. December had been full of work and the usual Christmas cheer. The twelve months of 1997 promised to be busy. With major trials scheduled for May, June and October, we were going to be at full stretch. I needed and had a lovely family Christmas, quiet, reassuring and traditional. The holiday season is all the better for a game of soccer to escape to after the commitments of Christmas Day. We were drawn at home to Bristol Rovers on Boxing Day. A cold, biting wind chilled the occasion, but we got a win nevertheless. In the season of good cheer it was the only thing to smile about. A perceived lack of direction and control at the football club was highlighted in the press, and by the absence of information in the programme. A good result against determined opposition lifted the spirits.

New Year's Eve had been one of the most pleasurable. Mandy and I had gone out to Corfe Castle over on the Purbecks on one of those beautiful winter days when the sky is clear blue, transparent and thin, seeming to stretch forever. We had wandered in the brisk, chill air before finding comfort beside a log fire and eating a full cream tea. As light faded, as it does depressingly early in the middle of winter, we headed back for the warmth and security of home; a New Year's Eve spent in peace and happiness, whatever raged in the world outside. While we sat long into the evening at our favourite local trattoria with our good friends Michael, Jackie, Daniel and Emma, out in the darkness others were being made to work late into the night, others who would soon become part of our lives. Unknown individuals who would shape my future.

For all those who have played sport at any level, there is always a memory of that try, that goal, of the winning boundary or the athletic dash to the line in the under-14s 100 metres school challenge. For me, those memories (17 goals in 15 games for my university team, a touchdown when concussed in under-16 rugby and an unbeaten 27 in a drawn cricket match) are prolonged by continual attempts to play a sport at any level that age allows. The beauty is that no matter where, or how, a goal is scored, it is important to that team. Sport is hardly about professionalism. The teams in the media spotlight represent only a tiny proportion of those in the game. I had played soccer for the last season and a half for Kinson Reserves in a small suburb of Bournemouth, a middle- to working-class environment on which the team makes little or no impact. On bleak Wednesday nights we could be found under a dim solitary floodlight that sought to illuminate, if not the tactics, a half of the training area, a patch of frozen grass between the back of the goal and the wooden shed used for archery.

Dave Pixton, a northern chap in his fifties, bearded and sandalled, alongside Stuart Lanham (a curtain designer and aspiring male model), led our rag-tag bunch of footballing talent in rigorous and enjoyable training sessions. They would turn up week in, week out, to inject their enthusiasm at no cost – save for a substantial amount in terms of their income that they gave up to support football at this level. I was thirty-one and my knees told me soccer was not much longer to be part of my sporting life, so I had resolved to play in games whenever I could get them, through training on Wednesday and playing on Saturday, dashing to watch Bournemouth when our game finished.

On Saturday 11 January, our game had been postponed, so I

went to Dean Court. As usual, I had still bought my AFCB season ticket, even though more often than not I'd give it to a friend or my sister-in-law, Kate (my brother hates football). We were at home to Rotherham: not the most attractive of fixtures even to the most ardent fan, but it was very rare for me to miss a match when I had the opportunity to go. The conscious decision to watch the team play is often born out of a singular belief that they would benefit from my going, the result depending on whether I wore my lucky shoes or held the programme in my left hand. That Saturday had to be one of the most dismal of days. By two o'clock, when dampness reached into the bones, it was clear that this would not be an afternoon to savour.

We no longer needed to arrive early. My dad could not stand, so in recent years I had bought him a season ticket seat every Christmas. I must have been mad – but the club needed the money! How often do we as fans watch from afar wondering about the affairs of state in the boardroom? At Dean Court we had our chance to find out if we paid £650 (more than twice the usual price) for a seat in the directors' box. Ken Gardner, our cuddly bear-like chairman, had promised us a new stadium. Seats like these gave us the chance to move in the wondrous circle of directors, guests and players alike, a view into the inner sanctum, a private privilege for the few.

All week the papers had spelled out the growing financial problems at the club. Although these were neither explained nor specified in exact detail, the situation cried out for a compromise. Only two directors remained, the others had by then resigned. I thought I could help. I was a lawyer with eight years' experience of City practice. A client does not come to a lawyer expecting to be charged thousands of pounds for a detailed legal brief. He wants to know the basic merits of his case and the tactics to achieve the best possible outcome before racking up too much expense. Litigation is a process of bringing conflicting parties together, attempting to have them concede points; the art is to obtain more than you are entitled to while leaving the other side believing they have a good deal. In the adversarial nature of the situation developing at AFC Bournemouth, I felt those skills might be of use.

The vice-presidents' bar area at Dean Court had that particularly seventies shade of yellow covering the wallpaper, the result of years of ingrained smoke. It was a soulless, mute, gathering place. (The game itself was a grey and unmemorable draw.) I was nervous, not quite sure who to address, or what to say about my fanciful notion. Maybe it was the sheer implausibility of it all. I eventually took courage and spoke to Diane Edwards, a familiar face, a petite, elegant assistant in the marketing department with a winning smile. She suggested I speak to Terry Lovell, the commercial manager. After some time, he eventually came to see me. Smart yet bumbling, with a ruddy, moon-shaped face, he listened patiently and said he was sure I could be of help. He would speak to the appropriate people and get back to me. As I left the club that day, it was almost dark. The whole day, the whole game, had been like a voyage on the *Marie Celeste*, empty, hollow, drifting, no direction, no purpose.

My working days were frantic. I was on the road to London by 6.15 a.m. I didn't mind driving in darkness along the dual carriageway, rabbits' eyes gleaming from the side of the road: it gave me plenty of time to think about the day ahead, the cases to be handled, the remortgage to be completed, the friends to be seen, how to work out where life was taking me. Returning home in darkness with just the radio for company was the price of a City career. Sleep, eat, journey, work, journey, eat, sleep – the week an interminable, vain pursuit of satisfaction. That in itself played havoc with a personal life. My conversation with Terry Lovell stayed at the back of my mind. The next week and weekend came and went with nothing but speculation about rescue plans, and the severity of the situation. I assumed that those at the helm – or at least those left after the mass resignations at Christmas – had the best interests of the club at heart. I was sure of that. I thought they must be doing their utmost to save it as creditors pressed for payment. The courts had given the club until the beginning of February to devise a rescue package or be put out of its misery.

A 'company doctor' was appointed by the last two directors to help save the club. By 20 January the local paper, the *Daily Echo*, was announcing his appointment as a third director to join Brian Willis and Norman Hayward. Roy Pack, a former footballer now company rescuer, was known to his friends as 'Crocodile Dundee'. A man of fifty with an overhanging paunch and afro-style haircut, he would not have looked out of place at a seventies retro evening. He came with plans for turning the club round but a curriculum vitae only to be released on suitable assurances being given, due to ongoing litigation.

He represented a beacon of hope; we will all cling on to hope when that's all there is. There he was on the back page of the *Daily Echo*, in living colour: rotund, with his broad Australasian grin and hands firmly placed on terrace railing. Another 'saviour' in the long list of those who were to guide us to a better future.

Four o'clock on a Monday afternoon is not usually my most invigorating time of the week. Sitting at my desk in the shadow cast by the interior lighting at Lloyd's of London, I made a call to Terry Lovell. He had forgotten about our conversation ten days previously – 'Oh yes, I wish I had known about your offer to help previously. I'm sorry I forgot. I need another lawyer and we're trying to think of one we could use.' He had spoken to Pack, who was keen to meet me. This was to be the following evening, not at Dean Court but at the Berkeley Hotel in Bournemouth. The owner was a long-standing and dedicated follower of the club, often putting players up for £15 a night – and that was bed, breakfast and dinner. Could I be there at 6.30 p.m.? 'Of course,' I replied.

That night, I experienced both the thrill of embarking on holiday and the dread before an exam. My sleep was restless, punctuated by excitement that I might be able to assist in some way and by the prospect of what I might find out. The newspapers had given me the background. We owed the bank a considerable sum of money – £2.35 million – and, not surprisingly, they wanted a solution to ensure they got it back, without wanting to put the football club out of business. We also owed the Inland Revenue and Customs and Excise £650,000 and they, too, wanted a plan for payment. Directors had loans outstanding, the players' wages had been met by their union. The total debt might be as much as £5 million.

Yet it wasn't all gloom. There were assets. We owned the land on which the ground was built, and had planning permission for a new 12,000-seat stadium. We also had a squad of players. As a lawyer I was certain there could be a negotiated way out. To try to make Tuesday pass quickly, I threw myself into detailed work, then I left early.

It didn't take long to find the hotel. It sits in a leafy, tree-lined avenue, a mirror image of hundreds like it, a backwater surviving on the meagre trade of the holiday market but offering exceptional value. Within minutes, Mr Pack emerged. A swarthy individual, his girth was at odds with his sporting background (which he said had set him up perfectly for the task of saving Bournemouth). The stereotypical image of beer-swilling Australians consolidated itself in my mind as he greeted me with a smile, 'Hello, mate. Glad you could come. Fancy a beer?' I attempted to explain a little bit about myself but swiftly found that, far from being interested in me personally, he really wanted to get to the nub of explaining his involvement and how *I* would play the major part in saving Bournemouth.

He rambled on about the need to involve me as soon as possible, how my offer of help had come at just the right time. I sipped my lager (Foster's for good measure) and listened politely. Suddenly he apologised and retreated into his 'office', promising he would swiftly return. I was left to savour the ambience of this brightly lit hotel, the nerve centre, the HQ, of the taskforce headed by this previously unknown Aussie.

Working within one of the better known law firms we had built our achievement by developing relationships of trust and confidence with clients and following our instincts. For the most part, my clients are not only business contacts but people I would count as friends. Mostly defending professionals who get sued by (former) clients, much of my time is spent trying to ascertain the truth. I was getting uneasy here. It seemed I was waiting for hours, but twenty minutes later, Pack pushed open the swing doors and waved me over.

He ushered me through. There was a unique level of sophistication revealed in his operation as he welcomed me into his 'war-room, mate!'. No more than a converted bar devoid of till or computer, papers in carrier bags were stacked deep everywhere. The chain guard was drawn down. The single light bulb swung without a shade, starkly illuminating the bare walls. In the middle, around trestle tables, sat a disconsolate group. I recognised some of the faces. Brian Willis, vice-chairman and long-time supporter of the club; Norman Hayward, ex-chairman and scrap dealer. Pack introduced Mark Liddle as 'a forensic accountant' who had been uncovering alleged, unspecified and unsubstantiated wrong-doings at the club, and his assistant, Terry Lovell, and Brian Hammond, Pack's silver-haired personal assistant and chauffeur who had previously driven round collecting lottery payments for the club.

Without further ado, Pack launched into an explanation of why he became involved. Having left his last, successful, venture, in August 1996 he had been brought into the club by the then chairman, Ken Gardner, who had asked him to look at restructuring to avoid mounting debts, in particular the millions owed to Lloyds Bank. Pack had concluded that, although the problems were deep rooted, much of the blame should be placed at Gardner's door. Gardner denied this. Pack claimed he had turned to those he believed really cared about the club, Norman Hayward (who had not been to a game or a board meeting in three years) and Brian Willis.

While Gardner was on holiday, Hayward had sent in Mark Liddle's firm, Bell Neville, to look at the books. Liddle confronted Gardner with his findings on his return and 'within three hours' Gardner had resigned as chairman due to ill health. A chain-smoking, ashen faced character, Liddle suited the role of investigator. Within weeks the other directors resigned. Pack argued they had no choice as he thought the company was illegally trading while insolvent. The club was in serious trouble and faced winding-up petitions by the Inland Revenue and Customs and Excise. Without a feasible rescue plan the club would now die in two weeks.

It was, however, the bank that he saw as the villain. Rather like *The X-Files*, it all seemed a little too far-fetched for me. Two hours had gone by and I was still none the wiser as to how to resolve the matter. Norman Hayward personifies the benevolence of an old granddad on his last knockings. He had been chairman of a small local side, Swanage FC, working hard with his wife on a voluntary and non-profit-taking basis. As a successful businessman, he accepted an invitation to become a director of Bournemouth in May 1991. In return he gave a guarantee of £100,000 to Lloyds, who were then owed £2.1 million by the club. Five months later he bought 61 per cent of the shares, became chairman and increased his guarantee to £500,000. He also lent the club £400,000, shrewdly secured as a debenture on the assets of the company. By October 1992, he increased his guarantee further, to £650,000. He alleged he did so only because Lloyds promised to increase the club's overdraft facility by at least £500,000. They did not. Alongside Tony Pulis, the team manager, Hayward presided over an unsuccessful three-year period in footballing terms, but one in which the club dealt heavily in the transfer market. Substantial sums were made on paper. Three players bought for £235,000 went for deals worth £1.8 million; Jamie Redknapp had gone earlier for £650,000. The economic recession, a fall in property values and a change in bank manager created an impasse. Lloyds immediately issued an ultimatum in September 1994 – repay debts or refinance with new capital.

Hayward was incensed that Lloyds had reneged on their part of the deal. Norm thought he had been dumped on. He stepped down as chairman, selling the majority of his shares to Gardner, Geoffrey Hayward and Peter Hayward (confusingly, they are related to each other but not to Norman Hayward). I did not quite see, notwithstanding any personal arguments Norm might have with Lloyds, how that might affect the club's debts. There was no doubt the club had used £2.35 million of the bank's money. Pack believed

16

it was all a set-up to take money from Hayward. 'Packspeak' was circuitous, a series of repetitive conspiracy theories. His method appeared to be to create debris, throw enough dirt to muddy the water and obscure clear solutions. He reckoned that as Lloyds had 'duped' Norman, every transaction with the bank since 1992 was void. They had brought it on themselves, he claimed. Their dispute was at the core of the club's stricken state, interwoven, complicating a situation now twenty-eight months on.

I had come to try to help them to compromise. I explained my legal background, long-time support of the club and links through my firm of solicitors, Hammond Suddards, with Lloyds Bank as a client. I thought those contacts might help a deal to be done which would at least allow the club to survive in the short term. Pack was in no mood to negotiate with Lloyds. He felt the bank could not be trusted. They should simply write off a large part of their debt and then he and Norm would run the club. That was his position. No compromise.

Pack wanted me to replace Bond Pearce, one of three law firms being used. He was using them but now discovered they had previously been employed by Lloyds to advise on football-related matters. He saw it as another example of an attempt to set up his client, Norman. I was told to replace them. This was not quite what I had anticipated. I explained I could give my own time free of charge but not my firm's. This was not my area of expertise and others would need to help. There are rules governing instruction of solicitors by clients, particularly where more than one firm of solicitors is already involved. I needed to refer him to my colleagues if he would meet them. By now it was past eleven o'clock.

Lloyds had threatened to put in receivers – although Pack's panic was surprising as he was adamant the club could resist such attempts. In his view the move would be illegal. Norm was told to go home and get a new shirt. As if running a military operation Pack shouted that the following day was crucial, his entire 'office' was decamping to a new headquarters in London. 'Read this,' he declared, thrusting papers at me. 'It's my report, the Pack Report. It'll open your eyes. I'm doing it on the state of football, using Bournemouth as an example. It's my plan that the bank will have to accept. It has no choice.'

Carrying this bulky tome, I departed as Pack was arranging for Hammond to drive him to London. I left that meeting exhausted not just from listening to Pack's delivery, but because my day had started shortly after 5 a.m. Getting up and coming home in the dark made me long for summer days, and the events of the evening had done nothing to lift that gloom. He wasn't interested in saving the club. He wanted to save Norman.

That evening determined my future. Set back on a corner plot, our cottage was built in the 1920s, surrounded by mature oaks, stately beeches, cedar, holly and rowan in a garden that Mandy, my dad and I had lovingly restored. She had done wonders with it, making it a real home. Everyone had long gone to bed, and in the kitchen the cats were asleep against the wall where the log fire on the other side of the chimney warmed the bricks. As well as my work, I had Pack's daunting bundle of papers to read through. Here, after all, was the battle plan that was supposed to ensure the survival of AFC Bournemouth.

Bleary-eyed on the train to work, I opened the file. Much of the six inches was material in the public domain – the annual report of the Football Trust (the grant-aiding body for clubs improving grounds); the Deloitte & Touche report into the game that is available at all major booksellers; a whole section on valuing intangible assets (riveting reading!); extracts from a law textbook on directors' liabilities, winding-up and guarantees; and collected accounts for the club over the previous six years.

What little remained was much more interesting. It contained all the background documents and the various financial arrangements between the club, Norman Hayward and Lloyds Bank; Hayward's share sale agreement with Gardner and the other Haywards, Geoffrey and Peter; documentation relating to winding-up petitions against the club and there, at the very front, the Pack plan, completed on 1 January 1997. He had told me with pride that members of staff had come in to compile this report for him on New Year's Eve and New Year's Day, working long into the evening. Lloyds had it the very next day. I wondered why a proposal now three weeks old had produced no agreement. Reading on, it was clear why.

Pack wanted a new management team in place on and off the field. He was to be managing director, supported by Lovell (previous experience: product manager for the Milk Marketing Board and corporate sales manager for a hamper company). He proposed sacking three coaches (and possibly the manager), six players and half of the youth team squad. He appeared unaware that the Professional Football Association and Football League do not let this happen without good reason – financial difficulties not being one.

Pack also proposed increasing Lovell's salary by £5,000 to £30,000, employing a new joint managing director called Malcolm Pickhaver at a salary of £30,000 and giving himself a fee and shareholding. In Pack's view, the company was 'heavily insolvent' and had been for ten years but was now in a 'worsened heavily insolvent' state. Quite what this meant, I don't know. The meat of the proposal was that Lloyds should cover its debt by swapping it for a new class of shares in the company and a mortgage on the land at £500,000. All guarantors – that is to say, Norman Hayward and Brian Willis – would be released from their liabilities.

Lloyds Bank's lending was secured on the assets of the club. Why would they discount their debt? Pack's reasoning was that if the football club folded, nothing would happen to the land. Lloyds clearly hoped to build houses on it. On two sides there are pleasant houses with large gardens in a favoured residential area. If they could do that, the land itself might be worth as much as £2 million. Why give anything up for a sentimental vision that gives you 30 per cent of the money owed and lets others get away for nothing?

I simply failed to see why Lloyds would agree to reduce its potential recovery to £500,000 plus a handful of shares in a company losing £800,000 per annum. The whole programme only appeared to be a way to provide a solution in which Norman and Brian were not called upon to meet their liabilities and Roy got a job. All other creditors gained nothing. It made no proposal for payment to the Inland Revenue or Customs and Excise, only that the new management 'would endeavour to pay PAYE tax'. On realising his plan, Pack would sell Matty Holland (the club captain) for £250,000, Ian Cox (regarded as one of the best central defenders in the division) for £150,000, Steve Robinson (another key central midfielder) for £150,000, and a further four players valued at £50,000 each, totalling £750,000. Easy!

My view? The whole scenario lacked credibility. It referred to hope without any workable plan. As a fan, I reasoned that Pack, Hayward and Willis were the board, but Pack's own intentions were far from clear. He was unconvincing and evasive, never answering questions he found too probing. I found a further document dated 28 August 1996 headed 'Royston J. Pack, Corporate Strategy Consultant, British Columbia House, Regent Street, London'. At the bottom, the slogan 'RJP – my word is my bond'. It referred to his negotiating a 'strategic alliance' deal with Hayward in August 1996. Pack argued that Norman might lose over £1 million. In helping him Pack would receive ten per cent of any savings made by him for Norman, payable to him or his nominee irrespective of Hayward's liabilities. Hayward was also to meet his expenses including board and lodging.

As I read on, Pack's plan became clearer. The strategic alliance with Hayward and Willis would eventually put him in overall control of the club and net him a not inconsiderable amount. Pack's CV was only available subject to a confidentiality agreement because of 'sensitive employment contracts in court cases in progress'.

Again and again his notes were adamant that the bank could do nothing. The overdraft had been put in place in 1994 for a nine year period, to continue so long as it was reduced by a certain amount each year and interest payments were met. As no interest payment had been missed, Pack believed there was no way Lloyds could suddenly demand its money back, the argument he was to repeat *ad nauseam*. What I couldn't understand was why it had dragged on for so long. Lloyds had demanded their money back three years earlier, and again five months ago, freezing the club's bank account. His plan referred to him and a chap called Brian Perry negotiating contracts with a club in Odessa, Blasco FC. It also set out his intention, now achieved, to collect the resignation of all directors bar Norman and Brian. Gwen Griffiths and Tim Pope of our corporate and banking department met Pack and Hayward the next day, but felt no bank in its right mind would agree to what was being proposed. Tim dismissed it completely.

I returned to my office and cracked on with real work. (Contrary to popular belief, as a City lawyer I did not enjoy long lunches – home-made sandwiches were customary.) The phone went. It was Hayward. 'I am outside my barrister's chambers. I don't know whether I should be trying to stop the bank appointing receivers. I am not really sure if I am getting good advice. What do you think I should do?' By now, I was wary of the whole Pack plan, warier still when asked to give advice without fully understanding where the request was coming from. Like being sued for passing a general comment over a drink in a bar, I wasn't about to say a word. Knowing that he could not be with a barrister unless it had been arranged by a solicitor, I suggested that he ask his own lawyer.

By 4 p.m., three hours later, he and Pack wanted to come over to meet my colleagues, but they eventually turned up at 7 p.m. Tim diplomatically questioned why a bank with security would be prepared to write off most of its debt on the whims of three individuals who did not wish to inject any money of their own. Pack's response evaded the question: 'We haven't breached the loan facility terms so they can't do a thing.' There was no suggestion from either man that they had the wherewithal or the ability to inject money. Tim told them bluntly that there was no way the bank could be stopped from sending in the receivers unless a restructuring was agreed. When Tim and Gwen pointed out that merely blowing your nose could trigger the bank to reclaim its own money, Pack exclaimed: 'You're all in it together. We expected as much before we came here. You are lackeys to Lloyds. This is a snow job. Come on Norm – we're wasting our time here because they don't know what they're talking about.' We rang the bank one final time to get them to change their mind. No way, they said. This was high noon – find new capital and pay back the guarantees within twenty-four hours or that would be it.

Norm joined in the tirade, threatening injunctions to prevent the receiver coming in, and the pair were shown the door. Gwen and Tim told me that if the club were to have any chance, it was best not to leave it to Pack and Hayward to sort out. They were happy for me to offer the firm's services, but only on strict terms that no other lawyers were involved and that we ran the show. It had become clear that lawyers to Pack and Hayward might be played off against each other and perhaps sued if the result was not to their liking. Thanking my colleagues for their time, I left for home in a depressed state, rolling in at midnight. It didn't look good. If only Pack and Hayward were not so anti-Lloyds, but on Pack's terms with Norman, they needed to be. It meant more work for Pack. He wanted a cheap solution for his client, one that got him a post as chief executive and an income from the club. He and Hayward needed to retain control. They had to avoid a receivership because if the bank did that they would put in an accountant to run it and sell it. A receiver would have no obligation to work with the directors. He would sell to the highest bidder. I began to feel that this course, a receiver who would look to ensure the business would survive if it could be sold at a reasonable price, might be a blessing, rather than what we had now – even if it was a voyage into uncertainty.

In the programme notes for the opening match of the 1996–97 season, Ken Gardner declared that work would start on the new stadium on 1 January 1997. He would be driving the digger. We had crashed out of the Coca-Cola Cup and crowds had plummeted to 2,500. The team had gone from the dizzy heights of sixth place after three games. And the club was losing money hand-over-fist with nothing to stem the flow. Now I knew the whole optimism of a new season had been a sham, no money in the bank, no hope.

Sitting in my office on Thursday morning after another long journey in, I was dazed but would not countenance defeat. I drafted a letter which would at least give Pack and Hayward the opportunity to see my terms to instruct a top law firm to sort out the tangled web of problems. They needed a negotiated solution and to give ground, but would they listen? No one at Hammond's had any faith in Pack's ability. I didn't think they would. Clearly he was running Norman's show and advising him. What we were saying was at odds with his plan. We were looking to save the club. His purpose was in conflict with that. It was no surprise when I received a call from Pack telling me under no circumstances to do anything further to assist him or Bournemouth on any official basis. He muttered about having to contend with the 'flying squad'. Maybe he feared, justifiably, that I was stronger, more ready to question him than his other 'advisers'. I had no loyalty to him and Norm. I believed in AFC Bournemouth and saving the club. I also knew now what he was about and what he wanted.

CHAPTER 3

Let Us Introduce Ourselves

With three heavy cases going to trial in the coming months, I was glad to be shot of worrying about Pack. My workload was onerous enough, and I was gladly looking ahead to the weekend. But this particular Friday in January was to be very different, a day to change my life. Having heard nothing further, out of curiosity I rang Terry Lovell mid-morning. He was in a state. At 7 a.m. accountants from Arthur Andersen had arrived to 'take control' as receivers appointed by Lloyds. The place was in turmoil. Receivership? The legal definition is easy. But practically? I got home early that evening and found the club was the local media's main story for the first time in years.

Lloyds' PR angle was that there was no option but to put in receivers to save the club, to take it out of the control of Pack and Hayward. The month's grace given by the court was almost up. The Inland Revenue and Customs and Excise wanted their money. Closing in for the kill in ten days, they would be back before a judge demanding payment or the end of the club. Unless a credible force was put at the helm, Lloyds felt the club would die. Unsurprisingly, Pack talked about how disastrous this all was, not in the best interests of the club, the creditors and, by implication, him. It clearly threatened his grand plan. Lovell had claimed he had already received pledges from businessmen worth £100,000. They never materialised. On our very own Black Friday, 24 January 1997, I discounted any rescue Pack-age. After all the times the club had cried wolf, this was for real.

Within hours, most supporters were instant experts on receiverships. One of the players remarked that he had had no idea what it meant. A wholesale departure of players seemed likely. Many remembered clubs that had gone this way before, with gates locked and players sold. Week in, week out, we had always gone out for a drink on a Friday, me, Guy, Trev and Martyn, old friends, creatures of habit, in the ever expanding bars of Bournemouth. It is strange to think that this Friday evening was to be the last when I was able to go down town without somebody recognising my face.

Rolling home just before midnight, a message said Pack had called. I had nothing more to say to him, but Mandy told me he had been insistent. I asked him why he had not attempted to gain an injunction if Lloyds were so wrong? He claimed to have been misled. His lawyers had refused to help without advance payment and the club's bank account was frozen. Absurdly, he assumed the bank might be prepared to unfreeze the account to pay for an attempt by him to injunct them from appointing a receiver. The wages hadn't been paid that day. He was determined to get rid of the receiver, who had asked to meet him, Hayward and Willis the following morning. He did not trust him and asked if I would attend the meeting as an independent witness. Without hesitation, I agreed – it would give me the only direct inroad that I was likely to get.

Appointing a receiver on a Friday gave the Football League precious little time to do anything other than allow the club to play the following day, away at Bristol City. I had dealt with Arthur Andersen before and they with Hammond Suddards.

It was a bitterly cold January morning, damp and grey. How awfully quiet Dean Court was. I knocked boldly on the door of company secretary Colin Macmillan's office, and opened it to find Pack, Hayward and Willis on one side of a desk. I was immediately ushered out. Eventually asked back in, no one introduced me. In the absence of any introduction, I introduced myself. I shook hands for the first time with the receivers, Alan Lewis and Paul Whitehead. Both were people you could not find threatening; on the contrary, I warmed to them straight away. Alan was slim, not imposing or dominant yet clearly sharp of mind and possessing a steely resolve. His manner suggested he had already begun to tire of Pack and Norm. A Crystal Palace season ticket-holder, he was a receiver dealing with a business he cared passionately about. Football is about more than a column of figures – that is probably why clubs can get horrendously in debt and still carry on. The directors vehemently protested about the appointment of Arthur Andersen. Alan meanwhile stated his dual aims – to get Lloyds' money back, and to keep the club alive.

The Football League represents the interests of 72 member clubs as diverse as Manchester City and Hull, Birmingham and Torquay United. In the last ten years it had turned its back on the twenty member clubs who went off to form the Premier League. Foolishly believing it could do better on its own, the League had been left way behind in financial matters, negotiating its own TV deals. Premiership clubs got millions, the rest peanuts. And so the divide grew. Fifty-eight clubs make a trading loss, yet it does not like the idea of clubs in crisis during the season. It's inconvenient. What to do? If one disappears during the season, what happens to its results? Those who have beaten that club will still want to retain the points; those who have lost would rather have the results removed. So much for the family of football.

Our situation was unwelcome. Alan had met Football League officials the day before. We could play today but they demanded cast-iron confirmation by the following Wednesday that we could either survive to the end of the season or would bow out gracefully now. This was a business losing £800,000 a year. With the cut-backs the receiver intended to make (removing staff and lowering expenditure) he conservatively estimated that the trading loss would be £50,000 per month. The effect of a receivership is to freeze debts. The business carries on but needs to run in the black or have funding while a buyer is found. Alan's job was to sell for the best price but that would take time. With a bill for the players'

27

wages for January of just under £100,000 yet to be paid – and no certainty of its availability to do so – the cavalry were needed quick. The League needed evidence that we had £300,000 by Wednesday (one month's wages and four months' losses).

If not, the game at Bristol City that afternoon was to be its last. Alan wanted an indication from the surviving directors that they were looking for a footballing solution. Pack and Hayward responded along the lines of 'we've done enough, matey', talking about Norm's guarantee of £650,000 and the £400,000 owed to him by the club (albeit he stood little chance of recovering that given that it stood in the queue after three mortgages at a collective £2.3 million). Brian had agreed to give a guarantee of £50,000 to Lloyds Bank when Hayward did likewise – although he was the only one who could ill-afford to meet such a liability. So where was the money to come from? Lloyds were not prepared to foot this. Norman wouldn't either. Quite prepared to fund something under his control, the notion of letting Lloyds use his money to save the club rankled. Brian couldn't and Pack maybe didn't give a damn. If those who had the money wouldn't offer it, it could only be the supporters that now produced the money.

Everyone was about to disappear off to Bristol to watch the game. Today was the only opportunity to get the message out in the media if we were to have any time to work at raising finance. I was unsure of my position or authority, save as a concerned fan. I agreed to Lewis's request to contact Richard Williams, a school friend with whom I had worked at Radio Solent in my gap year between school and university, to put this message out on his afternoon sports show. Willis said he would get in touch with a range of supporters, the local media and other contacts of his for an emergency session the next evening at the club. He asked if I would chair that meeting as I would at least be impartial between the receiver and the board of directors, to the obvious displeasure of Pack and Hayward.

I telephoned Williams (for the first time in ten years) to tell him about what had become the story of the week on the south

28

coast. He asked me to go on air that very afternoon – my first, highly nerve-racking, radio interview – and I outlined the need to raise £300,000 by Wednesday and said there would be more announcements soon. When I eventually made it to the local match I was playing in at Kinson, a club ground where the showers are, if anything, better than at Dean Court, the banter was particularly amusing. Some of the players had heard me on the radio on the way in. The divide was there between those who believed Bournemouth could be saved and those who thought it had gone. We had a preference for the slow continental build-up from the back. With players like myself in the side, we probably had no option. That afternoon, we took a 3–0 lead only to lose 3–5. If you had sought odds then for the goalscorer holding the record for the most goals scored in any one FA Cup tie to be playing in the Bournemouth Hayward Saturday League division four, within two months, a bookie would have laughed at you.

The tranquillity of Sunday morning at home allowing aching muscles to recover was interrupted by Pack. He asked me to meet him at his hotel HQ for 'a very important meeting'. I was loath to do so, already feeling at odds with him and his purpose. Initially I declined but he then told me he had lined up Max Clifford, the celebrity publicist, to assist in his cause. (I did wonder whether he would be wearing a Bournemouth shirt.) Fearing the worst, I thought I ought at least to join Pack to see what move he intended to make next.

Pack was nowhere to be seen. The receptionist advised he was up in his room. The most intimate secrets of a person's lifestyle are hidden in their bedroom. A knock on the door elicited an Australian rumble and, moments later, it swung open to reveal a towelled, all too visibly overweight Pack. He motioned me in and suggested I sit while he finished his ablutions. Sit where? The thin curtains were drawn, newspapers were piled high everywhere. I gathered we were meant to be meeting Clifford in his hotel, the Carlton, up on the cliff-top.

A further knock at the door and Pack ushered in a man who was introduced to me as his new chief fundraiser, Giles Gash, a man in his late fifties, reasonably dressed but with a nervous shake and bleary eyes. He seemed a nice enough chap but not the kind to raise £300,000. With hindsight, the traits were clear then: Pack had told me I was 'his' key man; now Giles Gash as well as Brian Hammond were afforded that dubious privilege. Gash deserved better. The two of us and a semi-naked Pack sat in his curtained boudoir conducting business.

It was time to go to the Carlton. Soon after we arrived, Max Clifford's car pulled up and he was greeted by Pack's familiar outstretched hand. Amusingly, the master of public relations did not seem to know who he was. Pack was brushed off. 'I don't speak to anyone unless I have seen a file of papers first,' was the gist of the response, with the footnote that financial arrangements had to be in place before any discussion. Conscious that he was being shown up, Pack reminded him that they had spoken about the matter already. 'Send the papers and we'll talk. It's not really my cup of tea, banks and all that,' said Clifford. The truth was that he was down on a family trip. This was no organised meeting, but an ambush. Flip-flopped and tracksuited, Clifford had returned to the hotel only to get his sunglasses. I had suffered enough time-wasting for one day. Sensing that the 'meeting' was falling apart, I struck up a conversation with Clifford.

He was clearly uninterested. Where was the sensation? I couldn't see anyone sucking the toes of the receiver wearing an AFC Bournemouth shirt! There were no politicians, actresses or babies – no tabloid angle. Having rather impolitely pointed these facts out to Pack, I, too, was summarily dismissed, leaving him beached at the Berkeley. I happily fled back to my garden to enjoy the sunshine and do something productive.

By 4 o'clock Lovell telephoned to say how angry Pack was. He was convinced I was a lackey of Lloyds Bank. I stood my ground. There was a football club to be saved and it was up to the supporters now. I guess Lovell must have called Pack straight away as another call from Pack followed shortly afterwards. I ought to keep my head low and do what he said if I knew what was good for me. Let him do the leading at the meeting while I follow quietly behind. He said

I was out of my depth. I did wonder whether this was something I should be involved in. I arrived at the meeting at just before 6.30, leaving it to the last possible minute to avoid any altercation.

My plan was to use the evening to find, among the thirty or forty people there, those strong enough to work towards the survival of the club, to outmanoeuvre the bitter ongoing sideshow between directors and Lloyds. No one had mentioned who was being invited, but I recognised some of the faces: Pack, Hayward, Willis, Paul Whitehead, Mel Machin, in his fourth season as the manager, Matty Holland, the twenty-two-year-old club captain, Jimmy Glass, the goalkeeper.

Brian Willis kindly introduced me to a number of people. There was Ken Dando, a dignified and loyal supporter, a man who lived for the club; Mick Cunningham, who looked like an Old Testament prophet but who was in fact the match programme editor and a house husband; two journalists from the local paper; a man from Radio Solent; Roy Matthews, the programme printer; and councillor Adrian Fudge. It was a sombre gathering. Brian said it was a brain-storming session to try to work out how to raise £300,000 by Wednesday. And then it was over to me.

'No one is going to help us, it's down to us,' I began. 'We have to raise money, lots of it and quickly. It will have to come from ordinary supporters. Neither the receiver nor the directors will put anything in. We need a fighting fund.' Everyone agreed, even Pack. It would be independent of the receiver and the directors. It was easy to justify, the very nature of a fighting fund lending itself to the creation of a trust to hold the money. This was something to which neither the receiver nor Pack could openly object. The greed, competition and practices of modern football are rooted in money. It is a powerful thing. As it could save us, so it could destroy. We needed an independent, accountable trust to receive donations and be run by trustees and a steering committee with no history, no skeletons. It would have the power to get what no one else had – the backing of the fans and the town while the others were distracted by extricating their own money.

My suspicion was that Lloyds might consider letting the club go under if it could be assured of building houses on the site. We owned the five acres on which the stadium was built. With that in mind, I had contacted David Atkinson, our MP, asking him to make a statement that this was not an option. Councillor Fudge said he would ask the Council to speak to the receiver. Pack, increasingly frustrated, stood up to recite his plan for restructuring. He identified himself as a company saviour who had been working in the background for some considerable time. It was a favourite ploy of Pack's to portray himself as the possessor of detailed knowledge, trying to place himself above those he addressed, when in reality he seemed to know very little.

With only three days to get the money many still wanted to look at why we were there, not how to solve the problem. We couldn't ask for an advance on our share of the TV money we received monthly from the Football League (£25,000 each month – nothing, of course, compared to those in the Premier League). It had already been given away.

We needed a dedicated show of support from the town, both in terms of finance and numbers by Wednesday, otherwise it was unlikely that the club would last beyond the end of the week. £300,00 was a lot to find. Even if we could not get that much we had to start. Or at least buy more time. Our initial target had to be to get Football League approval to play a further home game the next weekend – even if this would only be for an emotional goodbye. I made it clear countless times that a fighting fund, if established, would be independent, run by disinterested individuals, with money to be used at the discretion of the trustees. I didn't want to raise money the receiver would automatically be entitled to. It would not go direct to anyone, but rather would be kept to be used when necessary. Even if we were able to play the following Saturday, the club would have to be back in court (but this time represented by the receivers) to fight the winding-up petition to be brought by the Inland Revenue and Customs and Excise in ten days' time. Two huge hurdles to jump with only a rag-tag meeting of supporters so far.

Hayward had a money-raising plan: each Premier League club should cough up £25,000. Pack said he would ask his 'old mate' Bob Wilson, the TV presenter, for help. We all agreed that we needed to hold a meeting for supporters in the town. Fudge suggested the Winter Gardens for Tuesday evening, a 2,500 capacity hall. I was acutely conscious of launching a public campaign which might fail dismally. Only just over 3,000 spectators had attended the match against Rotherham. Who was to say how many would come to any emergency meeting? If we couldn't get a place like that busy in a crisis, what hope was there?

Predictably, Pack volunteered to take control of organising a committee. I countered with a suggestion that we form a working group of independent supporters which could meet the following evening to plan what might happen at the emergency meeting. Brian suggested that Ken Dando and I should become trustees of the trust fund. Five people volunteered to be committee members and others offered to help out when they could. Immediately, ideas began to flow: perhaps a 'Save the Children' type campaign could be launched and a local building society used for the collection of funds. Sponsored events could be held ... The momentum had begun.

I won't pretend that much legal work was done on Monday. As we all sat in the room that Monday evening, introducing ourselves, none of us could have foreseen the events ahead. The names I mention are now old friends, trusted and valued, but then they were anonymous: John Hiscock, a kindly figure, quiet yet practical with a successful record in business locally; Andrew Kaye, one of the most committed, honest and hard-working people I have met, who had supported the club for forty-two years; Andrew Noonan, a pillar in all that was to come, who immediately offered to be our note-taker, minute-keeper and general organiser; Ken Dando, of course. And then there was Martin Jones, blazered, respectable looking, a well-spoken man of similar age to me. He had been watching the club and apparently living the high life since his days working with Nigel Mansell in the late eighties. He now sold Spectre cars, fearsome-looking brutes that went like rockets. He pulled out a list of the 200 wealthiest people in the country and said he was going to write to them all, outlining our plight. It all seemed so easy to predict that money would roll into an area as well-off as ours. I mean, we were looking for only £300,000 . . . We were joined that evening by Chad Barrett, president of the supporters' club, a resolute, loyal and warm man; Shirley Delsette, who ran the Junior Cherries; Grant Coleman, the sports editor of Radio Solent; Kevin Nash and Neil Perrett, news reporters from the local paper; Jimmy Glass, goalkeeper and players' representative elect; Brian Willis and Terry Lovell. We needed to be seen to be fair until things became clearer.

We would be independent of the receivers and directors. Even then, we were conscious that any perceived relationship might tarnish our chances. Onerous obligations are imposed upon the trustees of a trust fund, yet it suited us to be totally impartial and independent. The root cause of the club's problems appeared to be a power struggle between individuals, Hayward and Gardner in particular. Even now I wonder why Hayward didn't write out a cheque for £1 million, dispose of the assets and have a quiet life.

A thought had occurred to me in my bath that night – what if we ended up buying AFC Bournemouth? A fanciful notion but the receiver had to sell to someone. It had been done before in America.

I did not see the issue of raising £300,000 by Wednesday as the final stage in the journey. We weren't going to do it. There were no mechanics for even collecting the money. The Football League were going to tell Alan by Tuesday evening whether we could play on Saturday. Forget the money: our best hope was using people power to shame Lloyds and the League into keeping us alive longer. We needed time more than anything. The public gathering simply had to be a success to make it easier to get money in. There had already been a huge response to the announcement of the public meeting. The *Echo* was receiving notice of pledges.

Ken had arranged an account at the Portman building society to receive money. It was the simplest method of collection, although we were told any money received at the club would be directed into the trust account. With the public meeting twenty-four hours away, we went over and over again the coordination of the event, as well as practicalities like providing refreshments, and the laws on public collections. By now, Radio Solent had decided to cover the meeting live and the commercial station 2CR asked Ken Dando and me to go on air the following morning. This project was clearly going to use up my complete holiday entitlement!

The Junior Cherries would carry buckets for a collection outside the meeting. All the players were going to be in attendance, greeting supporters in the lobby. I decided it would have to be an evangelical-style meeting to get everyone going and to introduce the receiver to the supporters – if we were to have any chance of success, we needed his backing. If we were to be granted permission to play the following Saturday I would bring him on stage. If not, the whole meeting would go stone cold straight away. It was ludicrous, really, to think we could make a difference. Alan had already made sixteen staff redundant, most notably the assistant manager John Williams, a Liverpudlian who had played for the club in the late eighties, and Keith MacAlister, the one-armed club secretary and part-time dancer who had looked after that post for nigh on thirty years. The meeting broke up at midnight, leaving a core of Dando, Kaye, Hiscock, Jones, Noonan and myself now entrusted with the job of securing the club's existence. For them, they had all agreed to stand up and be counted, to become the public face of the supporters' campaign to save their club. It would mean putting their personal lives to the side for however long it took and giving their all.

What had I got myself into? We were just a motley collection of football supporters about to begin the ride of our lives. An article in *The Times* suggested I had been given time off by my employer to run the 'Save the Cherries' trust. Not exactly – I would have to fit it around my day job. Those with influence in the town such as the Council, the media, residents and supporters alike needed to be drawn together in support, to make it increasingly difficult for the club to be shut down. On the flip side, the infighting between the warring factions that had previously controlled the club could erupt at any time.

Early on Tuesday I spoke to Chris Griffin at the Football League, who was responsible for overseeing the financial affairs of clubs, particularly those who got into trouble. He was busy – Brighton & Hove Albion, Hull City, Doncaster Rovers and Millwall were all under serious threat of extinction. He was softly spoken and ever the diplomat, impartial and fair to all those involved in these bitter wrangles. I implored him to let us play on Saturday, to give the supporters a chance to say goodbye to their team at home. Off the record, he told me that the next board meeting of the League would not be until 13 February and it was unlikely we would be thrown out before then, guaranteeing us a further three matches. Now we had a fighting chance but to announce it would have removed the urgency. I wanted Alan to be able to tell the fans at the close of the meeting.

We had decided the previous evening to limit the committee's media contact to one person and it was suggested that this should be me. I was the only one with any experience – albeit limited. (My previous firm had represented Asil Nadir, a benefactor of the Tory party and head of Polly Peck International who had fled to Cyprus. I remembered the wide-ranging questions which had been dealt with succinctly by a colleague, only for the reported stories the next day to bear little resemblance to what had actually been said.) Our first radio interview of the day went well, 2CR giving its own rallying call. Journalism's popular image of sophistication, high technology and proximity to society's movers and shakers does not ring true in local media. Most journalists work long hours in primitive conditions to do a job they love.

The next stop was Bournemouth Grammar School, where the former chairman and myself had both been educated (we had little else in common). Though I had not been back for a long time, the headmaster was happy to allow me to speak to two of the assemblies that morning. Walking up to the main door was strange enough – as a pupil, I never entered through the front. The building was much the same as it had been when I left in 1984, as were many of the teachers. Without doubt, my years there had set me well for university, my career and now this challenge that lay before me. It was a school where the staff looked to bring on well-rounded individuals who could survive in the real world. Their sheer dedication had always meant much to me. In his study, the headmaster had dug up a report card which showed my maths A level was a grade E against a predicted B and asked me what had happened. Standing on stage in front of two groups of two to three hundred students in the very place I had sat my exams, I was nervous. Yet they had already launched a 'mufti' day which raised £600 for the trust.

Amid all the emotion, there remained the basic need to protect the sanctity of the trust fund. Steele Raymonde, a Bournemouth law firm, would draw up a trust deed free on the understanding that they received public acknowledgement. Little questions like, 'What happens to the money if the club dies?' needed answering. Without their contribution, it would have been difficult to get the whole thing moving. Other more mundane matters needed dealing with, too. Did we have enough buckets? Were we insured for holding a public event? Where would we put the money at the end of the evening?

I had to plan the event. It needed to be balanced to represent the various parties. The most controversial figures were likely to be members of the Council and receiver Alan Lewis. Both were key to ensuring the survival of the club and both had to be made to feel welcome. I guessed that if Councillor Fudge spoke first, any hostility would be disarmed by his message of support. Compere Geoff Barker of 2CR would introduce us all on the top table – Councillor Fudge (no doubt to boos and cheers), Paul Whitehead (until Alan got there), Ron Hands (chairman of the supporters' club), Ken Dando, manager Mel Machin, Matty Holland and then me. I vetoed the idea of taking questions from the floor because the meeting could get out of hand: we had no idea how many people would attend and the depth of their hostility to Lloyds

Bank or the directors. With no hope of repaying £2.35 million there and then, we needed the bank's goodwill to keep the club alive. Bournemouth was very much a town where the zimmer frame and blue rinse were the best-selling items. Yet the influx of companies such as Chase Manhattan had brought new, younger people in and by now it was a growing centre – with more nightclubs than any town outside London. It was sure to be a gathering of disparate ages and behaviour.

That first meeting with Pack barely a week before now seemed like beginning a descent into a dark tunnel. For the first time, I realised that there was to be no turning back. A heightened sense of anticipation came over me. My hands were cold and numb. Inside the hall, there was a quiet buzz of preparation. By 6 p.m., Norm was taking his place alongside the banks of camera crews, resplendent in blue blazer and freshly laundered shirt, looking every bit the respectable pensioner. To many he was the returning hero. We were again the lead item on the local news. My interviews with the media were nerve-racking, but eventually I learned, and came to enjoy, the art of the soundbite – the thirty seconds of four or five easily repeatable quotes.

The queues outside were stretching all the way back into the square. People had begun lining up at five o'clock. In front of the theatre the crowd was six or seven broad. Down the hill, it wound on and on and on, old, young, disabled and fit alike with banners and red and black scarves, all there with a common purpose. Around 3,000 people were waiting in a hush, as if about to go into church. How would they all fit in? I pushed my way through, found Mandy and my dad, and brought them back up to where the players and some of the Junior Cherries were gathering in the foyer, buckets in hand. At seven o'clock the doors opened. How do you describe it? A team that usually plays for eighty out of ninety minutes in deathly silence before a crowd of 2,500 suddenly found itself with the noisiest, most passionate fans who streamed into the hall, running everywhere and chanting their love for the club in a wave of emotion that cascaded all the way to the stage. Within ten minutes the place was full.

Behind the scenes we were dealing with a demand from Pack that he, Willis and Hayward should sit centre stage. Eventually, with some prompting from Willis, he backed down. He still believed it was 'his' trust fund, even suggesting that the money collected that evening should be handed over to them.

I was the last to walk out on stage. The place was packed, my stomach was in knots. My brief notes could never have prepared me for this. The singing subsided, then there was silence. I searched for the right words with which to begin the evening: 'This club will not die.' Cheers rang out. I said that our team was here to survive not until the end of the season but until the end of the century, our centenary. At that point, the players came in from the back of the hall to rapturous applause, followed by John Williams, the gentle giant sacked by the receiver. I had to call order to explain briefly the seriousness of the situation we were in, the need to raise money and the hope that by the end of the evening, Alan Lewis would be there to tell us whether we had permission to play again or not. Why did I care? Years ago, my father took me to watch the club play. I was six years old. Now, twenty-five years later, I was taking him, buying his season ticket each year so we could spend a little time together each week. I told the audience that I wanted the opportunity one day when I had my own children to bring them to the ground, and then my grandchildren.

We had already lost too much in our town – an orchestra, ice rink, swimming baths. The demise of the football club would remove another asset which would not be replaced. Yes, the club had abused its position in the community but we could not afford to let it die. We were not there to discuss the past or wonder why we had got into this mess. We had to look to the future. At that point, I introduced Councillor Fudge. Within moments he was heckled with shouts that the Council should be doing more to bail the club out. The crowd was not prepared to listen to him. After a few moments, however, and a plea by me that he had come voluntarily to speak, he went on to explain that the Council, in an emergency session, would be looking to give whatever help it could.

A promise of £3,000 from Ron Hands of the supporters' club

turned out to be a rent rebate that never materialised, yet it got a popular response on the night. It was good to have the kindly, avuncular Ron up there. The supporters' club had become unable to generate substantial profits. Any money it had passed to the football club had been poured into a black hole. Ken Gardner had tried to close them down by force to redevelop their building. With little respect from them, and perhaps with much disdain, his plans had been thwarted. Now we had a chance to build together.

We moved on to Matty Holland, the club captain, who at twenty-two was bearing a great weight on his shoulders. The fact that the players had gone ahead with the fixture against Bristol City without promise of pay was significant. They turned up that evening with no assurances about their wages for January, further testament to their commitment to the club. Matty was so nervous, but managed to deliver an emotional plea to the supporters to get behind the team. Then it was the turn of Mel Machin, a quietly spoken, dignified individual who will probably go down as the only Manchester City manager to be sacked within days of trouncing Manchester United 5–1. He had seen his playing career reach the heights after a spell with Bournemouth and we had been lucky to take him on as manager four years earlier. He had come to a club in turmoil, where his best players would be sold from beneath him repeatedly without consultation while others would arrive, signed without his knowing.

In his first year he had taken on a team that by Christmas had amassed nine points out of a possible sixty-six and, on the very last day of the season, achieved a victory that kept us in the second division. From then on, we had improved our points tally every year. With a quiver in his voice, Machin asked a hushed audience what it would be like to sit in a deckchair and read the football results without seeing the town's name there. Looking at the crowd, he paused, tears welling in his eyes, and said: 'You wonderful, wonderful people.' The previous day had been his worst in football, when he had seen sixteen good people sacked, one of them his close confidant and assistant manager, John 'Willo' Williams.

With that the crowd erupted, chanting for the shy Williams, who finally came forward and after much persuasion thanked the crowd for their support. Nearly all of us on the stage were on the point of breaking into floods of tears. With all this furore going on, many had not noticed Alan Lewis coming in. He couldn't understand all the 'sackings'. He had asked Pack to compile a list of non-essential staff and it had included club secretary Keith MacAlister. Without Keith it would be virtually impossible to organise any game as he was responsible for ticketing and police. Alan was mortified. The penny dropped. Pack had since told Paul Whitehead he would be able to assist in running the club and there would be no problem in organising matches. To his credit, Alan said there and then that he would have Keith reinstated the following morning. But he saved the best news till last – the announcement that would win over the fans, make them realise he was on their side.

I introduced Alan, stressing the need to support him if there was to be any hope of the club surviving. I mentioned that he was a Crystal Palace fan (to various jokes about Lloyds shutting them down) – how ironic that two years on they found themselves £20 million in debt. He had come straight from the Football League with news for us. 'I am so pleased to tell you we are playing at home on Saturday.' The crowd erupted again. Perhaps this was another defining moment. Alan won the hearts of many at that meeting. The buckets came round. I stressed that we would take money in any form. It took a long, long time for the hall to empty that evening. I didn't notice how late it was, or how much energy had been sapped, as I went back to the counting room and discovered we had raised more than £33,000. Most of it was in small change. We had nowhere to keep it overnight until the banks opened. Finally it was driven off deep into the New Forest where it lay safe, up a darkened track in the back of a 4 × 4, until the next day dawned.

CHAPTER 4

Geoffrey and Harry

I can't remember how much I slept, but by 9 a.m. I was back at my desk in London. It seems to be extremely easy for the media to get in touch with people they wish to speak to and, within minutes of my arrival, the telephone was ringing with the local press and radio seeking quotes. Now it was getting national. I took a call from Andrew Longmore of *The Times*, who said he was trying to persuade his sports editor that I should be featured in the 'Face of Football' column. I am a regular reader of these articles, which are normally reserved for better known personalities in the game. Within an hour, he rang back to say this had been agreed and asked to come in and see me.

No sooner had I put the telephone down than it rang again and the caller introduced himself as Geoffrey Hayward. Sharing Norman's surname, but no relation, he had been a director of the club. 'You may not know, but it was my grandfather who founded this football club. Grandfather Wilfred is looking down from heaven today and he will be saying thank you for everything you did last night. A lot has happened but I will be delighted to help you in any way that I can to ensure that this football club survives.' Those few words immediately touched me. Whatever people were to say about the disputes of the past, I have never had anything but goodwill and support from Geoffrey Hayward. Another phone call, another conversation, but this was a pivotal point in securing the future of the club. Without his wise intervention we would have died.

Andrew Longmore came in. Another caring, compassionate journalist who was interested in a positive story, not in probing the murkiness that lay beneath the surface. He asked me why I got involved. I gave him the answer that I gave to the meeting. The truth was that I was just another supporter who wanted to help. With the board of the Football League not now meeting until Thursday 13 February, we actually had three games to establish our claim to remain a part of it. By now, the momentum was growing. Our three days had become thirteen in which to raise the £300,000. Already I had begun to see that anything might be possible. I was no Jack Walker with limitless funds to revive a club, but between the six of us we possessed endless enthusiasm.

Within days, the list of fundraising events had grown. Whitbread pubs agreed to hold quiz nights; a sponsored walk had been organized; a businessman set up a rock concert at the Winter Gardens. There were cakes to be baked, pocket money donated and services offered. We needed office facilities secure from prying eyes. A general appeal was launched and immediately answered by Adrian Howerd of Steeda Communications, who donated freephone numbers, telephone lines and furniture. Peter Aldersey, a vice-president and businessman in London, donated a fax machine (it didn't work but the thought counted!); John Hiscock gave transportation; and Julia Stone, a local fundraiser for the Stroke Association, gave up her annual holiday time to help coordinate our activities. We needed to run what was quickly becoming a large operation.

Support was not limited to Bournemouth supporters. Two Bristol Rovers fans had driven three hours to hand over £20, Newcastle sent a pennant and Sunderland a signed shirt. Even Leeds United helped – ironic given that result that relegated us in 1990. Their fans were organising a 'knicker-auction' to raise money for us. While no one would have taken seriously Norman Hayward's plea on television that all the big clubs such as Leeds should send £25,000 (less than a week's TV income), he, in his own way, had highlighted the imbalance that existed beyond the Midas touch of Sky television.

We were now determined to capitalise on the home game on Saturday against Blackpool to boost our attempts to raise money by a collection to prolong the club's existence. Meanwhile, I had the pleasure of a work trip to Doncaster. When my mobile phone rang and it was Luther Blissett's personal assistant asking how he could help, again the strange turn my life had taken struck home. Luther had played at the highest level, for England and AC Milan, but had also played for us, banging in four goals on his home debut. The fact that my dinner was interrupted provoked wry amusement among my colleagues, as did Radio 5 Live's attempt to get me on to their investigative sports programme that evening. For an ordinary fan used to picking up bits and pieces of information out of the local paper, Ceefax and Teletext, it all seemed rather odd. My whole involvement in professional football had been one of shouting pearls of wisdom from the stand at players who could probably neither give a toss nor hear a word I was saying. Anyhow, it made me feel better. Now, suddenly here I was having to speak like a lawyer while wanting to act as a supporter.

It was somehow refreshing to be out of the loop of madness for a few hours. Ken Dando interrupted that reverie by calling me to say that he had been asked to release the thousands of pounds we had collected to Pack and Hayward to enable them to fund a legal challenge to have the receivers thrown out. It was suggested that this would be in the best interests of the club. Ken's reaction was the same as mine, that we should politely decline and not publicise this request to avoid an open disagreement with club directors.

I had a lengthy conversation with Alan Lewis late on Friday. For him, Pack had become more and more of an irritant. He had continued to try to influence the day-to-day operation of the club. Luckily Alan's discretion meant even Lovell, as commercial manager, clearly did not know a great deal about what was going on. He was getting most of his information from our Clubcall line, as the premium rate phone bill showed. Pack had been stung. Given Pack's tendency to explode (usually when you highlighted the flaws in his arguments), we decided the best thing to do was to provoke him in a confined space, light the blue touchpaper and retreat. Alan wanted to sideline Pack. There was talk of Hayward walking out on the pitch to be hailed as the saviour of AFC Bournemouth.

It was one of the coldest February mornings that you can imagine. A leaden sky with that yellowish tint that often hints at snow, dry, but with a biting wind that cut through my woollen pullover and (slightly unfashionable but warm) Calvin Klein corduroy trousers. At a pre-match meeting attended by Diane Edwards, the marketing assistant, with her boss Terry Lovell, Paul Whitehead, Alan Lewis, Brian Willis, Roy Pack and Norman Hayward, Alan pointed out that no one would be going on the pitch to address the crowd. With that, Pack was off. Ken and I could have slept through it, it was all too familiar. Ken and I were accused of being lackeys of Lloyds Bank, and much else besides; meanwhile, receiver Alan Lewis had no right to be there. He was totally dismissive of the club.

After that, Pack went on to inform us that the trust fund had his money and it was his right to do what he wanted to do with it. Almost foaming at the mouth, he was like a man possessed. Maintaining his calm air, Alan asked whether Ken or I would like to say anything before the game and that he would be happy for us to address the crowd. An even bigger red rag to Pack's bull! He told the directors that he expected nothing more of them than their best behaviour and, at that, called the meeting to a close. Ignoring the bemused expression on Pack's face, he turned and left.

As the others began to file out, Norm started to speak to me. 'Don't bother,' said Pack as he thrust himself in front. Hayward got excited: unless we handed all our money over, they would get very upset. Ken emphasised there was no question of that – there would be uproar if we were to agree. We didn't think those who had sacrificed benefits, wages and pocket money wanted to see that happen. Then they were off again – the same accusations that

46

we were all in cahoots with the receiver and Lloyds Bank . . . Pack turned to me with his usual line: 'Look, mate, you don't know what you're into or what you're messing with.' He said he had asked me to do a simple task and I couldn't even do that! 'It's a snow job, mate. Just stay out of it. If you've got any intent of taking this club over, forget about it. We know who's out there and who wants this club. You can see one of them in the press tomorrow. I'm gonna make a call in a minute to my mates on the *News of the World* and they'll sort it out for me. You just stay out of the way. Right? We've got our plan.'

With that, Pack went off downstairs. With Ken beside me, Hayward continued the theme: 'You'd better listen to him, mush. We have our plans and you'd better not get in the way. I ain't going to lose out. F*** the football club!'

My heart was pounding. I wasn't quite sure how to react. Ken was silent too. I certainly didn't want to provoke things further, realising we might need his cooperation at some point. Perhaps his comments were the result of frustration more than malice. Genial on the surface but tough in business, Hayward was sharp and shrewd. We had no choice but to walk out of the room. What confused me most was why he was so insistent that we should not stand in his way. Could money alter the attitude when he had clearly thought so much of the club in the past?

A long time ago, Mandy had persuaded me to take in (as part of our ongoing fitness campaign) a cycle ride of some thirty miles of Dorset. Approaching Steeple Hill at Creech, you reach the bottom of a huge hill and find yourself, as I did, only making a hundred or so yards up it before having to push the remaining nine hundred. Down below to the right a house and garden open up to view. Creech Grange is a magnificent property, stone-walled with a long gravel drive to a mansion with lakes, shrubs, trees and animals. Only much later did I discover through a feature in *Dorset Life* that it belonged to Norman Hayward. The man who would have you believe he had given his last penny from his pension to the club was, in fact, worth millions. With one cheque, I believe he could have done a deal which would not only make Bournemouth debt-free but put it in a position of strength.

Love of the club? No, this was about money and getting even. Why else was anyone so worried about a small group of supporters who were trying to save their club? By then I knew Norm had made enquiries about the cost of demolishing the stadium. A loose-tongued local demolition expert relayed his enquiry to a good friend of the club who tipped off the trust fund.

Down in reception Pack was glued to the phone. 'If it hadn't been for him,' he was saying, 'this club would always have been successful. Anyone looking for reasons for this mess need look no further than his track record as manager and what he took out of the club. Don't concentrate on what has happened over the last few years.' Under Alan's management, hidden problems had come to the surface. Safety officials had only allowed the game to go ahead with crumbling sections of our South End terrace cordoned off – the same section that had been used all season. Built on a pile of mud, rubble and rubbish, the stand – if that is the proper term – had reached the end of its useful life. In the supporters' club, with its ambience and original Formica of a 1970s working-men's club, a slave auction was taking place with a camel race promised to raise funds. The prospect of camels careering through the park in sub-zero temperatures only added to the surreal atmosphere of life at that moment.

Did you ever see *Field of Dreams*? A sentimental, maybe thin film, but what the heck, I always enjoy it. A man hears a voice telling him to build a baseball pitch on his cornfield. He doesn't know why, but he does what the voice says, even though it could ruin him financially. 'If you build it, they will come,' the voice tells him. Moral? Just one person can make a difference. I really hadn't believed it to be the case, yet as I had stood up to be counted only a few days before, many more now followed on. In the spirit of that film they did come in their thousands that day – three times as many as on a normal Saturday at Dean Court. Bands played and the crowd roared as on to the pitch came John 'Willo' Williams, the assistant manager redundant yet determined to play a part, even if unpaid. I took the microphone and said my bit, repeating what had gone on since Tuesday and stressing the urgent need to keep things going. The local radio station, 2CR, presented a cheque for £4,000. Willo and I were probably as nervous as each other, although he had played in front of thousands. He gave a rousing speech, thanking everyone for coming, for their tremendous support at the Winter Gardens and asking them to get right behind the team as it came out on the pitch.

The only problem was that he had deviated from the script. As we walked off, he asked me if I knew what Hayward had asked him to say. It started off in similar vein to Willo's own comments but went on: 'I would ask you, ladies and gentlemen, to welcome on to the pitch' – to what was anticipated to be huge applause – 'the man who is here to save Bournemouth, Mr Norman Hayward, together with his business associate, Mr Roy Pack.' Willo had been uncomfortable with this and had shown it to Mel Machin, our manager, who had advised him to leave it out.

The back page of the *Echo* that day had a picture of Ted MacDougall, who was prepared to fly over from Canada if he could help the club in its hour of need. He would give his time free if we would provide his plane ticket. Now fifty-one, he had scored 150 goals in his first spell of 165 appearances between 1969 and 1972. He actually played with Mel Machin and was the most successful goalscorer in Bournemouth's history, eventually playing for Manchester United and Scotland. On the day it was great to see many other old players ranging from Ollie Norris, who took part in the great Cup run of the 1950s when we lost to the Busby Babes, to those from recent years such as Tommy Heffernan, Paul Morrell and Tony Funnell. People might not even know them beyond Bournemouth, but others like them who had given their all at one time or another came back. Yet our departed manager, Tony Pulis, who had 'worked' with Norm as chairman, said: 'I am convinced that now Norm has got back into the club, it will be saved.' I don't think he could have realised how.

The match itself pitted two mediocre sides against each other. The football was an irrelevance. Excitement gave way, before our biggest crowd of the season, 8,200, to the drab tedium of the previous match against Rotherham. With only seconds to go, a spectacular drive from Mark Rawlinson, a young player off-loaded to us by Manchester United a year before, rose right into the top corner, only for it to be disallowed for a foul elsewhere on the pitch. Still, another day over and our fund had topped £50,000.

CHAPTER 5

Is Anybody Out There?

If the pledges were to be believed, we would top £100,000 within a week. The sum in the bank was substantially less, but to the world at large – that included the directors and the receiver – it needed to appear a tremendous success. The match receipts enabled the players to be paid, heading off any imminent threat of a mass walk-out. With the additional money from the huge gate, Alan didn't need to call on our fund yet. We were suddenly getting more coverage than clubs outside the Premiership normally do – if only it had been for our football. The Sunday papers highlighted our plight and Sky did a feature. Ironically, if the Football League had not asserted its independence and instead accepted the Premiership's initial offer of 20 per cent of any Sky money generated, this may never have happened. The League would have £42.5 million a year rather than the £25 million secured in its own deal. This book would never have been written and, most probably, AFC Bournemouth would still be punished by the affairs that drove it into receivership. It is my strongest argument that securing yet more funding per club to cope with debt is no solution unless the money is applied in a proper, reasoned and sensible way. Not in wages.

That Sunday morning, given Pack's threats, I bought a copy of the *News of the World*, which, I must admit, is not my usual choice of reading. There he was, in all his rotundity, with his mystery man to nobble revealed as West Ham boss Harry Redknapp, Bournemouth's most successful past manager. Pack laid the blame for this mess at his door. It was sensationalism at its worst. However, the immense warmth the locals still felt for Harry meant that Pack had picked the wrong target.

Eric Peters, a diminutive Irishman, hosted a late-night radio programme every Sunday on Wessex FM and invited Brian Willis and me on to his show. This meant driving out to Dorchester, forty miles to the west through sleeping villages in rural Dorset along roads unlit save by the moon and the stars. Hardy's Casterbridge appeared to have shut for the evening. An alien invasion could occur on a Sunday evening and no one would notice. Plenty of Bournemouth supporters lived out there. Indeed, two coachloads of supporters make their way to Dean Court for every home match. In a studio in an old terraced house we had a jovial chat interspersed with records selected at random by computer, listened to by goodness knows how many (or how few) people. After an hour or so of Johnny Cash and Alisha's Attic we moved on to the pub across the road, which was empty save for one old boy and his dog and a slot machine flickering in anticipation. Brian and I could both have done with winning a fortune.

Brian was clearly upset by Pack's blast. He had contacted the paper but failed to stop the story being published. He was very worried about having to honour his £50,000 guarantee, money he didn't have. We discussed how difficult it was to find out anything about Pack. The man seemed to have no life outside what he was doing for Hayward. No friends came calling, he seemed to have no buddies to go drinking with in the evening nor, save for the minions he surrounded himself with, did he have any contact with other people. On Christmas Day, Brian recalled, Pack got Hammond to drive him to his mother's house in London, only to take him back fifteen minutes after arriving.

Monday again. The start of a new week – I was grateful that my adrenalin levels were helping me carry on through the pressure and too little sleep. Now the shake-down began. With any failing business, its prized assets are scrutinised by circling vultures. Already there was talk about how much might be raised from the sale of one of our players. With Customs and Excise and the Inland Revenue looking for £500,000 at the sixth hearing of the winding-up application, now a week away, money needed to be found fast. There was a constant need for momentum in the public eye. Donations were coming in at £5–8,000 a day. There had been a slow-down in funds. We decided to 'allow' the income to grow – in the public's eye – so they would keep faith with the project. Otherwise, it might come crashing down, or at least we would lose the initiative. A local brewery started making a 'Trust Fund Ale', Jimmy Greaves agreed to come and make a speech at a reduced fee, the 'Blues Brothers' said they would appear and the slaves who had been sold at auction performed their functions in servitude to those masters who had paid over £500 for them.

Already we had received reports that impersonators, claiming to represent the trust fund, had been out knocking on doors and seeking donations. People had given money and it clearly was not coming to us. We were also receiving money from those who could least afford it – people prepared to give up their invalidity benefit, the old, the infirm, and parents who wanted to make a contribution because they felt their children had benefited from the club. How could we resist their attempts to give without causing offence? The trust committee didn't want to see anyone give money who could least afford to do so. And we did turn away some, only a minuscule amount of the sum needed. Although all contributions made a difference, I strongly believed that divine intervention would get us there if it were meant to be.

I began to realise that while we raised money for survival, we needed to look for a consortium interested in taking us to a secure future. Easier said than done. Geoffrey Hayward offered to buy me lunch to explore the possibilities. He had been involved with the club one way or another for years and, as a director, was one of those who had resigned at Christmas. There had been an unbroken line of Hayward involvement in the ninety-nine years of our history. Lunch was hastily arranged at Chewton Glen, a splendid redbrick country house. Geoffrey had already concluded that the trust fund could be the key to saving the club and a catalyst for change. He would back us all the way, even to the point of buying the club. At the very least he felt we should play an integral part and wanted me to begin thinking about how that could be achieved.

Given my own overdraft, credit card bills and mortgage payments, I hesitantly explained that I did not feel I could contribute financially. Geoffrey, like a kindly grandfather, placed his hand on my arm and said, 'Don't worry. I will help you and make the introductions, but above all I want to see the football club saved and secure.' Geoffrey felt our two best options were to approach Harry Redknapp, our ex-manager and now running West Ham United, and Mel Bush, a rock promoter who had been on the fringe for many years without quite getting involved.

Harry certainly had other contacts that would have money at their disposal to assist. He was still firmly rooted in the area and was building a new house. Geoffrey thought he might want to consider a more permanent involvement in his local football club. Bush, meanwhile, had always intimated that if he were to get involved he would do it on his own terms with no help from others. Given the reaction to the trust fund, however, we both felt that he would have no option but to work with us. We knew we would have to move quickly before there was any possibility of any other creditor trying to get their money back or asking a court to shut the club down. Right then I began to really believe the whole thing could be saved. Geoffrey offered his house as a secure place for a meeting between Harry, Mel, Alan Lewis and the two of us to see what could be thrashed out. A few phone calls and everyone agreed that we would meet on the evening of Sunday 9 February, something that would have to be kept secret from the media and released on a need-to-know basis. Then I remembered Mandy and I had a long-planned weekend away. I knew we needed it. Bush could not meet before then. Harry, on the other hand, invited us round straight away.

He was seething. Pack's story had hurt, hit him hard and opened wounds; he had even called, telling Harry to ignore the article and suggesting the two of them could get together to present a joint show on football. Harry wanted to do all he could – anything to help save the club. He offered to contact friends like Dennis Roach, the original football agent, and others, if only to gain an introduction to those who might have the £2–3 million it might take to do a deal. Harry had always continued to help the club after his active involvement ended. On normal commercial terms, he had allowed us to have on loan a young Rio Ferdinand and had sold us Matty Holland, our club captain (who was to be important in our fight for survival). Harry still bore the scars of a tragic car accident at Italia '90 that had claimed the life of Brian Tyler, our managing director. As we talked, his son, Jamie, popped in with girlfriend Louise (now his wife), the pop singer. No airs, no graces, but genuine concern to help us. What was impressive was the warmth and close ties between all the Redknapp family. They had their own problems – West Ham kept losing and Jamie was injured – but they put all that to one side. Harry was adamant that Norman should not be allowed to get his way.

Norm kept on trying to get us to give him the trust fund money. It was Pack who was instructing the lawyers and I believed it was Pack who wanted us to make payments to keep them happy. Lawyers are usually comfortable with clients they trust and know and make regular billing. Norm said that more than £40,000 had been incurred in legal fees within the month. We decided to keep the trust money intact. If the winding-up attempt by the VAT man and the Inland Revenue was successful the following week, then it would be pointless to give money to anyone (not that we would have!).

Receiverships, winding-ups and other court processes were all confusing to me. I was not used to dealing with complicated insolvency practices. I just wanted to see the club saved. We were working hard around our jobs to raise money. Alan Lewis, running the club on behalf of Lloyds Bank, would get their money back by selling the assets at the best price he could. Certainly, he had a duty to maximise the price as he was obliged to pay any surplus beyond what Lloyds was owed over to the other creditors for distribution. If he did not maximise the sale value, those other creditors could sue him. Meanwhile, the club had to keep alive until a buyer was found. It could not run up new debts. Until Alan's appointment, it was making a trading loss. Neither Lloyds Bank nor the directors were going to fund that loss.

While everyone hoped that the severe situation might continue to produce higher gates, more receipts and extra income, there might still be a shortfall. That was where we came in. The trust fund would meet any shortfall prolonging the club's existence, but only for so long. Public patience and interest dwindles the longer a campaign continues. Too many last games, brink-of-extinction announcements and no one would take it seriously when they needed to. Other creditors were watching the situation. They knew what Alan was trying to do but had their own concerns. They in turn had demanded money from the club, but had not been paid. The Inland Revenue and Customs and Excise had asked a Court five times previously for this to happen, for the club to be wound-up. On each occasion, the club had been able to persuade a court that there was some reasonable alternative to putting the club out of business that might still allow creditors to be paid. Now it would come down to what view each creditor took of what was the best outcome for them. They could force the issue despite Alan's efforts to sell.

Under Alan's control, if he had to, he could make money by selling players. If the club was wound up the most valuable assets, the players, would immediately be able to walk free. The only asset left that was worth anything would be the land. Only Lloyds Bank would get their money back, the money would not be distributed equally between all creditors. Some creditors, however, were adamant that they were not content to wait any longer. Their previous attempt had been at the beginning of January, but then Pack and Hayward had persuaded the Court to allow an extra month's grace. Now the creditors were going back again, and on 10 February we would have another fight. We needed more time to prepare. Luckily the Inland Revenue decided they would allow us a further fifty-two days to find a buyer. At last something seemed to be going smoothly.

Pack had made his mark with the supporters' club – they banned him. In contrast, 'Willo' agreed to give his time freely to the club. Mel needed him, not least to boost the morale of the players. He even signed up with the local paper to write a column. Well over six foot tall and barrel shaped, he was certainly larger than life, a real gentleman and master of the quiz competitions. Among all this, after the dour 0–0 draw on the Saturday, the team had to pull themselves together and travel up to Notts County. Looking back at any season and trying to explain lost games, one can always argue that we had played opponents who were in a fine spell of form, or opponents who had been through such a poor spell that it was bound to come to an end – and that change began when they played us!

Our financial troubles did not fit in with the splendid facilities at Notts County's Meadow Lane ground. Our youth team set-up had not generated many stars for the first team but it is a vital part of the community and maintaining links with schools throughout the area, particularly from ages six to sixteen. Occasionally, though, a player comes through and, on that evening, twenty-year-old David Town scored a magnificent goal in the last minute of the game – a rasping strike to add to a goal by Ian Cox, commanding in defence but excellent at set pieces. It was our third undefeated performance in a row – and we had not conceded a goal. The receivership was certainly starting to pay dividends on the field, if not as yet off it. Alan was beginning to take a liking to the football management lark. Better than trying to sell coalmines in the US or holiday camps in Devon! In contrast, the following evening our young players met Tranmere Rovers in the fourth round of the FA Youth Cup. We lost 0–3, but the fact that we were the only professional football club in Dorset showed the void that would be left if we closed.

Another win and more time to deal with the debts. A good start to the week. We had not counted on the honourable intervention of our local Tory MP, David Atkinson. David told me he had read about our plight and had asked the Treasury Minister to tell his minions down in Worthing to lay off.

Strangely this only had the opposite effect. The Crown creditors refused point-blank to concede any more time. What's more, Acheve, a little-known private company, was latching on to the Crown creditors with their own claim of at least £100,000. They had lent the club £75,000 to pay wages, repayable over four months at £25,000, making £100,000 to cover costs and commission. Paul Whitehead, Alan's assistant, asked me to try to persuade Acheve to hold off. Andy Noonan, our note-taker, had previously been helping the club with the plans to build a new stadium. He remembered that Acheve had been introduced by a guy called Leitch, and told me about visits by a pony-tailed and bodyguard-protected man from Monaco. Not a typical sight in sunny Bournemouth. Acheve sounded normal enough on the phone. They didn't care about the club, they wanted their money back – now. They wouldn't accept that they would get nothing if they wound the club up. With neither them nor the Inland Revenue ready to play ball and give us a chance, we knew we would have to fight them in court the following Monday.

Alan was having some luck. It looked likely that Steve Jones, a former player, was about to be transferred by West Ham to Charlton, with our getting 25 per cent of the fee over and above the £215,000 that had been paid on his transfer from Bournemouth.

Meanwhile, my home and social lives were pretty non-existent. This whole saga was draining. The constant need to guide, direct, motivate and control strategy meant that everything else was put to one side: little things like remembering to pay credit card bills, having the ceiling repaired or cleaning out the nesting boxes for the spring. I had intended to plant out the Christmas tree, but it still stood in a bowl, dead and brown. Mandy and I had long planned a trip to Lisbon to see friends that weekend, but the BBC needed me to contribute to a documentary about our sorry mess on the Friday morning. Gardner and Hayward presented various segments throughout the programme, extolling their own virtues and sniping at the other. I was to give the 'people's view'. After filming was over Mandy and I were able to escape, albeit missing our flight and arriving late in the evening.

Warm winds, blue skies and forty-eight hours of sunshine. I sat in the breeze and walked by the sea with not a football or a receiver in sight. Save for Radio Solent, who tracked me down by phone to do a live interview about Monday's hearing, and discovering we had lost at Bury, it was almost a normal weekend. Not many of them were left. I knew Geoffrey Hayward, Alan Lewis, Mel Bush, Paul Whitehead and Harry Redknapp would be meeting to try to formulate a rescue package. Perhaps I should have been there but I needed the break for mental stability, health and for Mandy.

Monday dawned. Were we to be dead and buried or did we live on? I called from Lisbon airport. I did not want to pick up the phone. Fear gripped my hands, a windswept seasick feeling in my head. 'It's one more month,' Alan proclaimed. After a fraught twenty-one-minute hearing we had got a month to get things sorted. With Alan having no choice but to pay the January wages, there would soon be a shortfall in trading. Our projected tally of £100,000 within two weeks had not materialised. With barely £70,000 in the bank, it was like collecting rainwater in the desert. I would only release money for the trust fund if I thought we had a fighting chance. We had goodwill but that alone would not be enough. Alan cut costs down to the bare minimum, which meant making an early start on a long journey north to away matches in place of the usual overnight stay. Hours of cards, quizzes and battles over the video player on a bus with a dodgy heater and no proper rest before a match.

I returned home to hostile fire locally. The word was that I was in this only for personal gain, put up by Lloyds to do a job, in return for which I would have my political aspirations rewarded. At that time I was ward chairman of a third of a constituency in Christchurch for the Conservatives. Their principles at that time were ones I believed in. I had been privileged to meet John Major, impressive in person, yet roundly slated in the media. I didn't renew my membership. Norm was the favoured one, heralded as a 'white knight' with popular opinion in his favour. He had contacts, was monied and influential. Yet now the chinks in the armour were beginning to show. His crown was slipping.

CHAPTER 6

Buy a Club? Why Not!

Geoffrey telephoned me late on the Monday evening. Everyone had got on wonderfully well. He, Mel Bush, Harry Redknapp and Alan Lewis had spoken for hours. Mel was certainly interested in buying the club, Harry keen to play a part in ensuring it survived. Geoffrey had stressed the importance of Bush dealing with the trust fund. He had said he would listen.

I had been daunted by the prospect of phoning the wealthy and influential Mel Bush, but I found him friendly and chatty. He was looking to take complete control of the club and sweep everybody out. Bush thought himself successful in his businesses, all of which involved family in key positions. That was how he saw the club operating. Unless and until he had control of it, he saw no reason to talk to us but acknowledged he might be prepared to hand over the funding of, say, the youth operation to enable us to maintain a role in the future of the club. He wanted a new stadium, and a smaller stadium alongside for other sporting events. Coming to watch the team should be more of 'an event', and the manager should go as he didn't think he could work with 'seasoned professionals' (i.e. anyone over thirty). For example, he should never have let Alex Watson (then of Torquay United) and Mark Morris (then of Brighton & Hove Albion) leave the club even if these players were among the highest paid and possibly past their sell-by date.

What else would he do to revitalise the club? Sign up Chris Waddle and Ray Wilkins to put 'bums on seats'. His grand plans for a Victorian covered market in the car park ignored the fact that the land did not belong to the club. I implored him to think carefully about working with the trust to save the club. He was not interested. He was his own man and did things his own way. I got the feeling he thought we might be doing more harm than good by prolonging the agony of the club. Perhaps even then he would have preferred the club to die. He talked about £500,000 as his bid. Courteous throughout, he didn't inspire the confidence or the vision that perhaps his more famous clients, David Essex and Vanessa Mae, might have seen.

But it was the trust who had the power of the people. If we could give them a dream, a vision of a better way, then any alternative would leave a bitter taste. And I knew that Geoffrey would back us. With no other buyer on the horizon I began to think there was only one option. We could buy the club!

Another terrific performance (a 2–0 win at Dean Court against Preston) brought about a third victory for Alan Lewis, a fourth clean sheet in five games and we moved up the table. All that was disappointing was the size of the crowd. In the second home game since receivership, why had it dropped back under 5,000? Maybe there was a complete lack of faith in the club; maybe it had abused the community for too long. The six of us on the trust committee all gathered in the dug-out by the side of the pitch, the rain falling steadily. Did they think Bush's proposals were right for the club? To a man, they said no. Then I outlined my vision. Our task was to create an alternative to the cult of personality. It was no longer enough to save the club; we had to buy it for the town. We made a pledge to each other, a commitment to ourselves. We were to create the first community-owned soccer club in Europe. Quite what that meant I now needed to work out in detail.

Alan Lewis delivered a letter asking me for money. But now, with our new project to buy the club for the community, we were even more reluctant to part with any. The Blackpool game itself had grossed £49,694. Having made our decision, we needed three days' planning under our belts before word got out. Rather like buying a house, I figured we could probably work out some sort of payment plan if the deposit were large enough. In theory we could just pay Alan a cash sum for the asset as he was under an obligation only to get the best price. Norm didn't want to pay and Bush was saying £600,000 was top whack. I thought that at least £750,000 would be needed if we were ever to get this idea moving.

With three weeks almost up, the Football League had asked to see Alan at their monthly board meeting to review our situation. Alan asked me to attend, although there was some consternation within the League as to my right to do so. We left it that if I turned up they might just ask me a question; then I could be invited in. I prepared a brief, estimating what we might raise by the end of the season. I worked late into Tuesday evening and all day Wednesday, devising a strategy, a structure for how the supporters could buy the club, one I could show to the League. There was such potential to protect the club for the long term. My simple solution was to buy all the assets from Alan and put them in a new company in which the trust would have 51 per cent of the voting rights in two golden shares. The rest of the shares could be sold to raise capital. I also promised continuity, loyalty and integrity, both in the employment of the manager and the careers of the players at the club. Directors would pay for match tickets. There would be no wholesale stripping of assets within our control. This, I believed, could be a blueprint for the future of the game. I sent it off by fax.

The League were the only ones who could let us do it. I knew Bournemouth deserved a football club – why should the town be made to suffer for the acts of others? We had created the prospect of a people's co-operative and there were no viable alternatives. Surely they would not pull the curtain down before the final act, even though we had nowhere near £300,000 in the bank?

I'm not sure what I expected at the Football League, at its unprepossessing modern HQ near Marylebone. All I know is that it was another lunchtime used up. Alan was in tough-guy mode, having turned up with Lloyds' chief banker, Colin Grant. I was neither a director nor the receiver – everyone knew that letting me address the board would get Pack going. It was like a gathering of the dead and the dying. Millwall, who were in a similar mess to ourselves, came out and Alan went in. This was the first time I had met Colin Grant, his gold tooth glinting and with his robust Welsh accent. He was in no mood to give the League anything other than an ultimatum. Lloyds would put the club under if they had to.

They were in for quite some time and then Chris Griffin (League financial controller) asked me to pop in and answer one quick question. It ended up being seventy-five minutes of questions. The board of the Football League had a lawyer on hand as well as Griffin. Ron Noades, then chairman and owner of Crystal Palace, backed us but they needed two weeks to consider the issue. Good old Ron, who eventually 'sold up' at Selhurst Park and became the owner of Brentford, sacked the manager and brought players from one club to the other for 'considerable' fees. And here he was helping us. Northampton and Gillingham had gone out of business but had come out of receivership to re-establish themselves, while Aldershot and Accrington Stanley had disappeared from the League. Despite Ron Noades's agreement with what I had said, the answer was not that clear-cut. They hadn't explained how we could achieve salvation, did not accept my strategy. There would be terms and conditions to obey and they would dictate the process. The only solace was that we were not to be booted out of the League just yet – we would carry on for at least two further games. The prevailing mood of the meeting was that nothing would be done unless the main creditors were in agreement and the other clubs supported our proposal. Yet as the Bury chairman said on leaving, 'I haven't got a clue what all this means.' At least we were still in business. Two more weeks. Really it was like one battle ofter another, always fighting for more time against different opponents.

In any other industry it would have been straightforward for Alan Lewis to agree to sell the assets as a going concern to a buyer. Alan could sell to whomever he chose and not worry about the other creditors. The League didn't want anyone left high and dry. We had offered a compromise: a deal to Alan to buy the assets and, over time, money to the other creditors. The Football League did not seem to like that. They wanted someone to buy the club intact, not just the assets but all its baggage. To have to buy the existing shares and pay off the existing creditors – impossible! That meant getting agreement with Ken Gardner (with a 24 per cent shareholding), and Norm, Geoffrey and Peter (each with 12 per cent). We wanted to put the assets in a new company free of interference from Norm, Ken and Pack. The League did not have a precedent to deal with it and that worried them. We needed a swift resolution to avoid having to throw money in directions where it might not be best used, but now there was more delay. Two more weeks

My days were developing a familiar pattern: 5.30 alarm call, wake up, get in shower, shave with eyes shut in shower, dress, grab sandwich, give Mandy cup of tea, say 'hi and 'bye' to cats, 6.15 leave house (dark and usually wet and windy). Catch 6.52 train from Southampton airport, sleep, 8.03 scheduled arrival at Waterloo (8.15 actual arrival), wait for drain train to Bank, buy large Seattle Coffee Company café latte, 8.45 into work, eat sandwich – work – 4.55 run to tube, 5.15 train leaves, work, 6.25 Southampton airport, 7.00 home, 7.30 trust meeting, 11 p.m. home, make sandwich, say 'hi' to cats and Mandy, midnight, sleep. So that's why I was so knackered! But I couldn't give up now.

In the 'luxury' of our own trust offices, eating KitKats and drinking coffee out of plastic cups as the evening darkened, I knew now it was no longer a question of counting the pennies. We needed to obtain money, and lots of it. We had unanimously committed ourselves privately to go out to reclaim the club for the town and now needed to know how to go public. We decided to give a press conference at the club. We also had to understand the nature of the opposition. Both Pack (through Hammond) and

Perry were careering round in AFC Bournemouth cars. Terry Lovell was continually on the phone, unsubtly probing to find out who we were talking to, and what information we had been gathering. He was obviously trying to please everyone to protect his job, whatever the outcome. He came round to see me one Sunday afternoon. Pack was telling him the fraud squad was going to arrive shortly, that he would be for it. Terry had hidden lottery money in a club safe to pay bills and was scared Pack would commandeer the funds if he knew. Unless I disconnected the phone, Lovell would contact me every few hours with some sensational news about what was to happen. Nothing ever did.

Money coming into the trust fund would go to charity if the club died. Potential big investors didn't want their money disappearing into a black hole. I proposed the creation of a second trust account simply to collate investment money. If the deal was done they would get shares in a new company, if not, their money back – it was ring-fenced. I knew we'd have problems just taking money because of the Financial Services Act.

Our three days' planning were almost up. We had no money to employ glossy PR, agencies or consultancies – we did it all ourselves. James Worsley, press adviser to Arthur Andersen, offered us his time, advice and experience. He let the media know that on 15 February, we would announce details of our plans 'to secure the future of professional football in Bournemouth'. The *Daily Telegraph* had already picked up on our story, identifying no corner of Britain in greater footballing difficulty than Dorset. It compared the 5,000 crowd we drew out of a local catchment area of nearly 500,000 people against our opponents that week, Preston, who had an average attendance of double that from a population of just 90,000. And these were supporters for whom Manchester and Merseyside were but a short drive away. Robert Hardman concluded that with a decent ground and a few sound players, there would be many borderline fans who would be ready to return to a revitalised club. I believed that, too. And so it has proved.

We would never have made such progress if it had not been for the cross-party support given to us by our local council. From the start and allowing us to use the Winter Gardens all the way through to the present, they have given what they can to ensure their football club survived. It has helped considerably: from being a public voice, to addressing the Football Task Force, and then for every assistance in moving towards a new twenty-first-century stadium. For any club, any organisation, being able to work together with its council in partnership for the benefit of the local community is vital, a strong foundation upon which to build successfully.

I always prefer to pick fights that I believe I can win. Representing a client, there is no point in going to trial facing a heavy defeat. Cut your losses at the earliest opportunity because it will eventually cost you less. Once we had met Mel Bush and decided his aims were unsupportable, there was no alternative but to go for it ourselves. Geoffrey Hayward and I had spoken at length about the level of funding required and who might participate. We had agreed that it would probably need three or four substantial investors to follow his lead of £100,000. Quite understandably, he did not want to be left on his own and he had, of course, already given significantly to the club in the past. Harry's support reassured him. Now where were the others? The main occupation of the Pack camp was to try to discover who it was that was backing the trust fund.

Most national newspapers, plus satellite and terrestrial television, came down to cover our launch. By now, even though only three weeks into the whole crusade, I was feeling much more relaxed and comfortable in dealing with the media. As with any innovation, those with most to lose pooh-poohed the idea that the fans might save the club. The local newspaper said the plan was thought to be 'over-ambitious' by several of the old guard of the endangered club. The process would be simple. Ask those prepared to put £10,000 or more into a new venture to save the club to come forward and register their name. We would have to prepare a lengthy document setting out the reasons, the way in which we would run the business and financial projections as to how it would perform. Once that was complete we would go back to those who had contacted us, ask them to re-confirm their interest and then send this prospectus to them with an application form. We could only allow a maximum of fifty to be released. Otherwise, to comply with all the new financial services regulations, we would have to spend a six-figure sum in getting it done.

Even within that first month, I, too, had been surprised by the influence of a football club within its community. The letters of support, dedication and commitment were unceasing. There was one poem I knew I would want to reproduce at the end of the story. It was written by a young lad, 'Bournemouth born and bred' as he put it, just seven years old.

My name is Nicholas Bevan, I am seven and a bit
I used to have leukaemia but now I'm fighting fit.
Lots of people backed me and helped me with my fight
And now I feel it's my turn to help you with your plight.
I've enclosed a little money to help in your campaign
Perhaps with all the little bits the Cherries can remain.
If we were all like pennies then together we'd make pounds
And if we stand united then perhaps we'll save our ground.
The Cherries are our local team and when I'm old and grey
I'd like to tell my grand-kids that I helped in some small way.
I hope with all your hard work the Cherries can survive
And you get lots of backing to keep our club alive.
If people hadn't fought for me then I would now be dead
So I hope more people think of this and try to look ahead.
It was mostly through donations that for me they found a cure
And with the same determination we can save our club for sure.

Some supporters, virtually house-bound through illness, had the local radio, newspaper and television to help them still feel a part of the club and community. Others wrote from their bedsides to say how the radio commentary had made them smile in the afternoons. A dad with his young son in a wheelchair was in tears on television as he said that the team was all his boy lived for, his room decked out with Cherries shirts and pictures. If the club was to go, he did not know how long he might survive. I am sure that the Manchester Uniteds, Liverpools and Newcastles of this world provide inspiration. For a club like ours, however, these letters were at the heart of what I wanted to achieve.

Within days our list of investors began to grow, as did the efforts of all competing parties to try to gain the information. When investors came under pressure to disclose whether or not they were backing us, they would inform me so that I could keep tabs on what 'the enemy' was doing. We were able to track rumours that were peddled about the town by the likes of Pack. The scaremongering failed to damage us so we could afford to laugh.

I have always defended professionals for insurers, so I am somewhat protected from the 'crank' element of the profession, the blusterers, time-wasters, malingerers and downright potty individuals, those that are often found mounting legal actions against wholly proper people. The club was a magnet for these sorts. Luckily, Alan fronted most of the enquiries. By his definition, 'a barrel load of wide boys' responded to his advertisement for the sale of the club in the *Financial Times*, but not one had come up with a constructive offer. Lovell was an excellent conduit for time-wasting leads. His heart was in the right place but his lack of discernment enabled him to be embroiled in any potential development. He had called me with a mate named 'Pinchin' who wanted to take over the club. He was hostile to what we were doing and that ended that.

Then there was George Maxwell, who knew Geoffrey; Ken Gardner had got him involved with the club in December but he had faded out because of the receivership. He tended to talk at length in his droll Scottish accent, but initially he sounded promising so he came in to see me. In his plan he was going to be chief executive and would make a lot of money – and I was going to help him achieve that. I listened patiently to tales of his success and how once he nearly bought Barnet. Eventually, I told him that I understood he could inject £1 million into the club, a line of funding arranged with a merchant bank. He was a little peeved that I wanted to know what he could do for us and not vice-versa. Telling me he would not be lectured to by someone twenty years his junior, Maxwell announced he was leaving. That was not the last we heard of him. I say 'we', I actually mean Mandy, because it was she who had to put up with endless phone calls and handwritten faxes from him. He was last seen a year later sitting on a late-night chat show advising on sexual harassment in the workplace!

He was not the first or the last person to come in with grandiose schemes. We had guys suggesting a reversal on NASDAQ, flotation on the Alternative Investments Market or a full PLC flotation. No one seemed to realise what a forlorn enterprise we were dealing with here. We were making it clear that any capital that was to be invested now would have little hope of receiving dividends. Although we were putting in eighteen, nineteen, twenty hours a day, all these people had to be seen, because if one pearl came to light from within the swill, all the effort would be worthwhile. The 200 supposedly most wealthy people in the United Kingdom to whom Martin Jones had written (or apparently knew) had not as yet made any contribution, nor had the Premier League come up with lots of £25,000 as requested by Norman Hayward. Yet we had a good £250,000 in promises already. And February wasn't even over.

CHAPTER 7

Return of the Mac

The common feeling among the investors was that if they were to put money in they wanted me to become chairman of the club. Neither I or John Heller, the senior partner of our firm, was convinced it would be a good move for my career. I had gone to Wembley the day after the Preston game. The contrast could not have been greater. One night 5,000, the next over 75,000 watching the World Cup qualifier – England against Italy – at Wembley Stadium. Walking up to the ground, the atmosphere electric, John and I debated the merits of the Bournemouth situation. As he was to point out, it would be impossible to even try to combine a successful career in the City with becoming chairman of the club, as the investors were demanding. Then I could not begin to wonder how true that would be.

But I needed to have the substantial investors on board. They wouldn't do so unless I were to become chairman and there was no one else from the past involved. Our credibility was rising. The rest of the board who had resigned were all supportive of what we were trying to do. We developed a 'buddy' system under which John Hiscock and Martin Jones were to speak with Ken Gardner and keep him informed, while Martin and I liaised with Geoffrey Hayward. He in turn would talk with Colin Legg and Peter Hayward, as a former director, while

Ken would keep an eye open as to what Norman and Pack were up to.

Norman was determined to fight on two fronts – against Lloyds Bank all the way on the guarantees and against the receiver, although it was now nearly a month since Alan had been appointed.

The full effect of the receivership on the club was only just becoming clear. I was sent a letter by Arthur Andersen requesting immediate payment of more than £50,000 to fund the trading deficit to the end of February. It had been a good month, but the impact of paying January's wages and now having to meet another month, too, would severely damage the club's cashflow and in one fell swoop halve the money in the fund. We had another committee meeting late into the night. We eventually saw no alternative but to prepare to release the funds. We now needed to convert all the pledges into cash. Of course we had first to prepare legally binding documentation, a share offer, an application form, details of what people were buying into. We had to issue what amounted to a prospectus that could be distributed to potential investors. The bank required a minimum of £1.4 million to fund any deal or they would close the club down and build houses upon it. While this put Mel Bush very much out of the picture, we had to decide whether this was a game of poker. I reasoned that we should agree the best price possible and then see if Lloyds wouldn't lend the money to us to fund a deal – if it ever got to that point.

In this scenario the bank would effectively be gambling its own money on our potential success as a management team. Martin Jones had been doing a lot of work on the flotation of his company, Spectre Cars. He reckoned it might cost £15,000 for the 'pseudo' prospectus to be prepared for us by Alan's deadline of 28 February. He would oversee the task. With the club actively being marketed by the receiver, we knew we had to move fast to get our bid in by the end of the month. In the meantime, while the team visited top-of-the-table Brentford, and lost by a solitary goal, Mandy and I went to Brighton for her sister Emma's wedding to Jonathan. A special day to remind me of life outside of football. At the reception, held at the bridegroom's house, one of the ladies remarked that the chap standing next to her worked for Arthur Andersen. It turned out that he was the person who was supposed to fill the position that Paul Whitehead took at the club – his other job had gone on a day longer so he had been unable to take up the Bournemouth appointment.

If I was going to go cap in hand to raise money I needed to have something to show. The financial documents we would complete would have to be specific. I had begun to prepare the basic information that Martin could use to complete the task. It was like searching for a needle in a haystack, really taking pot shots in the dark. How does one start calculating the likely performance of a business that not only required capital but was losing £1 million a year? Having spent considerable hours defending accountants when sued on the basis of projections they had prepared, I was well aware that it would be the reasonableness of the assumptions on which I made my calculations that was important. If I were to build in revenue on the basis we would reach the fourth round of the FA Cup, then arguably that would be unreasonable. If, however, I were to state that the average home gate was going to be 4,000 people because that was the accumulated average over the previous three years in the same division, then that would be reasonable. One is indefensible, the other not. I had to begin working through every single element of the club's finances. In some areas there was factual information available, such as the number of programmes sold, cushions lent, cars parked – but what else?

The biggest variable of all was just how many people might be bothered to come to support the club. It is not as simple as counting the people through the gate, either. In any one game with a 4,000 attendance, I would guess that as many as half are either season ticket holders, concessions or complimentary guests. That in itself distorts any financial projections. It is also invariably true that if a player remains with a club, his salary increases annually way above inflation. Similarly, the older a player gets, if a club is to retain his registration, then he continually has to be offered better terms. The art lies in knowing when to move a player on – that is, by maximising his value before he becomes too expensive to the set-up – and when to bring a player in. We also needed all the information regarding salaries of the manager, coach and other backroom staff, but there was no information pack to assisting in preparing our bid.

Alan had revealed more information about the transfer dealings that had been taking place. Until then, most of the activity at Dean Court had been on 'undisclosed fee' basis, a nonsense as each deal has its terms and conditions. Quite why clubs hide the details of their transfer arrangements mystifies me. Disclosure of information is honest, builds good will and can usually be achieved without harm. Things were progressing well; only the Football League were delaying. Then they delivered a bombshell. They would not agree to our proposal. They wanted the existing company to be bought rather than the assets disposed of; the buyer would have to satisfy all parties. Had they listened at all?

In other words, we could not simply buy the assets from Alan. They wanted us to effectively get the old company to sort out its financial problems. This would mean the remaining directors creating a proposal that could be voted on and agreed by the shareholders and creditors. In essence, Norman Hayward, Brian Willis and Roy Pack would, if the club were going to be sold to the trust, have to agree a deal that they were happy with which they could then recommend to the shareholders and creditors who would be asked to vote on it. To achieve that we would have to ensure that whatever deal was done was enough for Alan Lewis and Lloyds Bank, provided sufficient monies to Norman to persuade him not to try and do his own thing, yet also had good enough terms to placate the Inland Revenue, Customs and Excise and all the other creditors. What a nightmare! So much for innovation and lateral thinking by footballing authorities. Until then, I had hoped that we would be able to bypass Pack. It was Pack who would cause all the problems. I couldn't imagine how Pack would allow Norman and Brian to help us push our plan forward. I now needed to talk to all interested parties to find out what they wanted. What was their price for allowing us to go forward? Given that every other director had agreed to wipe out his debt – and Norman had intimated to me that he would, too – the question was whether he would do the decent thing.

Norm had once owned 61 per cent of the shares in Bournemouth. The balance was spread among disparate supporters. He had, however, sold all bar 12 per cent some three years before, 24 per cent going to Ken Gardner. The only problem was that he had paid for only half of them. Although they were in his name, he still owed Norm £20,000. Not being one to be left behind, Norm had seized on this and issued a writ against Ken, seeking payment of the £20,000 or return of the shares. Ken, by this stage, was impecunious. He had stumped up £250,000 (one way or another) to meet his personal guarantee, already having put a large sum of money into the club in the past. A Canadian packaging company claimed the money might be theirs.

No one balked at the course we had set. In fact, our determination strengthened while the League had sat on the fence. Despite the heightened problems, our endeavours continued. For light relief, one of our match-day presenters, Terry Baker, organized a sportsman's dinner for us at a local hotel. A couple of hundred people came along for a great evening with Jimmy Greaves. Mark Liddle, the forensic accountant, had collared Andy Noonan at the bar. Having ignored Norman, Mark was eager to suggest that we now turn to him for advice. He prompted the suggestion of a meeting with Norman to work out what it might take to get Norman's full backing. Like others, he disparaged Pack.

I was invited to say a few words to the guests that evening. I paid particular reference by name to the past directors and their commitment to assisting us in going forward. Having consumed the first course, I had to dash away to Poole for another event before returning for Jimmy's speech. As I left the room, Liddle followed me out. If we were to have any hope of Norman's support, he suggested that we never mention Ken Gardner's name in the same breath. It was delivered with an icy tone.

For what it was worth, we wrote again to the League, imploring it to consider giving us some leeway and stressing the impracticalities of what it was asking us to do. The whole fiasco in the delay over the League's decision meant it was the end of February and our month's grace to the next winding-up hearing on 6 March was nearly up. We needed more time. At least we could argue that things were becoming clearer. Luckily the court couldn't hear us until 20 March, judges' commitments and all that. Knocking a few heads together had not gone down too well in the Pack camp. He now planned to float the club on the Alternative Investment Market (AIM). One look at the suggestion would reveal all its basic flaws. Nothing had deflected us from our belief that we were in the strongest position and we were about to benefit from a significant secret weapon.

MacDougall was back! Four weeks after the *Echo* had announced his willingness to come, Ted MacDougall, an icon as the most famous player in the club's history, flew in from Canada for a ten-day visit to help to try to save the club. This was a man who had dominated not only the scoring records of AFC Bournemouth, at a time when we attracted crowds of 20,000, but those of the Football League in the early 1970s. He had struck the goal of the season on *Match of the Day*. His very presence gave us a new focus for our campaign. We had chosen his arrival to mark the launch of 'Trust Fund Ale' with him having the number nine bottle (his shirt number, of course, from his days as our centre forward). I could not believe the number of cameras waiting at Dean Court for him to arrive that chilly February day. It brightened the gloom of the previous day's Football League announcement.

The media's bright idea was to produce a ball and get Ted to take a penalty with me in goal. It was reckoned that the idea of him 'shooting for the trust fund' would make a very humorous picture. His first kick was blasted into the top corner, Watkins making no attempt whatsoever to save it. Media then egg Watkins on and MacDougall suggests ball is to go to bottom right-hand corner. Watkins encouraged to save. Ball duly dispatched to bottom right-hand, Watkins lunges full length and saves! Suit promptly ruined to much amusement of first-team players while Watkins demands new goalkeeping contract.

That night we had one of the biggest events in the fundraising calendar, 'Cherry Rock' at the Winter Gardens, which had been single-handedly organised by one of our supporters. He had managed to persuade many local groups, together with more famous session players such as Zoot Money and Howie Casey (who was the saxophone player with Paul McCartney and Wings), to come and play for nothing. Fifteen hundred people piled in for an evening of great music that raised more than £10,000 for the club. Ted's energy knew no bounds, even though he was jet-lagged. The reception accorded him at the game at home to Shrewsbury was tremendous. He was fifty-one, but many thought he didn't look a day older than when he played in the same team as Mel Machin. So it was an old pals act with Fred Davies and Keith Miller, both members of that same team in the 1970s and now the management at Shrewsbury. Everybody was given a boost, although yet again we didn't lose but we didn't score either.

Alan had given us more time to get our bid in. Sitting in Liddle's office on a dark Sunday evening we went over the terms he thought Norman would find acceptable to allow him to step aside. If we were able to support him on his debenture (£400,000) and personal guarantees (£650,000) by paying him £365,000 out of the £400,000 and agree to work out a deal with Lloyds on the personal guarantees, he would support us publicly. The details of any benefit to him would have to remain private. He wanted us to succeed, so he said, but would still 'protect his interest' by looking at other possible deals in case 'anything should happen'. We were reassured that we should not worry about that. The money was to be paid over a three- to four-year period, some funded out of transfer deals as and when they occurred. Mark had emphasised that Norman was unsure whether or not he should try to buy the club or just let it go. He had convinced him that the latter was preferable.

We had stubbornly refused to recognise the need for professional help. Now the project was too large. We would need finance.

Without a bean to our own names, what bank would support our deal? We needed credibility to lend foundation to our plans. Lester Aldridge, with thirty partners, is the foremost commercial practice this side of the New Forest. It dominates Dorset but has a national and international client base. They were the only local legal option. We needed accountants too. Grant Thornton were well known to me as clients; they also had small-business expertise and local offices that could give us the protection of a reputable voice of approval for our plans.

It was strange going to an office as a client. I'd never done it before; waiting in reception, being shown into the lift and taken up to the boardroom with its views of the ocean and Purbeck Hills beyond. With most of the partners having City experience, Lester Aldridge were adamant they could give us the advice we needed in raising the money we needed *legally*. That was the first time I met Kevin Heath and Malcolm Niekirk, now my colleagues. Malcolm would give us the insolvency experience, Kevin would cover the banking litigation angle. They would be our rocks, our objectivity. Writing this now it is funny how things have come full circle. Were it not for this story I would still be working in London – I would not work in Bournemouth and Malcolm, Kevin and I would not now be colleagues embarked on our crusade to advise clubs in similar straitened circumstances.

Lester Aldridge would handle all drafting and negotiating of the details of the various agreements we would now have to put in place with the different creditors. Grant Thornton would back up our business plan, the bid that we would make to Alan Lewis and the prospectus. Alan knew we wanted to use our money to buy the club. To help raise funds Southampton had agreed to play a friendly. Late on that Friday afternoon I completed and handed over to Alan our bid of £800,000 to buy the club from him. It set out in detail the way in which we believed the club would operate. The staff we would appoint and the costs involved in doing so. He was polite and courteous but in his eyes I could see that the figures might not be enough. Anyway, we had a big game that night.

Normally, a fixture like that might attract three or four thousand.

If we could persuade Ted, even at his age, to put on his boots once more in Bournemouth colours, who knows what kind of crowd might attend? I had spoken to Mel about the possibility and he had no concerns about him being named. Dads who had watched the maestro now brought their kids to see their hero play, albeit for only eight minutes. We won, but Ted wanted to know what he could do for me. I was slightly embarrassed, but asked if he would turn out for Kinson Reserves at Muscliffe recreation ground on Saturday. It was about time I put my boots back on. I think he was a little worried about being chopped down from behind but readily agreed. A man who, by modern standards, would be worth millions of pounds, playing at real grassroots level. Real community football. Having almost scored in front of 9,000 the night before, now before 150 he was given the utmost respect. With just a few flicks and a tremendous shot against the bar the magic was still there. By Sunday he was gone, back to Canada, leaving a legacy of renewed hope.

Then, quite suddenly, all that optimism evaporated. We knew we needed to bridge losses. Now the bank wanted interest paid on the sums owed to it. Our offer was rejected out of hand. They wanted all their money back. The bank had put the receiver in, said debts were frozen, but now would not deal with us unless we had Norman Hayward on side co-operating with the payment of his guarantees in full. Where their legal manoeuvres had failed they now wanted us to succeed. I was furious. The news came as we were about to complete a 3–0 drubbing of FA Cup semi-finalists Chesterfield. What was the point in putting the onus on us to try to sort out Hayward's guarantees and persuade him to pay when there was virtually no chance of that happening? All of a sudden, a simple step to agree a price with Lloyds was not what they were looking for – they wanted everything wrapped up and sorted at once. To me, it appeared almost an impossible situation. Within minutes of the game finishing, I went on Radio Solent to express my anger. The bank's demand had in my view sounded the death knell for the club. Alan felt our offer was too low and didn't reflect the potential development value of the ground. This was nonsense.

Their own reports suggested it was worth only £500,000, and they had previously indicated that £800,000 would have been acceptable. Now they wanted the whole £2.35 million. My words were clear and concise and aimed at the bank, who appeared to be giving us no hope whatsoever. With no other offers on the table and the deadline gone, I could not believe Lloyds would risk the deal with possibly fatal consequences for the club. Lloyds had always maintained that they were immune to whatever the community might think. Two days later I had a call from a partner of some seniority in our firm. He and a colleague had been at a presentation the day before, pitching for work from Lloyds Bank. It had been suggested that one Trevor Watkins should not carry on making such comments.

I ushered Hayward into the car park. He knew what the bank could be like. He would settle for £265,000 on his debenture – a reduction of £100,000 – if we sorted out the guarantees for him. 'I can't do fairer than that, mush,' he said.

I needed a break. Harry Redknapp had been very firm in trying to entice me to come to see a West Ham game. He is, without doubt, a very generous and exceptional man who makes every effort to make you feel relaxed and welcome when speaking with him. I can be shy – believe it or not – and am wary of taking up offers made, but the prospect of going to see Chelsea play at West Ham was one not to be turned down. Mel and I met at the ground. I found myself privileged to be in a lounge full of luminaries at Upton Park, all of whom really wanted to speak to Mel to find out his opinion of what was going on. Worried about me, he had given me his ticket to the directors' box and gone to stand behind the goal. Here I was, an ordinary fan, in the directors' box. Stranger still, I was called to sit at one of the press tables to do an interview on Talk Radio as the crowd filed in. The programme that night asked whether Rio Ferdinand, who had played for us on loan, was about to begin a career that would rank alongside the great players of West Ham's past. In goal that night for Chelsea was Nick Colgan, who as fate would have it, would become one of the signings that we made. The game was a thriller, West Ham winning, through an injury-time goal, 3–2. To sit downstairs with Harry, Mel and Frank Lampard, and see Ruud Gullit drifting by, made it a very special evening. They were perfect hosts, dropping me at my hotel in town as they sped home to Bournemouth.

The bank needed us and we needed them. We were the ones they wanted to put a deal together. If they were serious about wanting to secure the £2.35 million they were owed, there was no way we would be able to do so without some form of financing. The town would not raise anywhere near that sum. We would have to persuade them to lend us the money to pay them to allow us to buy the club! None of us had the assets to give personal guarantees. 20 March was close upon us. Nothing had particularly changed since the previous winding-up application. There was precious little anybody could add to try to persuade the judge for further time to sort the club out. As a trust we took the lead on the next application. What I needed was creditors to say they wanted us to have more time and to tell the court that.

There was a diverse range of other creditors, from the landladies who had looked after youth players and the BP garage that allowed us to have petrol, to the drain-keeper who had attended each week. If the club were sold, in the normal order of things, the bank would have first call on any money. Secondly, the Inland Revenue and Customs and Excise, Norm and the other creditors effectively came last. I explained what Norm had demanded and that the other directors had agreed to waive their debts. Would those who were to get nothing be prepared to swallow Norm getting most of his money back? If not, how much it was all going to cost? If the bottom rung got 100 per cent then all above would want that too – amounting to an impossible £5 million. Something had to give.

CHAPTER 8

Favourite Friends

The team had been performing heroics. We had gone to the New Den, Millwall's cold, clinical stadium, for the battle of the clubs in receivership and, thanks to a fine goal by John Bailey, 572 supporters and many more in the main stand went home extremely happy as we dented the promotion aspirations of the team lying third in the table. It was another victory in what was becoming a very successful period under the guidance of Alan Lewis as receiver. The following week we picked up another point, a 1–1 draw at home to York City, with young David Town scoring again. It was more like kick-boxing than football – most of the game had been played with ten men on each side – but it was a fair result, and was the first goal conceded in more than nine hours of football.

Even though we had not as yet bought the club, let alone agreed terms, Alan had kept us informed about offers coming in, allowing us to play a role in consultation with the manager about team affairs. Alan felt that as we were the only clear bidders we should work on contract negotiations with players. That meant my working with Mel, the manager – me, a fan! The Football League rules dictate that, after the third Thursday in March, no players can be transferred between clubs and perform for other clubs that season. Many will also use this deadline day to negotiate with players going out of contract in the summer, either to get them signed up or to cash in by selling them if at all possible. Any club in financial difficulty is going to be the subject of transfer speculation. Having said that, there were very few firm expressions of interest for our players and none that could be taken seriously: offers of £100–150,000 for Matt Holland and Ian Cox, players worth far in excess of that. The contracts of three players, Fletcher, Town and Rawlinson, were up in June.

As we worked together on the players' deals, Mel and I were probably weighing each other up, neither of us at that time knowing the other at all well. Mel advised me on the length of the contracts and the level of wages we should offer, and the talks went well. The players happily re-signed – a powerful commitment to the club and their faith in its future.

Until that time I had little day-to-day involvement with him apart from witnessing his memorable contribution on stage that night at the Winter Gardens. He is a quiet man, dignified and with a deep passion for the club for which he had played years earlier. He has a profound knowledge of football and of players and is widely respected throughout the game. He lives and breathes football, watching on TV, travelling thousands of miles a year to look at players, making notes and reading reports. Because of his utter commitment to the club his family life is inevitably entwined with football. There is no escape from it at the end of a season; during those few short weeks of the close season there is no time to relax on a beach – all thoughts go towards planning for the new season ahead.

Since those days Mel has been a great support to me, helping me come to terms with all that goes with my position as chairman. We have gradually built up mutual trust and loyalty. It is a balanced relationship – he benefits from my strength as a negotiator (I do it for a living!) while he patiently made generous allowance for my weakness, my lack of football knowledge. His good humour and optimism helped keep me sane in those difficult months when we were in the throes of the takeover battle. We realised that the relationship between manager and chairman – the public face of the club – would be crucial. With that weight of responsibility there needs to be harmony, unity and understanding. The fans and the media will ask us both the same question and scrutinise the answer for any difference of opinion.

He has taught me many things but above all that I know nothing about football! With our knowledge and experience at polar opposites, there was much scope for misunderstanding. How to react to suggestions of a player sale, to deal with a player making a direct request to me, to know when (and when not) to go into the dressing room. All situations that if handled clumsily have an impact on the manager's job of running the team, affecting morale and team spirit. I have learnt to interpret the looks of the manager!

Ken Dando and I were very conscious of our growing public personae. It was becoming more commonplace to be recognised in the street. At the same time, my ordinary responsibilities at work were continuing – none of my three major cases was near to being settled – and my days were becoming longer. Not wishing to lose my job nor let the cause down, it was home life that suffered. We were still trying to pin Norman down to his demands. Despite our 'understanding' it was difficult to get him to agree to it in writing. He had now offered his services as an 'agent' to buy and sell players on the club's behalf on a commission arrangement, while also asking that in deference to his late wife the main stand be renamed in her honour and for a guarantee that no former directors would be on the new board.

As each game had gone by, the strength and character of the team had become more impressive. Of eleven games, we had won five, drawn four and lost only two, conceding four goals. We arrived at Watford, a team with promotion ambitions, on 29 March. Yet again a terrific display and a goal from Ian Cox brought about victory, ensuring the team moved up towards mid-table security.

I spent that weekend compiling all the background material for our business plan and the cashflow forecast. Designing the corporate image, looking at what needed to be done to make the ground more comfortable, who was to be able to go into a boardroom – indeed, whether we needed to have one – how to establish our credibility, what the management structure was going to be . . . there were so many things to consider.

We were building for the long-term future. What was of more immediate concern was that Alan had received a further bid for the club. It certainly had not come from Norm, given that Pack still appeared to be continuing to work behind the scenes to put together his own bid (as he had been doing for almost a year). I believed the bid had come from Mel Bush. I had tired of making phone calls that were not returned by him. Eventually I had my second prolonged conversation with him. He was none too complimentary about our having bid so much for the club. In his view, it would be better if the club went under, as he did not believe the League would carry out its threat to expel us. He was confident that their ruling that a club which goes under loses all its players would not be enforced. I asked him whether he had spoken to the League. He hadn't. He said he consulted lawyers who told him to let the club slip, so he could then pick it up cheaply. He had not sought to make any deal with Norman. The commitment of someone with his resources would at least give us far greater scope for implementing our plans for reform on a much quicker time scale. I implored him to meet us and try to work something out, but he declined. Two bids on the table. I was determined that ours would prevail. Investors were growing, although not with the large hitters we wanted. Ordinary people were offering hard-earned money to register for shares. Contributions to the trust fund, however, had slowed down: only just over £110,000 had been raised. If Bush had been prepared to do a deal which would satisfy the League and not put the club at risk, then we might have been prepared to back him if our own funds fell short. We had to spike Bush's gun.

We needed to get a deal agreed, to get a clear run. I was getting fed up. April Fools' Day seemed an appropriate day to lock ourselves in an office in London to thrash out a deal with Lloyds Bank once and for all, forgetting Bush. Serious stuff. While on the radio, our new benefactor Elwin Aals (a neat anagram of Alan Lewis) was supposed to have demanded we change our nickname from the Cherries to the Cranberries, which he farmed, if we wanted his £100,000 contribution.

It was hot and stuffy. Alan Lewis, Colin Grant, Malcolm Niekirk (our lawyer), Andrew Kaye, Martin Jones and me sitting round a table in central London. Proposal and counter proposal, endless rewrites on the blackboard, but eventually a picture emerged in which the guarantees were shoved to one side. Lloyds accepted that was their battle not ours. They still wanted their full £1.4 million (the net amount of borrowings minus guarantees) paid. With further negotiation, the bank was prepared to accept only £150,000 in cash, the balance coming by way of a three-year loan at a fixed interest rate, on the understanding that a further £200,000 would be repaid in the first year of trading. We would have to meet the cost of the receivership, a figure to be agreed but likely to be about £350,000. The bank would keep the £50,000 owed to the club through the sale of Steve Jones from West Ham to Charlton. By the end of that meeting, we had the bones of the sale from Lloyds to the trust fund – all that was left was to raise the money.

In all this, no one wanted to concede ground. I decided to make one last point: 'How about giving you £1 million down?' Eventually Grant caught my eye. 'If you are as successful as I think you might be I would be selling myself short if I were to accept that offer,' he said. For £1.4 million, we would gain freehold ownership of the five acres comprising the pitch and stadium, all players, the name and goodwill, plus all assets at the ground. The interest rate was agreed at base plus one and a quarter per cent. Any money owed to the club on previous transfer deals was to go to Lloyds Bank to reduce the debt. We next needed to agree a deal about payments to all other creditors. The longer the deal was delayed, the greater the funds that would have to be found to meet ongoing losses and the cost of Alan's time.

The cost of professional assistance was running into tens of thousands of pounds, drafting and approving all the financial documents. The League softened too. We at last received a draft set of conditions from them for the saving of the club.

Importantly it was now prepared to allow us to transfer assets to a new company. We would have to provide a bond of at least £300,000 to show we could guarantee the fixtures for a season, and a further bond to secure our debt repayment obligations to the creditors. The League demanded that the deal for all creditors was fully disclosed, with 'clean hands'. There were twenty-one conditions in all – non-involvement of past directors, credibility of future directors, a right to veto appointments, a list of intended shareholders – all to be compiled with before we would get final consent. The hurdles in the way seemed like mountains to be climbed. Above all, they still wanted a separate meeting and vote of all creditors and shareholders of the old company to approve the deal. That spelt problems.

We all left together on the train to Bournemouth. At last, we knew we could buy the assets, it was our deal if we could afford it. A terrific piece of news to announce on the pitch that night before the game, at home to Stockport County. Standing in the centre circle with flashbulbs going off all around, I was so proud of what had been achieved. There was lots of hard work left to do but it was a great blow to anyone else with designs on the club. Norman had been sitting in the stands; his face dropped as he heard what we had to say and he left hurriedly before kick-off.

Mel Bush was in Spain. Astounded to find we had become the preferred bidder, he phoned Alan during the game to ask how he could have done it. Once more he rejected our offer to work together. The euphoria of the fans was not, however, matched during the game, as we suffered another 0–0 draw. Our form continued to dip as we lost to Barry Fry's Peterborough and scraped a 2–2 draw at home to Gillingham. I cannot recall the details. The football had become secondary to the battle we were engaged in.

The next casualty in the quest to save money was Terry Lovell. Wages had to be reduced as the season was nearly over, protecting creditors should our plan to take the club over fall apart. Doing a deal with the bank was one thing, raising money another. Then there was working out exactly what we would have to do with the other £2.75 million of creditors, and how many demands the League would place on us. They had listed their twenty-one conditions. Now we would negotiate. By April, plans would normally be well ahead for the season to come. Who in their right mind would buy a season ticket for a club that might not even be in business next year? As well as planning the takeover, there was the question of running the business. Still Martin had done nothing on the prospectus, so the task fell to the rest of us to write it, to draw up a brochure for corporate clients, a season ticket leaflet and price guide. We would need a full Health and Safety manual, an employees' handbook, new contracts of employment, a complete reworking of all accounting practices. We knew that the Inland Revenue and Customs and Excise would demand (and we would want) that we be squeaky clean and have our accounts in working order. And I was still trying desperately to prepare projections for how the business might perform the following year, trying reasonably to show a profit to avoid having to provide any bonds – we just would not have the money to do so.

We had invited people to subscribe for documents with an indication of investment levels. By mid-April our list of interested parties included Brian Willis and Norman Hayward, each of whom wanted a copy of the prospectus, although somehow I did not believe it was for the purposes of investing with us. The rough and ready figures told us that we probably had £200,000 from two individuals, Geoffrey and Harry, the likelihood of an additional £200,000 from others, plus trust fund money of approximately £120,000, which, on our calculations, would evaporate before the end of May. It had to be hoped there would be more on top. The prospectus was prepared on the basis that a minimum of £750,000 would be raised. The document was a *tour de force*. Even though those who were looking to buy shares were all die-hard fans, we still had to verify every single fact in the fifty-page document. Even that Ted MacDougall was once a goalscoring hero of the club and had scored nine against Margate!

It was somewhat ironic that the last but one home game of the season should be against Gillingham. An unfashionable club from Kent, but one where Paul Scally and his pop singer wife would always give us a warm welcome. Apparently in recent times a close friend of Norm, he had rescued Gillingham a few years before and now found himself on the board of the Football League, deliberating on our fate. He had taken our previous manager, Tony Pulis, to run team affairs at the Priestfield Stadium. Norm and Roy Pack had visited Scally recently, no doubt looking to try to get the League to prevent us from doing as we intended. Alan had wryly observed the resulting heated exchange.

I spoke to each of the potential investors personally, persuading, chatting, asking for money. They were fully aware this was a paper transaction in something that might well prove to be a lost cause. Yet in the background, Roy Pack was still beavering away. God knows what he was doing. We just tried to focus on what we had to do.

CHAPTER 9

Eighteen Minutes

I had gone through the League's conditions one by one. They wanted 'football' creditors paid in full. Penniless, the club had paid December's wages by borrowing £65,000 from the Professional Footballers' Association. The Football League wanted us to pay back what we owed them. Until then, we would not be able to sign any new players, even though we could sell them. I spoke to Mick McGuire at the PFA and took the chance to build bridges and learn a bit more about contracts. Players are paid fifty-two weeks a year. A weekly wage is basic. Some get a lump sum paid over the length of the contract too (a signing-on fee). Most get appearance fees, maybe about £100 a game or a week in our league, but as much as £3,000, £4,000 or £5,000 a game in the Premier League. Then there are extras – win bonuses, cars, accommodation, relocation, a share in transfer fee, and, of course, money to agents!

Mick explained to me how most clubs were operating in our division. Northampton Town, for example, were not at that time paying signing-on fees. The average wage in the second division was £600 a week with extras such as appearance fees for those clubs keen to retain particular players. Our wage bill fell within the middle to upper part of the table. Although that surprised me, it was not encouraging. We faced competition to keep our players and clearly we were having difficulty balancing the books.

How much do you charge for entry to a game? What principles do you apply? As a supporter, I wanted to see value for money. I had been irritated no end when buying my season ticket each year that I only received a miserable 13 per cent discount for investing my money up front. Effectively, this would mean I would gain free entry to three home League games. It seemed nonsensical not to allow season ticket holders into at least some friendlies. We knew prices would have to go up considerably, although perhaps in stages. From our enquiries, we found we were one of the cheapest clubs in the League for watching football, but we recognised we could not suddenly hike the prices up to levels other clubs charged. So we hit on the idea of categorising games much as Premier League teams did. That would allow us the flexibility to put a higher gate price on the premium games while reducing it for poorly attended games such as the last Saturday before Christmas or weekday nights in cold months during the winter. We also introduced a family season ticket, and the seats which lacked the best vantage points were considerably cheaper. Slowly a working vision came together.

Within days of having gained another point, against Wycombe Wanderers, we had our victory. We were able, after hours of toil, to send out letters to investors who had made their formal registration with a prospectus. We were, at least, able to start preparing the draft contract to buy the assets from Alan Lewis. The close season (i.e. no income) loomed, so we searched desperately for worthy opponents to give us an end-of-season friendly (and friendlies before the next season) to generate further income. For years Mel Machin had been friendly with Alex Ferguson, who had been constantly supportive. The contrast between our two clubs could not have been greater: Manchester United were a powerhouse on the pitch and a huge commercial venture off it. I figured they sold more shirts in their club shop in one day than we might do in a year. They had no need to play us, but Alex promised Mel he would send a team down pre-season. Club secretary Keith MacAlister wrote to them to seek confirmation of this, and the game was set for the Friday before the Charity Shield.

It was finally one of our old friends, Jimmy Quinn, manager at Reading, who agreed to bring a side down to play us on the

Wednesday following the end of the season. With only one further home game, against Wrexham, to come, this was another boost, another lifeline. Every day the need to rely further on outside professional help became greater. Meanwhile, we still had to contend with Roy Pack and his hired AFC Bournemouth Metro in which Hammond had driven him to Plymouth for a reserve/youth team game. He had expressed keen interest in their set-up, looking to reproduce it at 'our' club. Pack was seemingly unaware of the private discussions we'd had with Brian and Norm. It was one of those weeks in which he had told Brian, who had told Ken (a familiar chain) that the Fraud Squad was about to descend yet again on Dean Court.

After the journey to Wycombe – another chance to look at a modern stadium – we were down to our last two games. Mid-table respectability meant my mind was elsewhere. How to create a structure with sufficient staff in place but without high costs was taxing me no end. We knew the staff who were already employed would be a part of any deal and a coordinator was required who could command respect yet wield authority. I had grown up with Andrew Dawson, having met him at Bournemouth School when I was fourteen. Our adventures when we were young were the basis for our friendship: a summer on the Costa Brava, a voyage of discovery. I had always thought my other life might have been as a travel organiser. It was the summer when Frankie went to Hollywood and we were mad enough to play an hour and a half of football against the local waiters in ninety-degree heat. He had forged a career as an accountant, was a keen sportsman and good with people. He was one I had in mind for the coordinating role, although I realised that as an old friend I could not play a full part in his selection.

We would need more revenue than the uncertain gate receipts could provide. We had to revamp the lottery department, for it was almost non-existent. That was the future. As of now the kitty was down to £80,000. We had already given Alan Lewis £50,000. He wanted another £25,000 to cover the wages for April. In three months, over £60,000 of bank interest had accrued and a trading deficit of £110,000 run up (£500,000 a year), even though costs had been cut dramatically. The League still wanted creditors and shareholders of the old company to approve the deal at a meeting. They were sticking to company law, insisting it was proposed and recommended by the directors of the old company – Hayward, Willis and Pack.

I figured we were on course to raise only about £500–550,000. Ideally, we needed a bigger player but bar Geoffrey and Harry there were none. It seemed best to approach Mel Bush again and try to get him to listen now that we were in the box seat, but he still would not join us. I spoke to him on a couple of occasions leading up to our final home game on 26 April but got nowhere, although the conversations were cordial and respectful. That game against Wrexham came on a wonderfully warm April afternoon and, as I left home, I had an unnerving feeling that it might be for the last time. We played well and won, denting Wrexham's aspirations of promotion – something we had become good at since the receiver was appointed.

I was in no hurry to leave. There was only the sound of the silence and the sprinklers on the pitch. The whole afternoon had been tinged with the seeming inevitability that this was the last game. I had always tried to be frank throughout the months of fundraising and, when Radio Solent had suggested a question and answer session from the supporters' club live before the game, had been very willing to agree to that. For the first twenty minutes it was a positive affair, or rather an affair of positive bravado. Then, rising up at the back, the crowd parted and there was Mel Bush, confronting us live on air. He implied that no one had seen fit to contact him to discuss our plans for the future, and now demanded to know our plans and our backers. That latter question was the most popular, but one to which I carefully refused to divulge the answer. He came not as a man who had written a blank cheque to save a club, but one who picked holes in those who had little they could give. As someone who always looks for the good side in human nature, I was surprised that anybody should keep on thinking we were in this for personal gain. We had all put our businesses at risk, our careers in jeopardy.

Our final game of the season took us to Plymouth, who had been having problems of their own. They were just above the relegation zone and had a chairman, Dan McCauley, who had banned the local newspaper reporter from the ground (he now watched from a crane) and become a target for abuse from the fans. For this last game, everyone turned out: the trust fund members, Alan Lewis, Norm and Brian, all sitting in the same row. The game itself was not particularly interesting – yet another goalless draw – but the off-the-field antics were. On the motorway on the way down, Andrew Kaye and I found ourselves trying to overtake a Transit van. It was full of Bournemouth supporters who, in the fashion of fans everywhere, jeered and abused us before, with looks of horror, recognising us and giving us a salute, waving us past. Rather than engage in pre-match hospitality, Andrew and I went on to the terraces in jacket and tie, offering as much hope as we could.

The first half was undistinguished, and it was bloody cold. Desperate for a hot cup of tea, Alan suggested that Andrew, Ken and I should go into the Plymouth boardroom, which he reckoned was five times as big as any other he had seen and had very few people inside. Ken had known Brian and Norm for some considerable time, so we let him lead the way in. He had reached the far side of the room when suddenly a voice bellowed out: 'Who the hell are you? Get out of here!' It was McCauley, that benevolent, kind, silver-haired chairman. We froze. Alan attempted some diplomacy. The implication was that, as potential new owners entrusted with the care of the club, McCauley should grant us due hospitality.

He was having none of that and we were man-handled out of the room as he remarked, turning to Norm and Brian, 'We have friends in here and you are not welcome.' Throughout the second half the vast majority joined in the cries of 'If you all hate McCauley clap your hands'. Once the game had finished, this side-show continued, with lumps of turf thrown at him while endless presentations were made for player of the year, barman of the year, steward of the year, car park attendant of the year.

The two headlines in our local paper that week, 'Pathetic Pilgrims' and 'Red card for trust chiefs', summed it up. Another draw at the end of a season in which we had improved our points tally, finishing with sixty in sixteenth place. This had been our 3,000th League game and, with luck, would not be our last. Fittingly, on the journey home, we were sped on our way by the occupants of the Transit van – not to another game but, perhaps, survival.

Norm and Brian were becoming something of a double act in my everyday life. Ken and I met them at the Carlton Hotel on 5 May and made it clear that either somebody had to give ground or the club would go out of business. Any deal presented by them as directors of the old company which materially benefited them was likely to be overruled. The other creditors at the meeting would be most upset that Norm and Brian had been given preferential treatment for no good reason other than that they believed they had done enough for the club in the past. What was to be done?

Brian thought quite simply that everything could be put in a letter. We then had to endure the usual quizzing of who was involved in our investment scheme and where they might be (for information, naturally, not for the purposes of trying to persuade those investors to pull out of the trust). The suggestion followed that we could then lean on certain investors to make further money available. Another helpful suggestion was that if we were to sell a player, it would be reasonably easy to engineer the deal so that certain money might be made available. Ken and I discounted both theories.

Why did Brian and Norm believe they should be treated differently? The implication was that we needed them. Neither was prepared to budge from his demands. With an element of lost innocence, they explained that having been led to believe this amount would come to them, they saw no reason to forgo it merely because others might be upset. We were left with the agreement that the proposal would give them £600,000 out of the £775,000 I calculated we could afford to pay over ten years.

To come straight out of that meeting did not put us in the right frame of mind for the end of season dance, where we had booked Peter Osgood, the former Chelsea star, to give a speech, and an up-and-coming comedian to do all the jokes (his planned blue routine had to be cleaned up in deference to the women and children). The following evening almost 3,000 supporters turned out for our friendly against Reading – another £20,000 in the bank bought us a little more time. Goodness knows, we would just pay May's wages but there would be none in June. I had the prospect of a four-day trial in the High Court looming the following week. It was fair to say my tolerance level for the complications of court procedure and the legal system had been reduced to its lowest level. The hours of getting home from London at seven and straight out to a trust meeting till midnight, were taking their toll.

We gave Norm and Brian ultimatums in writing. If the club were not to be wound up on 15 May, they would have to support our deal in every respect if they drafted their demands as they wished. Norm would receive £565,000 and Brian £30,000. The balance, £180,000, would be distributed between the rest of the creditors. If they didn't like it, they risked getting nothing.

So much had happened since the previous winding-up application that I could not believe a court would now put us out of business. The judge had, however, declared then that that was the only extension he would grant. We had failed to complete the rescue package within the allotted time, but that was not the fault of any party. Thankfully, this time we had a different judge and that instead of merely not opposing our application for yet more time, the Inland Revenue and Customs and Excise were actually coming out and supporting us. In turn, Norm and Brian also had their solicitor write confirming their support for an adjournment.

For the first time in months Pack got in touch. Perhaps he feared we might actually carry out our takeover for the benefit of the town. I had deliberately avoided any contact with him, knowing that any conversation would usually be prolonged and a complete waste of time. On this occasion, curious as to what he wanted, I picked up the telephone and heard him offer us his help, he wanted to be a friend and ensure we were successful. He explained how his wisdom had grown over the months and that he had information which might be of great use to us. I thanked him, cautious as to his motives.

The Conservatives had, by now, been ousted from power. Before the General Election, we as a football club had been courted by all candidates in the area. Indeed, the Labour candidate for Bournemouth East had suddenly donned a club jersey and asked if she might take penalties at half-time. David Atkinson, the Tory incumbent, had been returned. I had been unable to give anything like the help I wished to my own ward in Christchurch. This had, however, been the only place in the country where the Conservatives had regained a seat. My political aspirations had probably been the first victim of the demands of the football club, the first of many.

Another day, another court hearing. Like the prisoner waiting for a volt to surge through the electric chair, the blindfold was removed and we were led back with a further reprieve. One more month and this time it was final. Alan was now facing the prospect of having to pay the wages for May and I knew that paying £50,000 to him would effectively wipe out all of the trust money, leaving a balance that would just about cover the costs we had run up. The time was coming close when we might have to call it a day. There was no hope of further incoming sums that could be used readily. I couldn't touch money sent in for shares, it was only there once the deal was done. If we could survive until the creditors voted for the deal on offer, we could then unlock the investors' money.

Looking ahead to when we owned the club, I figured we might just be able to get away with working capital of between £120,000 and £170,000, even though that might necessitate an immediate sale of a player. For now, however, our liabilities just about matched our assets in the trust, without any recourse to the funds being held for those who wished to invest in shares. I knew the club could still go under even though the likelihood was that a deal was almost done.

Malcolm finalised the proposal that was to be put to creditors and shareholders. By law a 75 per cent majority vote was required by creditors, and 50 per cent required by shareholders. That was what made it so damn difficult. Even though it gave most money to Norm and Brian, I hoped we would be able to convince people that saving the club was paramount and vote in favour. There was doubt about the Crown creditors and football creditors, whom we could not control or influence in any way. We needed that majority vote or we were finished. We needed it completed and lodged at court by 3.30 p.m. on a Friday. Otherwise there would be no time to call the meeting and have a vote before the League decided our fate for us.

Tiredness got the better of me that Friday morning. I needed to be in the office early, but did not leave the house until 6.20 a.m. There, under one of the bushes, were two baby blue tits. One was cold, beak up as if fast asleep, but dead. Beside him was probably his brother, alive, looking forlorn, not quite knowing what to do with himself. Mandy took him into the house, where he was to take up residence in one of my trainers. He died later, too. It all seemed so much more worthwhile trying to save his life. I had lost touch with my ordinary life in trying to do my bit to save the club and now it could go under, thanks to the whims and machinations of those who, with one flourish of a pen, could have written a cheque to end the suffering.

Ken was at Brian's offices at 9 a.m. as arranged. Norm was not. He had decided he could not make the meeting until 12.30. To validate the proposal document, it needed to be in the post that day and also to be lodged at the High Court in London by 3.30 p.m. We were unsure whether a faxed copy would suffice, and instead had a bike ready to go to London. Even though everyone had legal advice, Norm turned up at the offices at noon, read the document and said he did not agree with it. Pack told him to leave. He wanted the payments upped, to ensure he got more money straight away.

Ken exploded and, screaming at them, told them they had bloody well better get a move on, otherwise there would be nothing left to fight about. There and then, just before 12.30 p.m., Norm and Brian, with Pack in attendance, agreed to the proposal. No one could now stop the papers going to the High Court. We got them there with just eighteen minutes to spare. By early evening, all notices were being sent out to the creditors and shareholders who would decide the future of the club. That the proposal gave nearly everything to Norm and Brian was exactly as those two wanted it. The creditors and shareholders would then decide if that would be appropriate. For me, there was no time to celebrate, but merely to turn my mind to the raising of finance and the preparation for the meeting on 9 June. Each recipient would also get a letter from the trust fund, imploring them to return their vote for the chairman to use in the way he saw fit.

Dean Court was quiet now, the players on their holidays not knowing if they would have jobs to come back to. No great interest is shown in the commercial side until the players report back in July. For Brian Perry, travel agent and tour operator, to make an appearance with 'guests' on the basis that he would like to see some of our boxes was odd indeed. He proclaimed the trust fund was doomed to fail, which suggested he knew something we ought to know. Having heard how he had been forced out of pocket by the outrageous behaviour of the former chairman, as he put it, I contacted him. Taking a wild guess, I put it to him that whoever he was showing around was no doubt trying to put together a bid to buy the club. He agreed and said he understood it was up for grabs to the highest bidder. Surely we knew that all along Pack had been planning an alternative takeover bid. That was why he had been so quiet. 'But, Brian,' I said, 'only we have the contract to buy the club.'

CHAPTER 10

Sundays Were Made for This

Andrew Kaye and I had an appointment at Chase Manhattan, whose European headquarters are located in Bournemouth. They were keen to involve themselves in what we were doing for the new season. As we pulled into the car park on the Friday, 6 June, before the meeting, Brian Perry rang me on my mobile, anxiously enquiring whether I had heard from his connections. He again questioned whether we had an option to buy the assets of the club, because Pack was still leading him to believe that that was not the case. I truthfully explained that we did and also had the funding in place – slightly less true. Within minutes the phone rang again and Paul May introduced himself. He had been dealing with Roy Pack for a couple of weeks in trying to sort out a takeover of AFC Bournemouth. I remarked that we already had an option to purchase the assets and no one could upset that. I asked what, particularly, he was interested in and he confirmed that it was the building of the new stadium. I pointed out to him that unless the proposal was approved on Monday at the creditors' meeting, there would be no football club and no stadium to be built. He said that he believed a new deal was to be put forward to the creditors at the meeting and that the trust fund was to stand aside. I again told him that it was impossible. If he would care to check the documentation, he should be dealing with us rather than with anybody else if he had a genuine interest in working towards a new facility. He seemed shaken by what I was saying. Every retort was a question hesitantly delivered as the carefully laid plans he had been making collapsed like a sandcastle cut from underneath by the next oncoming wave.

I popped into the supporters' club that night. There was the usual group of ten or twelve, but this time Martin was there with Ken Gardner. I asked Ken what he knew of the consortium and he suggested that there was a meeting to take place at the Berkeley Hotel over the weekend and that he would keep me informed. In his view, Pack was not particularly dangerous but ought to be taken into account. If he believed there was anything we needed to know that might interrupt our plans to save the club, he would contact us. He assured both of us that despite the extreme personal pressure being brought to bear on him by the Pack camp, he would stand firm and always do what was best for the football club. Regular phone calls during the course of the weekend, particularly from John Hiscock, Martin Jones and Geoffrey Hayward, reassured Ken that he would always be welcome at Dean Court.

All of the trust fund members came round to my house on the Saturday morning. This time we were looking at plans for the new stadium as well as all the operational and logistical arrangements for the forthcoming season. It was really quite exciting to be deflected from the true concerns over what would happen the following Monday. I didn't give this alternative bid a second thought. There was no way it was getting off the ground without the approval of the Football League, creditors and shareholders, and patently none of these had been canvassed. It was clear now that the Pack camp's primary aim was to let us do the leg work in the hope that they could then take this on and dump us. Maybe they thought that we were enabling the club to survive long enough so that they could finalise their bid. What they hadn't realised was that Monday was the conclusion of the end game.

I always hate killing time. Saturday afternoon was spent revising figures. Come the evening, Mandy and I took a drive out into the country beyond suburban Bournemouth. We are blessed with a grand array of beautiful landscapes – and a number of excellent pubs where you can eat well outside in the warmth of a June evening. Whether pubs at Sway, or Romsey, or Sopley, or for that longer journey, at Kingston, near Corfe Castle, we were spoilt for choice. But, no matter how I tried to distance myself in such pleasant surroundings, my mind turned to the gamble we had taken in trying to save the club and the dice that would need to be thrown and land the way we wanted on the Monday.

Sunday had not been a day of rest since 24 January. No matter my good intentions of getting fit, my love of food ensured that no matter how much exercise I took, my weight always seemed to stay the same. Popular rumour now has it that I was to have spent this day in lengthy meetings with lawyers. The truth was that throughout I had believed in openness. Of course, in any business, it is not possible to shout from the rooftops every single decision that is made or contemplated. Yet with the proviso that I was never to reveal the identity of any investor to save them from provocation and harassment, we answered as many questions as we could. I had a further two-and-a-half-hour meeting at the supporters' club. Martin Jones and I were supposed to be heading to London to meet a significant investor who, I had been led to believe by Martin, would provide the additional £100,000 that I thought we would still need to conclude the deal. All along we had to conceal the precarious state of our finance. Frantic phone calls backwards and forwards to the man we were to see eventually resulted in Martin admitting the meeting could not go ahead. By then it was gone two o'clock and Ken Gardner had appeared. He came bearing stories of how merchant bankers, accountants and lawyers were descending on the Berkeley Hotel in a last-ditch attempt by Pack to put together an alternative bid to frustrate the meeting the next day.

Interestingly, Ken did not believe that either Brian or Norman was fully aware of what was going on. In a moment of good humour, I had telephoned Brian the night before and left a message on his answerphone asking what the hell was going on with this preparation of alternative bids. It was not until early evening Sunday that he called me to say that he had no idea what I was on about. I trusted and believed him. He showed no awareness and promised that he would call me if he got any further information. A few minutes later, he told me that Pack was up to something, but it would not stop Brian backing the trust and the deal on the morrow. I also tried to get hold of Norman, but he was not at home. Eventually I spoke to his daughter. She sympathised with our having been caught in the middle of the dispute between the directors and I explained that we had done what we could. The proposal would go to the floor the following day but we could not control those creditors who had no particular allegiance to the club. She also feared the effect Pack was having on her father. I just asked her to convey my thanks to Norman for what he had done. Ultimately he had signed the proposal.

I took the extra time that day to look again at the figures and the money that we would need to complete the deal. With the knowledge that another significant investor was unlikely to come out of the woodwork, we were heavily reliant on the two we already had, plus a possible contribution from a third. We would not know the situation on that until at least the Tuesday. I took time to put in place an emergency meeting with investors, particularly the bigger players, for Monday evening. If the proposal put to the creditors was accepted, I knew we would have to act quickly and that would require further funds to be raised. If we couldn't do this through outside investors, we would have to call upon those who had already contributed to put more money in. We had the option to purchase. The club was ours for the taking. If we didn't raise sufficient money to do the deal then our option would lapse. I was concerned about the first three months of trading. If we could get through that period, I knew we would always be able to sell a player to fund any cash shortfall. The value of the players would go up once the club was out of receivership.

The story of the last supper has always had great meaning for me:

how those who had been through so much would spend one last night together knowing that tomorrow all they had worked for would reach its end. Whatever was to happen it would be a turning point, a new direction. All those on the trust fund had agreed that we should meet at 7.30 that Sunday evening to eat together, to relax, to share jokes, to reflect on the past and provide unity rather than each having to face a lonely evening. We invited Malcolm, our lawyer, to join us and forbade talk of the day to come. We ate curry and drank lager and laughed a lot. Then at nine o'clock my phone rang. It was Ken Gardner explaining that we really ought to go down to the Berkeley Hotel to see what was going on. He had, on good authority, found out that the alternative takeover was being hatched and, he thought, concluded, with all the advisers he had mentioned. Pack had told him this and he had stressed that the trust should be consulted by Pack.

Gardner claimed that Pack had tried to call me on four or five occasions over the last thirty-six hours but that no one had answered the phone and he had left a message on the answerphone. I said that we really had nothing to discuss and had no invitation. Thirty minutes passed before Ken called again. He had spoken with Pack and pleaded with us to go to the Berkeley as soon as possible.

By 9.30 on the Sunday evening we had all had just about enough of Pack over the last five months. We had time for Brian but were pretty fed up with Norman. We didn't know if either of them were there. Around the table there was great debate as to whether anybody should bother to go. We agreed that it was either all or none of us. If we went it was to be for a short while, to hear what they had to say and then leave. My dictaphone now took on a much more useful purpose. I suggested, and we all agreed, that Martin, who had kindly offered, should hold the dictaphone in his trouser pocket so that if there was any doubt at all over what was put to us we could use the tape as a bona fide record.

So, almost five months after I had first visited that hotel, we were back again now at 9.45 on a Sunday evening. It was much the same. We trooped into the reception area, where Ken Gardner, pipe in mouth, offered to buy drinks for everyone. A more properly attired gentleman came out through another door. Ken mentioned it was Paul May. With time ticking on, I wandered up to him and introduced myself, referring to our conversation a day or two before. I asked him how he had found the meeting. 'Bloody shambles, complete waste of time!' he exclaimed. I suggested that maybe he should have listened to what we had to say. He agreed and said that he would be happy to put his people in touch with us if that would be of interest. I said we were always eager to consider additions to our funding circle. He described Pack as completely off-beam. The alleged group of financial whizzkids, lawyers and merchant bankers were nowhere to be seen. He had had enough and was going. Pack had nothing left to offer.

No one bothered to to come out and meet us. Ken pointed to Pack's office and then to the doors to the left where he said the other members of the consortium were located. In we walked. Tables were arranged in a rectangular shape with a flip chart to one side, headed 'The Pack Plan'. There were lots of empty wine bottles on the table and, to the far side of the room, a group of five or six somewhat inebriated individuals. One or two sidled over and introduced themselves. One was an accountant. Another seemed to be along for the ride. One of the benefits of legal training is the ability to read quickly. No sooner had I looked at the flip chart and then read through the documents on the table, than this takeover was revealed for exactly what it was. This was a version of the proposal Pack had tried to persuade Lloyds Bank to agree to.

Sufficiently bolstered, I gave a summary to Malcolm, who by now thought it was time to go. Ken, still feeling there would be mileage in our meeting, went off to locate Pack and within minutes ushered us through. Leaving Ken Gardner outside, Ken Dando, Andy Noonan, Martin Jones, Andrew Kaye, John Hiscock, Malcolm Niekirk and I all trooped in to Pack's 'office'. Wearing a denim outfit, he was sprawled behind a desk in a bay window. To his left was Norman, resplendent in a daffodil yellow shirt and suntan. Channing, a director of Acheve, who had lent the club money, was sitting in a corner. I can also only recall one other chap being there. He was introduced as Paul Oughton, a partner in a firm of City solicitors. They all seemed to have had a drink or two bar Norman; Oughton, splayed in an armchair, pint glass in hand, appeared to be the worse for wear (or maybe just tired?) and had a beer-splattered blue T-shirt of the type we used to wear when we were kids. We rather pointedly asked what was the purpose of dragging us out at such a late hour. Oughton was very full of himself, confident in his opinions. His view was that we had significant problems with our bid and that unless we listened, everything would come crashing down. Pack tried his softly, softly approach. Explaining that the trust had been 'led by the nose' and that it was 'time for them to step aside', he claimed substantial backers were involved with him and Norman with a view to their taking over the club. Would it not be so much better if we were just to pass across all of our money to them so they could then use it as working capital once they had taken over the club?

Furthermore, would it not now be easier for us to reveal the identity of all those investors that we had lined up so that they could then approach them to establish whether they had the money they said they had? It was all rather audacious. It may even have appeared as basically reasonable. Norman was adamant that he needed to see proof that we had all of the money before he would allow the meeting to go ahead the next day. Pack then interjected that he was going to be at the meeting as a nominee acting on behalf of the Berkeley Hotel. He would be asking me particularly awkward questions that I would not be able to answer. To save me the embarrassment, he was prepared to sort everything out now. Malcolm seemed unperturbed.

Oughton started complaining about various breaches of company law. It was all rather pointless. Malcolm suggested that if they had nothing new to say we might as well go. That particularly irked Pack, who by now was getting quite excited. I mischievously asked if he felt done out of a job. Having read his original submission to Lloyds Bank, I wondered if he was prepared to acknowledge that he wanted to become chief executive. He said that Norman deserved to be able to come back as chairman because he was the only one who did anything for the club. When pressed, he would not confirm that he was to play any role, claiming, 'I'm here to do a job and when that job is done we will see what happens next.'

Andy Noonan decided that he had had enough and got up to go. Realising that our precarious hold on decorum was slipping, I decided to state that, unless there was anything new to be discussed, we were leaving as we had an early start the next day. This really did provoke an outburst (all on tape). Hayward shouted and screamed, frustration overtaking him as we turned to go. Pack suddenly got it into his head that one of us was wired, perhaps because we deliberately kept repeating the questions they asked before giving any answer. The man hadn't been able to give any details of figures, backers, lawyers, bankers, anything that would conclusively show there was some reasonable alternative. That was our cue to leave, led out by Martin, walking at a reasonable pace with Ken, Andy and the others following. I deliberately blocked Pack, trying to engage him in sensible conversation until I saw Martin was through the door.

Shambles? I don't know why we bothered. At least we were prepared to give everybody an opportunity to the end to make their views clear. And it confirmed Ken in his view that he must vote for our deal. Pulling out his crumpled voting paper he held it aloft and proclaimed the future of the club was in his hands. Heads spinning, hearts pounding, we all felt the same, but we had faced that together and now it was time for bed and rest in preparation for the momentous day ahead.

CHAPTER 11

On the 29th Day . . .

Monday morning was boiling hot. Lots of pure Colombian caffeine, a cold, tingly feeling in the hands and the need to be strong for what might be the performance of a lifetime. The aim? To guide the ship through the rocks to safety, wherever that might be. We had done our job, as agreed with Norman and Brian, to put forward their views but with our names attached. I truly hoped that everything would just go smoothly. I had already heard the early morning interviews live on the radio stations and now, just before nine o'clock the entrance to the Winter Gardens, bathed in glorious sunshine, was a media circus waiting for the acts to appear. Just as my whole involvement had started at the Berkeley Hotel and I had returned there the night before, so now we all went back to the scene of perhaps the most significant evening of the story so far – way back in January when the Winter Gardens was packed to the rafters. Yet again, it was the venue that would hold the key to saving the football club.

The day was to hinge on the performances of the main protagonists, all of whom were already around and about. Peter Hall (the overseeing accountant from Grant Thornton) arrived and asked that Malcolm, Ken Dando and I all be available to make submissions to the audience. Most of the creditors and the shareholders were passionate fans of AFC Bournemouth. They all wanted to play their part in a democratic process that they hoped would ensure its survival. Even the players had begun to appear with the manager. They came not because they understood the legal process but because they cared about the football club. It all made for great television but what they did was done out of caring and compassion. The creditors' meeting was to begin at 10 a.m. with the shareholders' meeting in the afternoon from 2 p.m.

The walk up on stage seemed a lot longer than it had been that night back in January. This time it was a great deal easier to see the faces in the crowds, but I chose to follow drama school advice and concentrate on a point in the distance where no one was sitting. My speech was very much geared to asking for the vote to go in favour of the proposal, because otherwise we would have no football club and no one would get any money. There were no questions and the promised bombardment from Oughton went undelivered. (The history of that particular side in what it threatened, and failed, to achieve had become quite commonplace.) Pack was nowhere to be seen. We were asked to remain while the vote was carried out. When Peter Hall invited comments before the vote, the Crown creditors revealed the biggest surprise. They said the deal was unfair and produced a set of modifications that they wished to make to the proposal. Everything was turned on its head, putting Norman and Brian back in the same position as all the other hundreds of unsecured creditors, ensuring there was an equal percentage pay-out according to how much was owed them. In turn, those creditors who ranked above the unsecured, such as the Crown creditors, would be certain to get their money first. After much reading into company law, I understood that this would be the usual way of dividing money and that all the Crown creditors were doing was seeking to re-establish the natural order. This did, however, completely wipe out the purpose of the proposal we had spent so many hours working out with Norm and his lawyers. It was put to a vote and carried; Norm was helpless.

Oughton looked as if his middle stump had been plucked out first ball. His client beside him looked distraught. Next his furious reaction led to an immediate adjournment, to allow Oughton a chance to regain his composure and consider his tactic. What he then demanded was a further forty-eight-hour period to consider what the Inland Revenue wanted. This was a non-starter with the imminent Football League meeting and their desire to have the matter resolved. Luckily, the League's financial controller Chris Griffin was there to confirm this.

When the meeting reconvened, the modification was again read out: 80 per cent in favour. Oughton asked for a detailed count – fair enough in the circumstances. The modification benefited all creditors save Norm and Brian and met with 80 per cent approval; leaving Norm, Brian, Acheve, Brian Perry and the Berkeley Hotel to oppose it. The mayhem we had feared had happened but not in the way we had predicted. I genuinely felt sorry for Norm and, more particularly, Brian, because if it had not been for Pack and the involvement of lawyer upon lawyer, it might never have come to this. What it did mean was that we had the creditors' vote in favour of a proposal. Oughton and Hayward left the meeting never to return.

Other members of the trust had popped in and out during the course of the morning. Now all we needed was a vote in favour by the shareholders. To block it Norm needed Ken on his side. Ken swung in just as the afternoon meeting was about to commence, pipe in mouth, delivering a wholehearted message of support for the trust. Perhaps it was his way of proving his independence and voice and that he was not shackled by the demands of Norman's agents. Vote he did, and vote in favour. By 4 p.m. we had what the League wanted, a completed takeover proposal ready to go, voted on by the shareholders and creditors. Amid scenes of jubilation, the TV crews descended for interviews. Already my mind had moved to meeting investors at seven o'clock and the residual threat that Pack might still try to worm an alternative bid in. As I had learned, the litigant can be dangerous, especially if he has funding at his disposal.

A quick flip to the Meridian TV studio and then on to a meeting of the whole of the trust committee and main investors. We were on the verge of success. We had raised about £400,000. Rather than ask everyone in the room how much more they might be prepared to put in, the question was: would people be prepared to find more if new investors were not forthcoming? To a man, they said yes. Geoffrey in particular kept repeating that too much had happened for us to give up now. Talking privately with him later, he was conscious that by agreeing to put in £100,000, his position was isolated. He asked to wait to see what was forthcoming from the others before looking to him to discuss what shortfall there might be, if any. Mel agreed to forgo an additional £15,000 that was owed to him under his contract and to take shares instead; three others put in £30,000 more between them; Phil Hordle, who had contacted me from Japan, had an extra £11,000; the group of international supporters put in a further £2,000; and Geoff Sharp, a businessman supporter from Nottingham, agreed to loan the club £20,000 for a year on an interest-free basis. Martin Jones was silent, his grand promises of being able to tap into some of the wealthiest people in the land had come to naught. He knew I was desperate for extra money. I went off to meet his Home Counties contact on a wing and a prayer. Without an extra £90,000 we could not do the deal and survive.

The person concerned was extremely decent, pleasant and charismatic, but within minutes of our meeting I knew that everything was not as Martin had outlined. I put it to him that I needed another £100,000 to give me the satisfaction that this deal would work. Without Martin's presence, I believe that money would have been forthcoming. This individual genuinely wanted to help, but for business reasons distrusted Martin. Of all the people involved, only Martin had been unable to match his promises – difficult though these were to achieve. I only wish he had admitted that he wasn't up to the task. There was no more money.

Yes, we could pay for the deal but had little working capital. My projections were showing that even with the money raised, it was going to be nip-and-tuck within a few months. Ken and I would be personally liable if everything came crashing down. I didn't want to throw good money after bad, even if we could attempt to flog a player as soon as we took over. I knew that I had, realistically, until midnight on 18 June to exercise the option to purchase. It would then lapse, throwing everything into confusion. Although we were projecting a recurring profit of around £100,000 on the year, that was for the end of May. Between now and then, I was sure the bank balance would fall below zero without an overdraft to cushion it. I did not sleep well that week. The *Echo* was still emphasising an allegedly new £2.5 million takeover deal. It fell for the sales pitch; any exploration of the reality behind this plan would have shown it to have had zero chance of succeeding. Probably unbeknown to Pack, the very people he was speaking to had no money of their own. What they had been trying to do was to find a financier prepared to give them money which they in turn could present as their own to Pack.

My first day-to-day experience of the Football League came with the chairmen's summer conference that took place in London four days after the creditors' vote. Alan, as the receiver, had the invitation, but suggested it would be good for me to go. We were not new boys quite yet, our fate still hung in the balance. The itinerary started with a black tie dinner, which seemed a daunting prospect; so we opted to arrive for the morning session. The first person I bumped into was Dan McCauley. Exchanging pleasantries, like a new kid at school I went into the hall where, I was to learn, not all the 72 League clubs were represented by their chairman, even though this was their summer conference. Much of the day was given over to reviews past and present, changes in the format of the Coca-Cola Cup, debates on the effects of Bosman (opening up freedom of contract for players over the age of twenty-four), changing of the headquarters of the Football League. Then there were the debates on the future of Brighton & Hove Albion and ourselves. Patience was thin on the ground.

The League had drawn up charts to show what would have happened had we been thrown out when we went into receivership and if our results were expunged now. It actually made a big difference to teams who finished in the top six and, indeed, to Crewe, who were promoted, who otherwise would not have been there at all. At the end of the meetings, Alan and I had a private audience with Chris Griffin and the League's lawyers who made it clear that it could not confirm our membership until the twenty-eight-day period during which any dissatisfied creditor could appeal had expired. The rumblings from the Pack camp were that they fully intended to make an appeal, but that they would leave it until the very last day to submit it, to cause maximum confusion and increase pressure on us to formulate a deal to clear them off. This was a straightforward but risky strategy. I guess they were working on the assumption that if we had already purchased the club (which we would have to have done to exercise the option) we would not want to risk having membership of the League turned down.

Our option expired the following Thursday. We needed to do the deal then or not at all. The time had come to return to those big players. Geoffrey's £100,000 was there. Others' contributions had suddenly been put in jeopardy. An independent financial adviser might regard it as madness putting £100,000 – or even £10,000 – into it. They are, after all, paid to give advice. Harry Redknapp could only put in £50,000, less than he had hoped to invest. We chose to accept Harry's contribution on a loan basis. Since then he has been wonderfully supportive, repeatedly declining our offers to repay it.

The end of the road came on 17 June 1997. A total of £540,000 had been raised, of which £140,000 from the town had gone in paying the receiver, lawyers and accountants. The loss of £50,000 from Harry dealt a significant blow to my view of whether we could finalise the deal. With one working day left to conclude it, I knew we would start experiencing cash flow difficulties within six to eight weeks without more funds. Sure, we would have Manchester United visiting, the influx of season ticket money, commercial sponsorship (insofar as we were able to achieve any at such a late stage), but all this would do would be to mask the cash deficiency and the inability to meet full receivership payments as they became due. Yes, I knew we could hold off paying certain bills, but I was not prepared to put

114

all the principles we had espoused at risk in the knowledge that I would have to barter with people soon after taking over. All the investors were good honest supporters. That they had come up with money didn't mean they had pots of it. I knew that the deal wouldn't work.

There was a certain relief of the kind one experiences when someone who has suffered a lengthy illness finally dies. A feeling that the struggle is over brings a certain peace before the distress and despair creeps in hours or days later. It somehow felt so much easier to turn and say the deal could not be done, to let the struggle for life slip away in the quiet of a close season. To try to make failure look like glorious defeat. Depressed, I knew I had to speak to others on the trust fund who might be around. I did not let on as to my conclusion, but asked if they would meet me at the supporters' club. For hours we sat on faded grey draylon seats holed by stubbed-out fag ends, playing with the figures. In our negotiations Lloyds had upped the price of the deal with an increased indemnity, £350,000 of receivership costs, but were taking only £150,000 as a down payment. I just did not see any flexibility, but they represented my only hope. If we were to create extra cash flow (and that in essence was what we needed) we had to reduce the price of the deal even further. If Lloyds accepted £100,000 down, we would save £50,000. Any saving on the indemnity, such as by including Steve Jones's transfer money, would save us at least another £25,000. As I left the club that evening I believed the dream was over, that AFC Bournemouth would not play again. With heavy heart and no peace of mind I climbed into the car and slowly drove away. I felt nauseous. The next day's dawn could bring the joy and pain of the previous six months to nothing.

The day had come. Within minutes Colin Grant was on the phone. His initial approach was to call a bluff. I think he assumed we were just playing poker. For the first time, he completely surprised me by immediately agreeing to reduce the down payment by £50,000 to £100,000 on condition that we did repay £200,000 in the first year of trading. He also agreed to count Steve Jones's money into the indemnity, so reducing our exposure there by £25,000. I had always understood that they were to give us an overdraft but again he refused. The only concession he would make was that if we were to deposit £250,000 in a separate account, we could have an overdraft for £250,000! At least I had the deal I sought. It was the one miracle I saw in the whole of that campaign. He asked if we then had a deal with which we could proceed and with great pleasure I confirmed that that was the case. Within the hour all the plans had been laid and I had notified the League that we were to complete the purchase and fully intended to start our season on 9 August – hey, the fixture list had been produced and we were in it. How could we disappoint by refusing to turn up for our first game, away to Northampton Town? That seemed appropriate, as they were the opposition who had given us so much advice on how they had dealt with their receivership a few years earlier.

To say Andrew Kaye was overjoyed was an understatement. We alerted the media and called a press conference for that afternoon. All of the signatories to the deal were ready. Word had got out of our announcement. That had spurred Pack to contact the League who still had to decide whether we had met their conditions. He let it generally be known that if anybody were to agree to complete the deal and allow the shareholding of the League to transfer to us, there would be trouble. No matter how much we were to debate that issue, we were not going to get the League's agreement to the whole affair yet. It was for me to make a decision in isolation as to whether or not we went ahead and purchased the assets. That within six weeks we might not have membership of the League to play in was on my head. Lawyers being lawyers, I was being advised of the risk in completing the deal with that uncertainty. I in return kept making the point that if we did not complete, there would be no club to worry about, anyway.

It was a calculated risk. The message I received from a majority of people I had spoken to at the chairmen's conference and, in particular, from David Sheepshanks, the chairman of the League as well as Ipswich Town, was that the plug could not possibly be pulled now. David had expressed his joy at our survival. Yet it was my decision, and was on my shoulders, to decide to take the risk, and I did not do so lightly. I did not mind that responsibility or the potentially fatal consequences. I knew that at Dean Court a large gathering of media and players was waiting for us to arrive. It took some considerable time to sign off all the documentation at our lawyer's offices. My strategy throughout – think up a couple of key quotes and build around it ad hoc – had worked for the most part, but now the BBC's presence was live. I needed to encapsulate for the supporters a sense of achievement.

There had been many obstacles put in our way to prevent this deal going through, I said. At last, though, I was pleased to announce that, 'Shortly after four o'clock this afternoon, the assets of AFC Bournemouth, the stand, the stadium, the name, the players, have all been transferred into the hands of the community club. The deal is complete and AFC Bournemouth has survived. We will be seeing you on 16 August at Dean Court against Wigan Athletic.' I said this with meaning and with honesty, despite the doubts in my mind. There was bubbly in abundance. Out we went on the South End terrace for the obligatory pictures of happiness, radiating across the papers the following day. I cannot believe now how joyous I looked. Front page news! All the planning came into effect. Season ticket leaflets, corporate ticket brochures, Junior Cherries plans – all were available to try to make up for lost time. We had to condense work that should have started back in April into the period between 19 June and our first pre-season friendly at home to Portsmouth on 15 July. And there was still much work that could not be done until we took control. For Bournemouth and Boscombe Athletic Community Football Club Ltd, we were in business. (Ironically, Mel Machin had hung on and on waiting for the deal to go through, but had eventually had to depart on holiday, missing the announcement.)

At the back of my mind was the concern that we could take money from people for tickets when there was still a risk that we would not start the new season. Conversely the more season tickets we sold, the better our chances of the League backing us. In private,

I stipulated that as much of the money as possible should be put to one side, so that if a decision was made to bar us from League competition, we should be able to return it.

The search was immediately on for a shirt sponsor as Frizzells had understandably pulled out. John Saunders at Seward Rover MG, a local franchise, was keen to be associated with our new business and signed a one-year deal. Patrick UK agreed a £60,000 shirt sponsorship deal over three years to provide all the first team strip.

My first and most important signing, however, was to ensure Mel Machin agreed to remain with the club. When one reads of hiring and firing, changes based on failure or success, one wonders how often people consider the need to have time to build, to impose a hallmark. Many of the past promises made to Mel had not come about and I was determined we would not let him down. His was a popular name to crop up whenever a managerial vacancy occurred elsewhere and yet he was prepared to commit his future to the club, on a three-year rolling contract. His assistant, John Williams, accepted a one-year deal. Likewise, Sean O'Driscoll (fourteen years with the club) was retained as youth team coach. I then had to deal with the Professional Footballers Association. It seemed somewhat ludicrous that they said we could sell players and yet not buy any for a decade. After lengthy negotiation, we reached an agreement, got the embargo lifted and Mel was able to make his first signing, one in keeping with our low profile: Justin Harrington, released by Leicester City on a free transfer. At £400 a week for a year's contract, it was a risk worth taking. By then, most of the better players who were available had been snapped up, leaving us to sift through what was left for any further additions. Mel had seen a Frenchman, Franck Rolling, another Leicester City player. A central defender aged twenty-eight, he would offer good cover. He agreed to play in a pre-season friendly so we could take a look.

Season ticket sales went better than expected. Within weeks, we had gone well past last season's 680 mark, heading for 1,000 – a huge increase on the previous year. On the financial side, I guess I spent most of the next six weeks liaising on an almost daily basis with Chris Griffin at the Football League, working through time and again the detailed figures we had prepared, and assessing the likelihood of their accuracy. We could have put anything in and tried to justify its reasonableness, but I felt we had made a fair stab, which was confirmed by Andrew Kaye's brother and his firm of accountants. We were conscious that the League wanted to be satisfied that we could survive as a business until the end of the season and fulfil our fixture commitment. Without that, when the summer was over we would be too.

CHAPTER 12

Beckham by the Sea

Amid the euphoria in the town that the club had been saved, we fell victim to an unpleasant side-effect of running a football club. We were the board so, *ipso facto*, we could not be ordinary fans. Convicted on the basis of wearing a jacket and tie! Within weeks we became a target for vandals, which was nothing new but a perennial problem. Martin took to sleeping at the stadium; he had developed a fear that someone might just try to desecrate it. I thought he was potty but Martin claimed he had heard noises in the night and had frightened off intruders. A grown man, resorting to sleeping in the ex-chairman's comfy chair? Yes, he had some of his belongings strewn around the ex-chairman's room. Yes, he had once turned up at the ground with a lorry loaded with mattresses and other items. He had explained he was just moving house. It seemed plausible, so we let him carry on.

In the second week of July the phone rang and a voice came on introducing himself as Theo Paphitis. 'Hello there, Trevor, I'm the chairman of Millwall Football Club. I've just taken over, rather like you, and wanted to have a chat about Matty Holland. What price are you asking for him?' He was prepared to come up with £150,000. With my fantasy football hat on, I figured Matty would probably be worth a lot more than that and told him so. 'That's all right,' he said, 'I'm not used to this.' He had rescued Millwall, who had got into dire financial trouble throughout the same period as us, during which both clubs had developed a mutual bond. They say transfer enquiries are like buses: none for a long while and then they all come at once. Next morning, in the middle of an ordinary day, David Sheepshanks rang to enquire about our progress and, at the same time, about the chances of Matty joining Ipswich. I talked a lot but said nothing.

Any manager will tell you that their stock answer is that the player is not for sale and, in an ideal world, a player would never have to leave if the manager had his way. Matty was a tremendous professional and possessed ability, which meant he was the last person anybody in charge would wish to lose. Within hours, David was back in touch, saying he was prepared to pay £380,000 plus a further £100,000 upon promotion, 'but there could be a little more if this is not enough'. I told him it was not. By this time I had contacted Mel, whose response was less than enthusiastic. His suggested asking price was £2 million! I carefully explained to David that our manager was not prepared to let him go, and his 'helpful' advice was that in our predicament, I ought to think about the financial implications for our club.

For Mel and John, there had been no time to chase players. Our French triallist, Franck Rolling, was too late to play in our traditional pre-season friendly at Ringwood, a market town a few miles outside of Bournemouth, who play in the Hampshire League. Spectators imbibed the local ale in a roped-off field that had all too little in common with the Football League. But we were in business. We performed extremely well to win 11–0 without really exerting ourselves. A year before, we had won only 3–0. On 15 July we staged our first fixture at Dean Court. The police turned up, the gatemen turned up, the stewards turned up, so did 2,500 fans and the opposition, Portsmouth! Who would have thought that within two years they would follow our path to financial ruin? We won 1–0 and Rolling played well.

By now, Martin was no longer sleeping in the club. He assured me he had got a grip on what was happening at the stadium and was implementing all the changes I had started. The traditional practices of having blank signed cheques in drawers, buckets of cash to dip into and endless petty cash outgoings had been stopped. Until the takeover, every part of the business had operated in isolation, empires within empires controlled by one or two individuals with little or no management direction or accountability. There was the Lottery, Commercial, Administrative, Junior Cherries, and then the playing staff. There were no written contracts for the off-field staff – at least none in modern form – no health and safety manuals, no formal procedures for disciplinary hearings or grievances, no signing-in of visitors. Out of the woodwork, alleged commercial contracts started appearing. One particular advertising company claimed a monthly retainer of £2,500. It was on £30,000 a year when our previous main sponsor had paid only £40,000. I was mightily glad I had insisted we had the freedom to drop the majority of contracts we didn't want to keep.

Roy Pack was still active. His latest attempt was to try to persuade the Royal Bath (a major creditor of the old company) to host a formal dinner in celebration of the achievements of Norman Hayward, Brian Willis and himself. He was rumoured to be calling companies with whom we were doing business, trying to dissuade them from putting their money into sponsoring the club, claiming we would be out of business in weeks. He wanted to fund a pamphlet, explaining the wrong-doings at AFC Bournemouth. I would have had no problem reading his booklet if it complained about the past. It didn't concern us and I certainly didn't want our sponsors to give him money. We had to be professional and move away from the amateur football culture. Our practice was, where possible, to use local suppliers and, step by step, companies came forward. Rawlins Davy, a local law firm, agreed to do conveyancing for players at a fixed fee, Homefield School offered scholarships for players' children and Bridgeland, a financial management company, offered to assist in financial planning to provide commission. Even the *Financial Times* did an article commenting on the turnaround. That in itself attracted publicity. Within a very short time I took a call from an accountant representing a Middle Eastern client. Would we sell the club? I knew we could always do with more money to bridge the cashflow shortfall that was looming. If the team did not perform, sooner or later we would need more cash. The client, his accountant and daughter visited the club late one rainy Friday afternoon.

The idea of one person having control of the club again was abhorrent. The deal was £1 million cash, 80 per cent of the shares and for me a job with a guaranteed £50,000 salary, signing-on bonus and recruitment of the staff I wanted. But the deal was that Mel Machin would be out. I rejected it out of hand: it was not my club to sell. Arguably the supporters who had saved the club should consider whether it was ever in the best interests to sell. I believed the club was worth more anyway. My suggestion was that £1 million might buy 15 per cent of the shares, but the Arab wanted overall control. Loyalty and integrity were our main platform and my ambition was to give an opportunity to all those who had put so much in to make the business work.

The next mysterious call was from a man professing to act on behalf of another client with some spare money to invest. This person didn't desperately want to run a football club, but felt he might have 'something of interest' to discuss. The entourage was fronted by a Yul Brynner lookalike prospecting new ideas for his boss, who wanted to diversify from the sparkling wine industry. This tubby, perfectly pleasant individual watched a game and then spoke of a million or so, but again the lack of control and concept of a trust fund somehow ruined the idea of their having a new plaything of their own. Suffice to say we have not received another bid since. For me, all these zeroes were beyond my comprehension – ordinary life consisted of an evening out at a pizzeria, buying a car on interest-free finance or trying to work out the best mortgage deal. Here was a new world in which normal business concepts seemed to go out of the window. The inspiring thing was the faith of those who invested so much in an enterprise in which they would only ever have a minority stake.

When we only narrowly managed to draw with Bashley, an amateur club, in a friendly through a late penalty from Jon O'Neill, our Scottish forward, I took a wager with Andrew Kaye. Jon is an intelligent, articulate chap with a tremendous dedication to succeeding at professional level, plucked by us out of Celtic Reserves. For a prize of a dinner for four at a restaurant of the winner's choosing, the wager was that he would score ten goals in competitive matches that season. Meanwhile, it was quickly becoming clear that in this brave new world of a community-owned club, everybody expected to have a say, and expected their say to be acted upon, as my burgeoning postbag showed: players, tactics, kick-off times, music played before the game, even the beverages on offer – all were the subject of our stakeholders' concerns. Democracy is important, but it can become unwieldy. The importance is in transparency, without being to the detriment of the business. Publishing a list of players' salaries, bonuses and transfer targets would probably ensure that, within a week, half the playing staff would have demanded transfers and we would never sign anybody in a million years, nor have any relationship of trust or confidence with any other club.

Where a community club, like a listening bank, can help, is in reacting and being open to change. For some time I had sat down with Alan Helm, the resident caterer but owner of a separate company, to work out a fair basis for providing facilities for the season. He offered us £10,000 a year for the right to sell food at set prices from our stadium outlets, while demanding the right to provide food for the supporters' club. He figured he would double the size of cups for tea and the price would be put up from 50p to 90p. There was a vast outcry at the hike in this price. So it came back down, as did the size of a cup! Behind the scenes, it was customary for staff who arrived two hours before kick-off to have sandwiches provided. A small cost, perhaps, on a match day, but it mounted up over a whole season. Providing twenty-four cans of beer to each opposing team also seemed a luxury that over time would cost the club good money. Both went.

It was a rude awakening for me to come across the small minority of people who complain about anything and everything, whatever is done. I am in favour of standing at football grounds for one reason above all others – it protects you from being stuck in the same place week after week. More complaining is done at football grounds every Saturday than anywhere else. I don't exclude myself! When we used to sit in the main stand, all around me I would hear voices (mine sometimes included!) criticising, complaining and moaning. Praise was a rare occurrence. Sitting in the directors' box as chairman certainly wasn't going to change my ways. Yet still these people returned the following week. The British are unlike the South Americans or Latins who can marvel at a fleeting moment of skill in a game and go home happy even if the team has lost. It is as if, by some God-given right, a professional footballer should be able to score from thirty yards with every shot. Maybe they should, considering the wages they are paid. But they are human.

Four days on, the phone rang again and Ipswich were back. I had worked out (I don't know how!) that if I could get £800,000 cash for Holland, it would be a good deal. David Sheepshanks was indicating that they might be prepared to increase their offer to £500,000 with a small bonus of £50,000 on promotion. There might be 'a little more money available' should we find this unacceptable. I said I would 'take instructions' given the frosty reception I had from Mel before. In reality, it was a question of settling it at the best price as we would need the money. One unsettled player, one unhappy manager and a fan base which had been promised that we would never sell our best players – I couldn't win. This had the potential for catastrophe, destroying our credibility, my relationship with Mel and the fans' belief.

A day or two later our programme of pre-season friendlies continued with a trip to Reading. This was my first visit to a League club in my official capacity as chairman. (It had been some years since I was a student in the town.) I decided to arrive in style, taking the train out of London and then the bus along the main London Road, jumping off at the eye hospital. With temperatures in the high eighties, the bus packed and little breeze, my ruffled suit and sweaty brow probably gave every impression but professionalism. Does one pay for drinks in the boardroom? I plumped for mineral water, bit my tongue as I waited to be asked for payment, and found no request was made. Call me the Innocent Abroad, but I was not sure of the etiquette. Isn't it strange that, even at that level, uncertainty came into my mind as to what limits of hospitality I might accept without compromising my integrity. It never crosses my mind when I entertain a client that this could in some way be seen as a bribe, an attempt to secure further work. It's not. Owing to the reputation of the past regime, however, we had resolved we would never put ourselves in a position of offering favours or seeking them in return. At Reading it was all very proper, and I was quickly out into the stand. I paid for my train, paid for my bus fare and would have been happy to pay for my entry, as I had the Saturday before at Ringwood. The culture of 'we pay so all pay' seemed simpler, one that we have continued. We still all have to line up in the shop to buy our season tickets!

We had been trying to contact Franck Rolling. Perhaps wanting to keep his options open, he had gone back to Scotland. Motherwell wanted him. Bizarrely, Martin Jones had told Matty Holland that Crystal Palace were prepared to offer £400,000 for him. Matty collared me, but I was able to deny it, perplexed that Martin had offered a figure and a club that were both untrue. By the next day, though, everything was blown open. Ipswich leaked their interest in Matty to the local press, in an attempt to force our hand. David Sheepshanks called me again, now offering £500,000 plus one of three bit-part players worth £100,000. Our local media wanted comments. Suddenly the player discovered what was going on and came over to me outside the ground. Mel had told him how much he wanted him to stay. But he said: 'I'd really like this move, Trevor – it's a great opportunity for me. You won't stand in my way, will you?' I spoke to the manager, who dismissed the players offered in exchange out of hand. One of them had actually been touted about a few months earlier and the others had problems of a personal nature in their careers. Funnily one is now in the Premier League, one still at Ipswich and the other in our division. Mel was still adamant that a figure above a million was appropriate, but it seemed highly unlikely that we would ever achieve this. With my £800,000 figure in mind, I let Ipswich know that Holland would be sold if they offered a package around £1.1 million.

Sitting at the commercial office department late that night, working on the figures, I heard a group outside. Having built sixteen corporate executive boxes overlooking the pitch, we wanted to use them to the maximum. Every extra pound would improve our chances of long-term survival. The previous year, all 160 occupants had the use of only one bar, which at best could comfortably hold no more than 90 people. The sweaty, crowded atmosphere did not enhance our image of making a fresh start. There was another room across the way, but until recently this had been used as a family room for kids at half-time and before and after the game. I knew that other accommodation was available beneath another stand for an ideal family room. It meant a short escorted walk around the ground, but was viable, vacating space for a new bar for half the box holders. From a business perspective, it would make sense.

For years, Shirley Delsette had run the Junior Cherries, organising and controlling it. Shirley worked part-time for just over £3,000 but with telephone bills paid and commission of £2 on each young fan signed up (and every time they renewed their £8 subscription). She ran the accounts. Now we had decided to move her room. I guess she must have been drinking in the supporters' club. She probably never suspected I was sitting inside the office and heard her every critical observation.

Ron Hands, president of the supporters' club, told me in confidence that they desperately needed us to take it over, as none of them was a businessman and it was running at a loss. This was a business that took more than £40,000 from its gaming machines, had a turnover of £200,000 and yet made no profit. It was the largest single underused facility at the ground. If you can imagine a warehouse site empty 90 per cent of the time, that was it. Save on match days, perhaps ten or a dozen people gathered each night. A large overdraft had been racked up by them as well as a loan of nearly £85,000 from Bass Brewery, £50,000 of which we had paid off ourselves on completion. One of the two managers employed by them (why two I shall never know) claimed they had got a much better deal on beer from other suppliers, so had not used Bass, who were becoming particularly anxious about their money. Either we ordered beer or another £35,000 had to be found to pay them off. Another unexpected pressure on our cash flow.

Kevin Heath had advised us on anything remotely litigious. A partner in Lester Aldridge but also a footballer himself, he did not waste time with flannel. Pack waited until the last day to try to overturn the vote we had got from the creditors and shareholders. Piles of paper with affidavits alleging this, that and the other. Most of it was irrelevant, a potted history of the life and times of AFC Bournemouth in the Hayward era. At the core were suggestions that the voting had not been counted properly.

We had bought the club knowing an appeal could put us under. We believed it was without merit, designed to frustrate, to inhibit and procure some deal from us to pay them off. They had been given twenty-eight days but had left it until the twenty-ninth to appeal. We could not believe it: a simple error and now they could do nothing. We told them so. They tried to persuade a court that we had miscounted. It was only Kevin's insistence that we go one court higher to argue our case when the first one found against us that saved the day. Now we would have a clear run through to finally getting on with the real business of playing football, so long as the Football League were happy. Pack would disappear into the ether only to surface when news of other clubs came to us on the wind, his offers of help seeing him appointed elsewhere.

David Sheepshanks never compromised his position as chairman of the Football League with his desire to sign Matty Holland. It was just that every conversation we had involved both subjects. By the end of the week he was telephoning me at home and we (me, David and his dynamic PA) were getting on fine, while in the press the war of words continued. We were furious they had leaked the deal. The fact that the names of the potential players involved in the part exchange, Tanner, Sonner and Gregory, had come out upset him as much as bringing the whole business out into the open had disappointed me. Ipswich's offer increased to £600,000 plus bonuses related to promotion of £100,000. My asking price dropped to £1 million. In the press David commented that this was his maximum. If unacceptable, the deal was off.

I had enough to worry about with our own squad. I did not know the players would expect to be paid a bonus if they won. Nor did I realise that it would be down to me to create a scheme. How much do you get if you win a game? What is it worth? I looked at the old schedule. Clearly some of the old provisions could never have been paid if the team had achieved the targets set. I mean, payments had to be less than receipts.

How much to win the FA Cup? Promotion? Top six finish? After hours of drafting, Matty Holland, still the captain, and I agreed the final version. It was his last major contribution to the club. Ian Cox was set to replace him. Hard as nails, telescopic legs that most attackers never got past (at least not with the ball), Ian is a wonderful player destined for higher leagues – with us, I hope. He was originally bought as a winger – the joke was always that Mel bought a player and changed his position. It worked though; he has the knack of turning cast-offs into million-pound assets.

Having a friendly at home against Wimbledon that weekend meant that I would be encountering both manager and Matty again. I was in a difficult position. Mel didn't want to sell him, believing Matty didn't want to go. Matty said that he would like to further his career at Ipswich if the clubs could agree terms. With wind of a better deal and a desire to leave, it would be very difficult to keep him content. We could not up his terms anywhere near to what Ipswich might offer. My first transfer was turning into a mighty long one. Yet even in the Premier League, as I gathered in conversation in the boardroom with Joe Kinnear, dabbling in the transfer market can send you to your wits' end. I was amused to hear of how he was told by an agent about a fantastic player he should buy. That had involved a trip to Norway, only to discover that he had been playing in the English second division some years earlier and been responsible for conceding a hatful of goals. Harry Redknapp was there and remembered the same player had also been peddled to West Ham by the agent and they too had gone to see him. For all clubs, the chance to secure the next Alan Shearer or Michael Owen – even a Matty Holland – means it is extremely difficult to forgo the invitation to look at an individual, even if this involves the expense of flying him in and providing his accommodation. Rumour has it that Lennie Lawrence at Charlton missed the chance to sign Uwe Rosler because he balked at a £1,000 air fare (too much for us). Clubs like Bournemouth are always looking for that elusive star, yet every time a trialist fails, more money is kissed goodbye.

On the following Monday, the papers linked Matty with Liverpool. Having agonised over the figures at the weekend, my conclusion did not alter. To be promised £800,000 would ensure long-term stability for us (well, at least eighteen months). We would have time to build and impose our own ideas. We had the team photoshoot that day – would we exclude Matty? I sat with Mel and explained that we would have no real option but to sell the player at the best price. There were not many words from him, not much encouragement, but I did not expect them. I left in silence.

David was now up to £700,000 all in. We were obliged to pass 33 per cent of any fee to West Ham, his first club. To make the deal more palatable, I wanted to try to agree a compromise with them. Everyone has always assumed that the close bond between AFC Bournemouth and Harry Redknapp was behind the frequent transfer activity between our clubs. These were all commercial deals done for West Ham's benefit; some have been good for us, others less so. Most transfers are based on talk, respect and friendships between managers, contacts and recommendations. Peter Storrie, managing director of West Ham, was in Copenhagen. He knew

I was asking him to do something he did not have to do, but he limited West Ham's claim to our profit on Matt's transfer, £175,000 up to £700,000, and 25 per cent of any balance. I called David, saying that for £800,000 cash he had a deal and suggested he meet me first thing in the morning in London.

That David spilled the coffee all over me probably helped. We were able finally to agree that Ipswich were to pay us £730,000 down with a further £35,000 on twenty-five games played by Matty, and another £35,000 on fifty games, with 25 per cent of any subsequent fee received by Ipswich payable to us. That effectively gave us £800,000 within one year, the payments to us of the £730,000 being divided into three over twelve months, so that we would have regular cash flow. It was security, the largest one-off deal the club had ever entered into. I was sad that it would break the hearts of many fans. We had put prices up and I had promised we would not sell players. This was money we could not refuse now. Pushed to all the extremes by the previous directors, court action was continuing and fees were racking up. Then came the hate mail and Mel and I did not speak for three days. If I had not sold him, another player would have gone or, without a sale, then the club. With only one new face in the side and our star player gone, the odds on us finishing bottom probably seemed the best on offer.

Holland's sale was like a death in the family. People avoided eye contact, not knowing what to say. I felt so depressed. Timing was everything. The cure was the long-awaited visit of Manchester United. These days, the top sides hardly ever visit the lowly clubs for pre-season friendlies because they have lucrative tours overseas. It was a tremendous gesture on Alex Ferguson's part. Of course, with the Charity Shield taking place only two days afterwards, they would not put out a star-studded first team, but it would still be a formidable line-up to match most teams. He had promised that David Beckham and possibly a Chilean World Cup star would be playing, as would Gary Neville and Ole Gunnar Solskjaer. The fact that the last two were injured did not affect the gate of nearly 9,000 people. How Manchester United, accustomed to the splendour of

Old Trafford, took to the confines of down-at-heel Dean Court, paint peeling and, notwithstanding new power showers, largely third rate, was something they did not let on. Ferguson and Beckham arrived together in a large limousine, which was swiftly surrounded by kids and adults, too. Both were content to sign autographs, Beckham smiling and chatting and not giving a hint of his superstar status or the arrival of his girlfriend, Posh Spice, radiant as ever, through a separate entrance.

Our boardroom, no bigger than my bedroom, is distinctly unattractive. As well as our six directors, there were those people every club has, long-term fixtures for whom the boardroom is probably the safest place to be. All are characters and long-standing fans of the club: Ted Keep, Dr Ogden, the Revd Fisher and our very own Lorraine Pardy. She is now in her eighties, frail, but enthusiastic as ever. Irrespective of her infirmities, she comes to every game, sponsors the first match ball of the season and resolutely forbids anybody getting in the way of her serving tea and coffee to our guests on a match day. You may not always get what you ask for, but you won't be forgotten.

I had often seen Alex Ferguson coming across as dour on TV. In reality, much like John Major, he was an invigorating, entertaining and charismatic man whose ability to talk to all people at all levels shone through. As he came into the boardroom and I took his coat, Lorraine came across and asked if he would like tea or coffee. She then offered tea and gave him a piece of fruit cake before he could reply. Taking his hand and, with that distant look at a stranger, she said: 'Now, who are you?' It was a magical moment. In the other room, one of our lounges, a dozen of my London clients had come down for the day and were enjoying a refreshing 'client development' day. I was delighted they were there as friends. Unlike the other clubs they would visit, everybody could walk from room to room, down the corridors and never hesitate to stop and talk.

It was an evening with a very special atmosphere. Old players, familiar faces and good friends such as Harry Redknapp came along to enjoy a game of football. Brian McClair and the Chilean international, Dante Pole, played alongside Beckham, who, with one moment of sublime skill, gave the whole crowd a memory to take away, feinting inside Robinson and bending the ball fully twenty-five yards into the top corner. To our credit, that remained the only goal of the game. Looking at their team now, all of them are either established at Manchester United or plying their trade with other Football League teams. In one evening, our takings were as much as for three League games put together, enough to meet the wages for a month, enough to be another long-term boost in our battle for survival. The irony was that Manchester United's last visit had been as FA Cup holders – and they were sent home defeated by our lowly side. In the boardroom, Mel and Harry chatted and joked with Alex. Mel and I spoke – our reconciliation had begun. Three days later the tables were turned: we were the big name team for Salisbury City's opening game at the new Raymond McEnhill stadium, winning 3–1 in front of perhaps 400 people. As United gave to us, so we were able to give to teams below us in the football ladder.

There were five days to go before the season commenced and yet we still did not have official permission to start it. Financially we were secure – the chairman of the Football League knew that – but Pack still loitered. With the loss of Matty Holland, the need to sign players became increasingly urgent. We had even gone to the lengths of organising special practice sessions for other trialists. During the entire season we would look at, perhaps, sixty or seventy players who would come to us for a number of these sessions, none of whom eventually made the grade. Windward Island internationals, non-League players or others who had just been seen playing in the park. French, Danes, Norwegians, Bajans, Scots, English, Welsh . . . you name it, we look at it.

We had a mysterious phone call from Italy, recommending a player with Genoa, Alessandro Turone. Southampton once gave, allegedly, a two-month contract at £2,500 a week to a bloke claiming to be George Weah's cousin. He appeared for 58 minutes in a Premiership match before they decided they'd had the wool pulled over their eyes. The appearance of Turone seemed to match it. When the olive-skinned, Armani-suited Italian brigade arrived, there was actually no doubting his credentials. His father was general secretary of Inter Milan and had played for Genoa, Inter, Roma and captained Italy. That his son was not up to it was one thing, but this was a far cry from the San Siro. Portsmouth Reserves at Dean Court in front of twenty-six spectators.

We were left trying to hammer a deal out with Franck Rolling, who by now had returned from Motherwell, claiming other contracts were available, and asking us to name our best price. His demands were £2,000 a week, way above what we might pay. Franck wanted a car, his accommodation, relocation expenses. All in all, a Premier League deal for a second division job. We haggled and eventually came to an agreement at less than half of the total demands. It had taken three weeks to sort this out. Negotiations are time-consuming and draining, but we had 'Le Galloping Gourmet' (his father runs a restaurant in Morocco) with a qualification in nutrition and diet. Possibly a half-decent player too. Alex Ferguson had offered a number of players who we might be able to take on loan from Manchester United. Graeme Tomlinson had scored sixteen goals in seventeen games for Bradford before a £100,000 move to Old Trafford. He had been scoring a goal a game in the reserves but had had an horrific injury. We agreed to take him, but could only pay £400 a week, a proportion of his wages. Certainly the bookies thought we needed him. We were now, at 66–1, long shots to win the league and getting even hotter as odds-on favourites to go down.

CHAPTER 13

Too Bloody Hot!

August. It was hot and the City was empty, Bournemouth full of holidaymakers. I was confused. No news from the Football League. Without advice to the contrary, we decided just to turn up at our first game on 7 August even if we hadn't got written permission. Northampton Town, our opponents, had been in a similar situation to ours some years before, but had fought back in partnership with the council, as, in a sense, we had done. They had obtained funding for a new stadium designed to cater for the needs of the twenty-first century. Located on the outskirts of town in a bowl ringed by food outlets, cinema and other leisure facilities, it had major development potential. The club had battered its way through to promotion the previous year: finishing twelve points behind the third-placed team (the equivalent of four wins), they had won through the play-offs to take their place in our division. It was a strange feeling to wear jacket and tie in 85° heat and drive up to the doors of the stadium and park right outside, then to find oneself in the boardroom rather than just paying through the turnstile. Never publicly, but privately, I had always thought the event which would define whether we were to survive or not would be if we kicked a ball in anger at the start of the 1997–98 season.

We are good, in Britain, at hiding emotions – but not on that day. I made my excuses – the lack of air conditioning pushed the temperature inside into the nineties – and Andrew Kaye and I went to our supporters' end. The wall of fans, more than 700, gave us immense pride. We then went back down the tunnel, quietly knocking on the dressing-room door. All around, the lads were finishing their preparations. In the middle stood Mel, John, Steve Hardwick the physio, Duncan the kit man, and Michael the vicar. I searched for words, but could not find any. A hug from one person to another, clasping arms round each other's shoulders, not a word spoken, but eyes glistening as the emotion of the moment took hold. In the main stand there was thunderous applause, warm waves of love, admiration and joy from those of us who had brought the club this far. My eyes welled up as the team ran out, red and black striped, immaculate.

In the blistering heat Northampton's kick and rush tactics – or at least kick and hoof – to the two huge blokes up front caused a few problems early on. Our players, who on average were perhaps the youngest team in the Football League, keep the ball on the ground with short, intricate passing movements of no more than ten yards. A tough game to play in searing heat. The game remained scoreless until the sixty-eighth minute, when the ball broke loose for Jamie Vincent, our twenty-two-year-old left back. He steamed up the wing, cut inside and let fly with a shot that crashed into the top corner of the net. Seven minutes later, Steve Fletcher, our lanky centre forward, scored a second with a ferocious volley. Not only had we played our first game as a community club, we had won it against a team tipped for promotion that year. Meaningless as it is after one game, the result put us fifth in the table (only devout followers of the sport will understand the pleasure after even one game of trying to predict the outcome of the season to come and to draw conclusions based on ninety minutes which will hold true for the next ten months). We were the only team in the top half to win away, so that had to make us better than all the rest!

Fate has a horrible habit of bringing you back to earth with a bang. Our League season is interspersed with three cup competitions, the most notable, of course, being the FA Cup. In the Coca-Cola Cup we were drawn to meet Torquay United in the first

138

round, played over two legs, home and away, just three days after the Northampton match. Torquay of the third division was a team which on paper we should easily beat. Those who reach the second round can expect to share rich revenues. For the cup competitions, the win bonus was greatly enhanced, as much as four times that of a first win in the League.

Barely 3,200 people turned up for what, in mid-August, was a particularly uninviting evening match. Despite having all the advantages and most of the possession, we lost. Football fans across the country all share the manager's nightmare of a player posing no danger whatsoever, yet being hauled down in the penalty area. It happened to us. We lost to that penalty goal. The atmosphere was less than electric, certainly compared to the 14,000 who had been outside the ground earlier in the day for a guest appearance by Jon Bon Jovi at the Radio One roadshow. Disaster struck when we could not play our new striker. Training ground injury? Recurrence of knee problem? No – Graeme Tomlinson had ricked his back sleeping awkwardly on the waterbed in his hotel room. Almost as strange as when Jamie Vincent was out for two months with a septic insect bite. The painful reality of a game like this, with European soccer on TV, was that our 45 per cent of the gate receipts (45 per cent going to Torquay and 10 per cent to the League) meant there was little left after costs. The total take was £14,000 with a further £2,000 in programmes and car parking receipts. Once VAT had been taken off, our net take of £6,300 barely covered the cost of policing and stewarding the game. We knew we had to do bloody well in the second leg to reverse the 0–1 deficit.

Footballers have a public existence but for most it's a career that ends before you or I reach the halfway stage of our own. Many are no more than bit-parts in a global circus. You have to earn their respect, or they will abuse it. The manager's art is in knowing how to deal with them and to bring out the best in diverse personalities. Those who will respond to praise, who are prepared to learn and sensitive to criticism – they're the ones who are accepted and get on in their playing life at our level. Within any set-up there will be those who will be automatic first choices, those who are young with much to learn, others at the end of their careers and some who will never be more than squad members filling in gaps from time to time. This last category is the problematic one. Some players will be insecure, others will have a desire to improve and progress to the next level whatever their limitations.

Most managers have undergone little or no management training. Their skills are gleaned from their playing days: a 'suck it and see' approach to dealing with individuals. Leo Cotterell had been signed by Mel on the recommendation of a scout, although he had seen him once or twice. Leo had played for England under-18s and been a member of the national sports academy. Throughout his initial year with us – on a cheap contract – he had a tendency to be injured. In pre-season training he had again sustained a number of knocks. He had not made the grade at Ipswich, had personal problems and now was not getting into our first team. His undoubted skill was affected by being shy of tackles, probably a cardinal sin in a defence-minded team. D. H. Lawrence suggested Bournemouth existed for the sick because it was like a huge hospital of old people. Leo had approached Mel and then me to ask what his future held at the club. The very next day he asked me again. The harsh fact of life was that he had chosen a career in football and was now faced with a dead end. The other side of all those newspaper stories about huge transfer deals is the unsavoury business of having to tell a player he is not good enough. Players have financial safeguards. You can't sack them for non-performance. To get rid of one you either have to pay their contract up in full or agree a different compensation package. I felt sorry for Leo but I had to learn to become as hard as nails. He was last rumoured to be setting up a window glazing company, playing part-time non-league like most we have to let go.

Mel and I got into a routine of speaking two or three times daily. Most business is done between the manager's arrival at nine o'clock and before training an hour or so later. We would review targets, existing players and admin for upcoming games. More often than not we would divide responsibilities, which meant that we shared all information. I, in turn, needed Mel's guidance on dealing with the lads who would inevitably talk to me. In those early days we seemed to have a party from week to week celebrating our survival. The following Saturday we were at home to Wigan, with the might of Dave Whelan, owner of JJB Sports, financing them. His multi-million-pound empire had already dished out over £1.2 million on the third division champions in the close season, and they had opened their campaign with a 5–2 victory at Wycombe Wanderers. As one wag put it, this was the recently bankrupt meeting the recently bankrolled. Ironically, the letters section of the local sports paper that day carried a missive from an indignant supporter criticizing us for alienating Norman Hayward and Brian Willis and their invaluable experience!

My playing days now over, match days for me were no longer a matter of turning up in the afternoon: they were entire working days. They kicked off at 9.30 a.m. and there was a three-hour board meeting at ten – jeans allowed – followed by a quick change to undertake all the official duties before the game – wandering outside to talk to people, sometimes visiting the disabled section, making announcements in the supporters' club, mingling in the vice-president's room and the boardroom. Then it was a matter of talking to the players' families, girlfriends, other guests, ensuring the officials were happy, checking on safety, seeing what scouts were visiting, popping into the club shop and offices, seeking out old friends in the crowd, liaising with the media and doing interviews where requested before watching the game, and doing more of the same afterwards, eventually collapsing in the boardroom around six or six-thirty, reviewing the afternoon's events with the manager and getting home around eight. Work? Yes, but extremely enjoyable.

In view of everything Geoffrey Hayward had done for the club during the course of the year, we had unanimously offered him the position of president, a titular position but one that would show our appreciation. He accepted, setting up his stall against the boardroom bar, where, with the board, he ensured visiting directors would receive a warm welcome. Even on that first home Saturday, there were seven scouts from clubs in higher divisions, there because they knew we could play good football. To think our own team had cost just over £200,000 to put together really hit home as they tore into Wigan. Our galloping gourmet did, as the local media put it, 'serve up exquisite fare' with a goal in the last minute to bring about another victory. Watching the TV screen in the boardroom, Michael the vicar jumped up and shouted 'Bournemouth top of the League!' It was so exciting to run from room to room filled with people shouting and screaming with delight that there, at 4.55 p.m., our club had appeared on *Grandstand* at the top of the table. It had been a strange afternoon, one on which we had to ask Air Traffic Control's permission to release balloons from the ground to ensure they did not interfere with planes, and Jason Brissett, our enigmatic winger, lasted only twenty-eight minutes as a substitute before he was himself hauled off ignominiously. There must be one such player at every club.

We had a good celebration that night at the Mandarin Chinese restaurant. Andrew, Sally, Mel, Jo, Mandy and I gorged ourselves on an excellent meal. Halfway through, Mandy nudged me and pointed out an old friend sitting on a table less than ten yards away, his companion merrily picking his nose with chopsticks while attempting to feed him seaweed. Not-so-young love. All that was missing that day was the presence of Martin Jones. While he was away visiting a friend in Scotland we had uncovered numerous inconsistencies which gave cause for concern. He had given guarantees of financial obligations to staff, had not organized the doormen as he said he had, and had agreed to provide cars to players without checking with everyone else. These were not fundamental matters but created a nagging doubt. He had eventually arrived at the ground that Saturday afternoon about twenty minutes after the final whistle, apologising profusely and telling us he was to start his new job the following Monday. Andrew and I had resolved to sit down and talk to him, but, rather than force the issue, decided it would be best just to carry on ourselves. In attempting to ensure the supporters' club became a fully funding part of our set-up, Martin had been designated the representative. His promises of new salaries did not help. Taking the premises over and running them as an enterprise would take a long time, longer than we had available at the start of a new season.

The logistical enormity of organising a home game is not much greater than that involved in going away. Travel, food, accommodation all need to be arranged. Luckily, there were several good agencies we could turn to who were able to sort out deals enabling us to stay in reasonable places at an affordable price. On average, dinner, bed and breakfast or a pre-match meal at a hotel of three- or four-star category would be between £30 and £40 a head. That first season we were plonked at the Britannia Hotel just outside Manchester for our visit to Oldham. For the team, there is no luxury other than a six-hour journey on a coach with basic microwave, drink facilities and two video screens. In the past, throwing bananas from the back of the vehicle over the driver's head may well have made driving the team coach a less than attractive prospect but, since Mel had been in charge, the discipline instilled meant this had become a fairly comfortable job. With his roll-up cigarettes and deft touch on the brake pedal even when on open roads with no other cars in sight, Roger became the sixteenth man on all our away trips. Our team, although admirable ambassadors, is also a good-humoured, spirited bunch with a fair amount of repartee to while away hours on the coach, so it's necessary to have a driver prepared both to give and take the mickey. For £8,000, Yellow Coaches, a local bus company who had previously sponsored our away shirts, gave us a vehicle for the year.

Our arrival in Manchester fitted in neatly with my need to visit my company's office there to discuss our North America business plan. Upon reaching the Britannia Hotel, I discovered it to be a huge complex boasting three nightclubs, swimming-pool, three bars, and restaurants – not quite the quiet country location I had envisaged for a pre-match stay. Routine for an away trip is usually for the players to eat dinner together before retiring to their rooms at 8 p.m. to watch a bit of television and sleep through to late morning, when the pre-match meal would be served. On this night we were lucky enough to be given tickets for a first division game at Manchester City, who were at home to Tranmere. Mel had been manager at Maine Road for two seasons, gaining promotion in the first of these, beating Manchester United 5–1 and then being sacked days later when they neared the top of the division. Although in the shadow of United, they were always one of those 'big clubs' that we dreamed of playing ourselves. Even then, at the start of the season, there was an air of crisis. It was clear how much Mel was respected from the number of fans who said they wished he had never gone. City had millions of pounds of talent on the pitch and yet could not prevent their defeats continuing in front of as many as 30,000 fans.

By contrast, our game the following day really highlighted the differences even between clubs who had been exposed to our level. Oldham had played in the Premiership, been relegated and now were pushed into the second division. I was not prepared for the state of the ground I found. Located among old stone terraced houses, it had an air of decay. The road ran right by the stadium, so you jumped on to the pavement and into the offices. The pitch had been used for rugby and was cut up. The stand, painted a garish orange and blue, seemed to have been put together higgledy-piggledy. Executive boxes had been built on stilts. Unlike a business producing services or goods, football is so much in the public eye that on a week-to-week basis the pressure on it can become intense. With failure, a club is still burdened with the contracts of those players bought and used in an attempt to stay at a higher level and now having to perform in a division below on salaries markedly different from most of their colleagues. For Oldham to have dropped two divisions in quick succession, and still having to pay extraordinarily high wages that they could not get out of unless they sold the players, was a path to self-destruction.

Nearly every club has a few famous supporters and yet in a survey we were found not to have many at all. I guess if we did, someone might have come forward by now and given us loads of money to help save the club. Over years of doing summer seasons in Bournemouth, Stew 'I could crush a grape' Francis of *Crackerjack* fame had come to love the club and, being based up north, was there with us that day, as he was at most games. Oldham had been tipped to go straight back up to the first division, but again we gave as good as we got. With fifteen minutes to go, the score was 1–1 and, as Kevin Keegan might have said, 'There is only one team in it.' That team was supposedly Bournemouth, save for the fact that the referee had not read the script. Bang down the middle goes the ball, McCarthy touches it on, literally, a little Gaelic football palming it into the area and a volley putting it into the net. The referee gives a goal, our very own 'hand of God'. When home is a six-hour coach journey away, one does not want it on the back of a defeat. Invariably there is a quicker departure time than if we had won. Early on I tried to make conversation before realizing I ought to follow suit and keep quiet until the manager spoke, as that seemed to be the catalyst for everyone to talk again. What surprised me was the level of introspection straight after a game. We had been given a video of the match, which was played on the coach, although it was stopped before we got to anything contentious, to avoid recrimination and debate over who might be at fault.

It was a Bank Holiday weekend and I wanted to spend some time with Mandy, my cats and Mum and Dad, who had been so patient while I concentrated on football and work. Mandy's birthday had come and gone without our being able to do anything special and I had not really known what to buy her. Every time we went to the vet or watched a programme about animals in distress, the reaction would be to try to help, to want to be able to have more animals. I once had a girlfriend whose mother had not gone away for thirty years for fear of leaving her cats on their own, having amassed quite a collection by then. We weren't quite that bad. Anyhow, I went out and bought a rabbit!

The more homely my life became, the more I loathed having to get up at 5.30 a.m. and go to London, as I did after the Bank Holiday. As each day went by, the contacts I made and the demands placed upon me increased the likelihood of leaving London and working on the coast. On my first day back, we had to play the return leg at Torquay in the Coca-Cola Cup first round in the evening. I had been undecided about going down there, knowing it would be a three-hour journey and a return at midnight, with another 5.30 start the following day. It may only be just over a hundred miles to Torquay, but in the summer it can take over three hours to get there. Having left at 3.30, we eventually found the Palace Hotel, where Andrew and Sally Kaye were having a relaxing afternoon tea. Plainmoor is just that, a small ground more in keeping with a non-League team than a professional football side. Mervyn Benney, the chairman, was a typically enthusiastic, zealous soul who could not quite contain his excitement that his team was ahead 1–0 after the first leg. As they attracted crowds of only 2,000, I knew it would be a hell of an achievement for them to get into the next round. Our view of the game was from behind one of the goals, where the directors' box had been placed. This was rather like Daniel in the Lion's Den as our seats were surrounded by Torquay fans. We levelled the aggregate score 1–1 but, four minutes from the end of extra time, we blew it: a complete defensive cock-up and goalkeeper Glass let the ball in. We were out.

Because of the extra time, my estimate of a midnight return turned into a 1.15 a.m. arrival home in thunder and lightning. Out of the cup and an away defeat: what to do next? Week in, week out, the whole world seemed to hinge on the result of one game. Suffer two defeats in a row, as we had done, and some would have us on the slippery slide to relegation, doom and gloom, fire and brimstone. Talk to those who do know about football, like the manager, and he gives you the inside line on whether he believes there is anything fundamentally wrong with the team. I had swiftly learned that if I were to make any comment to Mel on anything remotely connected with tactics or positional play, I would always start the sentence with 'I know I know nothing about football, but . . .' He had such patience with us asking mundane questions in those early days. Most of us could see that we preferred to play the ball down the right-hand side and had reasoned we could just as easily do so on the left. Having diplomatically put this to Mel, he then proceeded to show us on his board, using noughts and

146

crosses, exactly how the system worked. It was actually far more technical than that, involving players performing to their all-round abilities. Lesson over and suitably chastened, we could all see why we left the football to him.

For my part, I needed to see that the board set-up had been finalised and that a balance was achieved between the strengths and weaknesses of all the characters that were a part of it. On it were Peter Aldersey, managing director of Hibernian Insurance, and Ian Griffiths, whose background was in building and construction, both investors. I felt we needed a strong board of six people all having the ability to disagree vehemently with each other, yet respecting all views, prepared to accede to the majority and to give credit in arguments when it was due. Given that we were never going to be a money-making club, I felt it was important that the board would be able to act as a team and be able to speak to one another, be loyal, have integrity and honesty, and be a group of doers, not talkers. I knew there was bound to be criticism from a small minority of the public who would think they had a divine right to be on the board, or at least a say on who was appointed. What was I to do? There was no provision for rotation of directors in the articles of the company – deliberately so, to enable the team to have sufficient time to put into place their plans and implement them. The club had suffered for too long with changes in management every two years while letting the core business rot. I wanted to see a team of directors in place for three to five years, with the onus on the individual to be responsible and to step down if they were to abuse their position or become involved in financial impropriety.

Personal lives, personal lives. One can never tell exactly what is going on. We preached the values of loyalty and integrity and agreed we would be honour bound never to let the others down on a public front. We knew we would have to ensure the accounting and financial controls were tight, that the new stadium would be moved along. The trust would be maximized as a vehicle for democracy and consultation. We would be seen as leaders, not followers. Mel never had to ask what he could spend: rather, what we could afford. It was agreed that the manager should be backed

147

all the way on making investments if he thought that the return would be greater than the outlay. We would have to speculate to accumulate and recognize that the process of transition would take time. We knew, as fans, that Mel had the talent for spotting players and we knew now he would have a better opportunity to go out and see them before making decisions. He is a good manager on a reasonable salary committed to the club, and that, in itself, is a difficult combination to obtain. I sought the board's approval for the policy that we should not be seen as a hire-and-fire club. What on earth would we know about finding a new manager or coach if we were left to do so?

Having turned thirty, the days and months seemed to be slipping by. It seemed a sin to have wished away those hours of one's youth at school. The autumn was encroaching and I did not feel as if I had even had a summer. Our next match was against Blackpool, who had just knocked Manchester City out of the Coca-Cola Cup. We pulled in more than 4,900 spectators for a performance that Mel was to describe as our best since he had taken over. Tomlinson had recovered from his waterbed trouble and scored a goal on his return. We won 2–0 and, as Neil Perrit put it in the *Echo*, 'the thoroughbreds from Bournemouth dished out a good old horse-whipping to a group of donkeys normally found plodding on Blackpool sands'.

Even at this early stage of the campaign, with AFC Bournemouth standing astride the second division once again, it was clear that there was a pressing need to strengthen the team. For a club at our level, with limited resources and no bottomless pit to fund endless speculation on players, any purchase had to be carefully weighed up. And that was only for free transfers. To invest large sums of money, the onus was on the manager to make a choice that he was entirely comfortable with. The number of times I have heard other clubs suggest 'he'll do a job for you' would make me a millionaire for the proverbial pound. There is no exact science. It would be impossible to cover every game played in Britain. We might only scrape the surface having scouts watch four or five games every week. When dealing in players not at the top end of the market, it is a blessed game of chance – that freak occasion where you just happen to be at a reserve game or a non-League affair and spot someone interesting, picking the day when no one else is watching and tying up a deal. Sometimes you can tell on just one appearance. The fear for a club at our level is that if you invest all your money in one basket and this move doesn't work, you've blown it. As in law, business and now football, keeping options open seemed the best strategy. I quickly learned that it was more about other managers and coaches talking to our club than about any scientific form of scouting network. The 'he'll do a job for you' cliche would be typically disregarded if coming from an equal or lower division club but was paid the utmost respect if the recommendation came from higher up.

We came up with a list of names. Mel had seen John O'Kane play one game for Manchester United and come away extremely impressed. We were quickly able to agree terms for his purchase, a six-figure outlay taking in half the money that might be available for transfers. He had figured prominently in United's reserves and Mel felt he could be a star player. The only problem was that he did not want to drop down two divisions, preferring to take his chance in the Premier League. He was right. Within a few months he had been picked up by Everton and was playing first-team football. I lose count of the players we look at. The only criterion I set was that Mel must be happy and certain with his choices, which meant he would have to see them play rather than rely on the judgement of others. His days had regularly become eighteen or twenty hours long, driving to far-flung parts of the country in all weather, invariably attending a game where there would be a dozen or so other managers or coaches. People were raving about a young player who was knocking goals in left, right and centre. On three occasions we had tried to persuade him that a career in professional football might beckon, but he preferred to work in a local fish and chip shop. Eventually he decided a life in football might be more lucrative and yet failed to turn up for the training session. Week in, week out, fly 'em in, fly 'em out, bring them down to a hotel and training session, send them on their way. A constant process of evaluation that never gets into the media and is never seen by the fans. Even when the target is decided, there is then the process of checking his references, talking to those who have seen him. Then there are the negotiations to sign!

The fixture list had thrown up a local derby for us in early September. It was not like the north, where you find dozens of clubs within a small radius of each other. Our nearest clubs were seventy or eighty miles away. Bristol had long been the sleeping giant of British football, a seafaring city with two clubs, City and Rovers, both of whom were in our division. We were top, Rovers were in fourth place and nearly 6,000 filled the ground. I felt it was right that we should have a proper silence to honour the memory of the recently deceased Diana, Princess of Wales, and it was properly observed. The match was full of cut and thrust, aggression and skill. Sky TV televised highlights of the match, testimony to the turnaround that we had achieved and, for once, this was coverage for all the right reasons rather than negative ones. A 1–1 draw both pleased and disappointed. We dropped to fifth place and were never to return to the top three that season. The referee was marked one out of ten and we would always believe that a clear penalty was denied us. Rather like the day we played Crewe and Robbo hit a terrific shot from thirty yards into the roof of the net, only for it to cannon against the stanchion and fly straight back out again. The ref waved play on and we ended up losing the game. It did not help when, three days later, he called Mel to apologize, saying he had seen the video tape and could now see that the ball had gone in. In any other business you would be entitled to compensation, but not in the Football League – just a continuing sense that a majority of referees, though far superior to many in other countries, would be better off having this as full-time employment with at least the assistance of a fourth official looking at video tapes throughout a game in case it was decided to call on them. They say your luck balances out over the course of a season, but who believes that?

We suffered badly through not having competitive reserve-team football. Of a squad of twenty-four players, only fourteen could ever be involved on match days. To keep the rest interested, it is not sufficient just to practise every day. The previous year we had been made members of the Avon Combination League, a group of twenty-five or so teams mainly from higher divisions located in London and the Home Counties. For us to play against them guaranteed our players the opportunity to keep match-fit, to attempt a recovery from injury if required, and to try different formations against top-notch teams. We played all our reserve games on our own ground while other teams would use school playing fields and non-League grounds rather than damage their own pitch. I was outraged that, on a mere whim, the London clubs should decide we should no longer be part of the set-up, casting us out with other teams further west. I could well understand their desire not to travel to Torquay, Plymouth and Exeter given the distances involved and road conditions, but we were no more than an hour and a half's drive from London – all motorway and dual carriageway – and with good footballing style well suited to teams in a higher division. I am sure that if we were to get out of the second divison, we would be far more successful in the first, where there is more open play and less of the kick-and-run game. When we played some of the teams in our division, you would think we were pygmies in a land of giants. The game resembled rugby more than Association Football. Anyway, without reserve-team football to watch, which in itself would give us the chance to see players who might be available, we spent a lot of time at Southampton's reserve ground just twenty-five minutes up the M27.

I had this naive belief that we might in some way be helping if we were to go to such games. Knowing that Mel and John were spending most of their time in the afternoons and evenings traversing the country, I thought the least we could do was to offer moral support by joining them at some of the grounds they would be at. We had been interested in David Hughes of Southampton for some time. He was on a week-to-week contract and they were looking for £75,000. They had a new manager in Dave Jones, from Stockport County, and under the Bosman ruling, Hughes could leave on a free transfer at the end of the season. Southampton had taken a lot of flak because their board of directors had benefited considerably from selling out to a retirement home/leisure company. I had personal experience of that as during our troubles I had been telephoned by one of chairman Rupert Lowe's assistants to ask if we would consider a ground-sharing scheme based in Southampton. It would never have worked for us. Certainly clubs like Bournemouth rely upon the regional identity of being based in or close to the town – it gives a sense of community and bonding to the people. In any event, all credit to the Southampton board for actually going to the youth and reserve team games rather than just watching the first team play. I arrived just after the kick-off against Ipswich. (Mel was keeping a good distance from their manager, George Burley, for he was still a little unhappy that Matty Holland had been taken away from the club.) What surprised me was that twenty or so managers and scouts came down on a rainy night. It highlighted the immense competition among clubs for any talent that might be out there. A young lad with curly hair was standing next to Mel, so I found a space further up. Everything seemed very cloak-and-dagger, with mutterings and whisperings among those standing around. About fifteen minutes before the end of most games, there is a sudden exodus of spectators, in a knot. These are the scouts who turn up week in, week out, their love of football balanced against the belief that they will have seen enough in seventy-five minutes. It turned out that the young lad with Mel had been Hughes, who was keen to join us.

By mid-week, nearly every activity that was to take place that first Saturday in September had been cancelled or postponed, on account of the funeral of Diana, Princess of Wales. The Football League had dictated that clubs should either play their games on the Friday evening, Sunday afternoon or Tuesday evening. We were to play away at Gillingham on Friday, our least favoured choice but the only one the police would agree to let us have. Travelling down by train, I reached the Stakis hotel at Maidstone for our pre-match meal (the standard baked chicken, pasta, egg, baked beans) in time to share a pot of tea with Mel and John. Any reason for playing seemed immaterial when at six o'clock everyone moved to the TV room. Staff, team, guests and waiters alike stood and listened as the Queen addressed the nation. It seemed wrong for us to contemplate playing a game of competitive football that night. Concentrating on the task in hand was almost impossible.

I have pointed out already the links between our club and Gillingham – notably Tony Pulis, Mel's predecessor as Bournemouth manager, a charming chap off the field, who had taken his gritty, uncompromising midfield style on it into management at the Kent club. The Gills were a physical side who still retained many ex-Bournemouth players. That night, seven of those involved had at some stage played for us, too. Paul Scally remains one of the more flamboyant and charismatic chairmen within the League. His ever lovely wife, Lisa Marie, advertises on a full page in the match programme that she gives a 'singing experience', and is available for bookings at a 'reasonable price'. My own links with Gillingham were that one of the underwriters with whom I deal is a long-standing supporter of the club and a decent chap to boot. It did us no good to have John Bailey, our right midfielder, out for this game. He would have fitted well into the cast of *Oliver!* with his lovable rogue face giving the impression of a street urchin who might put his hand out, begging for money, while swiping your pocket watch. And he'd do just that on the field, stealing the ball and confounding the opposition. Only five foot eight inches tall but with the performing flea's apparent ability to jump twice his height, he dominates games for us. Moss, a great shot-stopper but prone to moments of coming some way off his line, had played for us in goal before moving to Southampton. On this occasion, he raced fully two-thirds of his own half only to find Steve Fletcher, our centre forward, reaching the ball just before him and lofting it high into the net to give us the lead. In the second half, though, we gave away another silly penalty as

153

well as a second goal to Gillingham. The long journey home was eerie, as on the M25 there was hardly any traffic. The funeral the following morning was the focus of everybody's attention around the country.

Our plan for integration and letting the club be run in a true community manner had hit a snag. The reasoning had been that the supporters' club and its management would be best placed to look after what it best knew about: drink. Both managers had expressed a firm belief in their ability to understand and run bars. Alan Helm, the resident caterer and licensee for the main bars in the main stand, had let us get on with this because we had said we wanted to do it. Unbelievably, we found that the stock ordering had gone somewhat awry. Over nine litres of Malibu had been delivered to the vice-president's lounge; I could not see it being drunk by the fifty or so local businessmen who had tickets on a match day. I had enjoyed this drink years before on the Costa Brava, but my sweet tooth had long since deserted me. With no Del Boys or Rodneys in attendance, the thought of our octogenarians knocking back vicious cocktails with umbrellas protruding out of them did not quite fit our needs. For all of that year, we had leant on willing volunteers who were very difficult to bring to account. We desperately needed to take on a full-time executive director to control what was going on. We considered a long list of candidates but soon came to the conclusion that my friend Andrew Dawson would be the most appropriate person for the job. He had the energy to implement modern management techniques. After much negotiation and reassurance – this, after all, was a business in its infancy after being £5 million in debt – Andrew, thinking of his young wife and two children, agreed to take up the position on 1 November.

In the meantime, we had little option but to make gradual progress behind the scenes. Our vision of a clean sweep, everything changing overnight, was idealistic but never realistic. In any business people can appear busy. Martin Jones was one such person and all the things he had promised began to unravel. We hadn't seen him since the Wigan game. Even his girlfriend Sarah didn't return my calls. In the accounts department we were beginning to uncover mistakes on a day-to-day basis from some of the other volunteers who had been helping us out. We asked the accountants Burnett Swayne to look after our affairs on a full-time basis. Simple matters such as going over to an automated system for paying wages directly into bank accounts took time. I think the players had been surprised to have had three months' pay paid to them on the due date, for as John Bailey told me, part of the adventure of being a player at AFC Bournemouth in the past had been to wonder just when the monthly pay would arrive.

The previous regime came up with the notion of building a bar under the South End concourse and above the supporters' club. A cursory examination of what was left up there revealed a collection of boxes, bags, a crash helmet, golf clubs and a briefcase. These were Martin's possessions which we thought had been removed to his friend's house at Ferndown. As with some mysterious treasure trove, we forgot to go back and open it, preferring to wait for him to return and collect the items. He had made much play of his hedonistic lifestyle, even buying a new Vitara for Sarah, driving her and a friend to Luton airport to fly to Scotland while he drove up alone. Very strange behaviour. I was worried about him; he was nowhere to be found. I decided to open all his post. The first letter was a demand from a hire purchase company for repayment of all money owed for the purchase of that Vitara. Then there were communications from banks, credit card companies, finance companies, stores – all seeking payment from him. Probably because he had become uncontactable. We never heard from him again.

Eddie Howe is one of the best players ever to come through our youth programme, clearly going to play at a higher level, either with us or, if we are not successful, a Premiership team. He is one of those people who will never say no, who is always willing to help represent the club both on and off the field. I was delighted that we

155

were able to give him a six-year deal, the longest ever awarded by us, giving him certainty in his future career and us the assurance that our assets were protected. If any club did come in to buy him, we would receive a healthy transfer fee. The effect of the Bosman ruling was that I knew we would have to revisit every contract with every player who we regarded as part of the core of our future success. We could never reveal details of every player's contract as this would create resentment among the team and inform other clubs of what they would have to offer to lure them away. I had to try to get across the message to the fans that we may have made money on the Matty Holland sale, albeit most of it used up in receivership costs, but that a percentage was being put to securing the long-term future of the club in establishing new contracts. We needed to get away from the endless process of always fearing that a player might be lost to the lure of another team without recompense. The plan was to look to four- to six-year contracts for those key players and to get those out of the way soon, securing one or two every month to spread the wage increases throughout the year. Each contract would usually involve a small signing fee of a few thousand pounds that would be payable annually. In the past, all of these fees had been paid in one month, usually July, adding as much as £100,000 to the wage bill in one month alone. To ease pressure on the cash flow, we wanted to try to distribute them during the year while trying to ensure the players did not feel they were being neglected when other contracts were being negotiated. Just because a certain player had not been spoken to, did not indicate we didn't think highly of him – the reality was that it was a question of spreading wage costs more evenly.

It was funny how voices from the past kept resounding. Terry Lovell, who throughout the receivership had tried to protect his sanity and his job, had continually pressed for a meeting. I was tired of raking over the past and, unlike the Pope, did not feel I could give him the absolution he wanted. I guess he was looking for somebody to tell him that he had done a good job and that everybody understood why he had behaved in the way he did. He complained that he was misunderstood and misguided because of the pressure put on him by those around him. I was just not interested. I had no time – no desire – to go over everything again and felt he was just looking for his old job back. He had spent his time criticising Diane Edwards, his assistant, who now ran the department, and there was no way we could ever countenance his return. I wish him well, but the past is a strange land.

We heard similar grumblings from the part-time staff who were shocked to find that under the new regime accounting to the taxman would be required for all their receipts.

We finished the month of September losing at home to another lowly team, Grimsby, by 1–0 (it was a month in which we gained just three League points from a possible fifteen). They were another side relegated from the first division who had started the season inauspiciously. As Neil Perrett had put it in the *Echo*, he only wished the programme had been longer so reading it would divert attention from the sorry display on the pitch. Mel reckoned Grimsby were one of the best sides he had seen in the division, which many mocked given their lowly position. How right he was proved to be when they achieved promotion at the end of the season. The only solace was, notwithstanding the sudden big-money arrival of Keegan and Wilkins, Fulham lost at Wigan, who we had beaten.

We were pressing lots of buttons to sign players. After much haggling with Queens Park Rangers, I was able to agree a price of £40,000 for Michael Mahoney-Johnson. Tomlinson had played for us against Grimsby and had been as ineffective as ever. We decided to return him to Manchester. Later that evening in a bar in London, Mark Lawrenson had been chatting to a couple of our fans, who without declaring their interest listened as he told them he had just been to Dean Court to watch a forward. It was Tomlinson, whom Newcastle United were thinking of signing.

They were as unimpressed as us and decided not to pursue their interest.

Mel and I then went to watch a reserve match between Southampton and Arsenal. Again Christer Warren impressed as he had in the other games we had seen. Southampton Reserves' leading scorer, he was giving the Gunners' defence a trying time. We knew he was available and he had actually grown up in Bournemouth before signing for Cheltenham Town. He was now going to cost us money to get back. Unlike most managers, Mel is extremely cautious about spending money, concerned as he is about the well-being of the club. He told me he thought Warren had something and could become a very good player, so I said we should go for him. We agreed a fee of £50,000 the following morning. We were delighted to find that within minutes of agreeing terms, both Oxford and Gillingham had made offers to buy him, too. Southampton detailed the package he was on and it fitted with our own wage structure. We knew exactly what we would be able to offer. Most players have agents, but Christer had the Professional Footballers Association working for him. It offers a free service, is comprised of ex-players and, of course, has ready access to all of the information about wages within clubs. My assumption was that everything would go smoothly until Mel called me. He told me no deal had been agreed and he had booted Christer and the PFA rep out of his office. Apparently the PFA had suggested Christer should have a salary package approximately double what he was receiving at Southampton. Their proposal was seemingly out of touch with reality. Mel had told them to clear off. A rather perplexed John Sainty, the assistant manager at Southampton, had then given Mel a call, heard what had happened and rather robustly told the player what he thought about it.

In the meantime, the intervention of the Jewish New Year meant nothing was progressing on the Queens Park Rangers front. (You would have thought it was a simple matter.) And we had a Norwegian agent asking whether we would take a Norwegian international player on loan for the rest of the season. Andreas Lund wanted to overcome a knee injury but could not do so in

158

Norway as their domestic season was almost over. We agreed in principle that he should come to us for five or six months three weeks hence. Our research had shown he was a highly rated player of Premier League quality whose manager knew we played good football. All the while I was preoccupied with the knowledge that I had to give my first seminar to a group of young business executives about my role as chairman, lawyer and 'never the twain shall meet'. I have no instinct as to whether or not this is at all interesting to an audience!

October began with a visit to Chesterfield – the first of two long trips in a week. I enjoy an early Saturday start, ripping through the countryside, empty roads and, hopefully, bright sunshine. Better than hours on a Friday night, dark, congestion and probably rain. Over 30,000 supporters had backed this town of the crooked spire when they reached the FA Cup semi-final the previous year. The team hotel seemed to be the only establishment of any consequence there and, looking at it, I was mightily glad I had not gone up the night before. It was a poky, dingy place whose character was embellished by two wedding parties who seemed to have arrived already. Mel recalled how, years before when he had come as manager, this had been one of the first away trips. He had not at that time been able to change the squad around to his liking and a number of outrageous characters still remained. To visualise the sight of bare buttocks sticking out from a couple of windows with various objects dropping on to the pavement below seemed a long way from the quiet discipline and good character now instilled throughout the club.

Chesterfield has a nice ground and, in James Norton Lea, one of the most respectable and clear-speaking chairmen I have come across. Not having been carried away by the success of the previous year, they carefully and quietly banked money and sold Kevin Davies, their striker, to Southampton for £750,000. That he was to move on from Southampton for ten times that sum within a year highlights the vagaries of football, but at least the money helped Chesterfield build a base to go towards a new stadium. Like us, they had found it extremely difficult to find players on reasonable wages. Jason Lee of pineapple hairdo fame had ended up at Watford, but when he had crossed Chesterfield's path a salary offer of £2,000 a week had not been nearly enough to secure his contract. With talk of Chris Waddle on £6,000 a week at Burnley, Ronny Rosenthal on the same at Watford and now Fulham's antics, clubs like Chesterfield and ourselves were quickly becoming the poor relations of the division. We both had marketable players, but where does that leave the likes of Rochdale, Darlington and Doncaster down in the bargain basement of our game? Anyhow, we achieved a 1–1 draw and raced back down the M1 for my secretary's wedding reception in east London.

Visual awareness was the main theme of our first year. We had to be seen to be more fully integrated within the community and ensure that people knew we existed and were part of the town. That there were only two road signs – probably twelve inches by eight in size and only on the dual carriageway from one direction – meant it was an extremely difficult task for anybody to work out where the team played. It is probable that every week and in every town a free newspaper is delivered to every address. Having spoken to our printers, who also looked after the *Evening Echo*, we were able to agree a strategy whereby we produced a quarterly newspaper to be delivered to 100,000 homes across the region. At least this would give us direct access, for a fraction of the cost of radio and TV advertising. Our social rehabilitation continued with the relaunch of the main newspaper, the *Echo*, as the *Daily Echo*, Andrew Kaye and I attending the business launch. The heightened need for articles meant our feeding of stories to the media increased, enhancing coverage of the club.

Meanwhile, I was becoming increasingly frustrated that we were unable to bring in any new players. Nothing had happened in a week on the three deals. To the fans this looked like inactivity or, at the worst, an inability to run the business, with my being equally frustrated at not able to tell everybody exactly what was going on.

160

Southampton's Christer Warren had received a bollocking from John Sainty over his PFA-inspired wage demands and sheepishly telephoned Mel Machin over the weekend to ask whether or not the deal we had offered was still on the table. Having spoken to him, he knew now we were telling the truth – that our offer was in line with the division and that he had been misled by the PFA. I was pleased he said he would join us on a three-year contract. As for Mahoney-Johnson, this saga became something of a joke in that he played in a QPR reserve game, going off injured. This was the second time it had happened. Mel and I were no longer interested in signing him until he had proved his fitness. Somehow the transfer never seemed destined to happen. By the time he recovered, QPR had sacked their manager and everything was thrown into uproar again. By the time they had decided they did want to sell him, Mel's interest had cooled and the player went to Brighton on loan, returning to QPR and not heard of since.

I was conscious that most of 1997 had been dominated by the events of the past, with everybody looking over their shoulders at financial insecurity and the battle to survive. There had been no time to celebrate or organize a party. Harry Redknapp had kindly offered to bring his West Ham team down to play a friendly, for which we pegged back the prices and printed 2,000 tickets for schools, hospitals and charities. We picked a day of incessant rain in October to play this match. On any other occasion, we would probably have called it off, but having invited all those who had participated in our survival – Lloyds, Arthur Andersen, businesses, lawyers and so on – we did not want to disappoint. In spite of injuries, Harry was still able to bring the likes of Eyal Berkovic, Andy Impey and Ian Bishop. It was a chance to have a laugh as well as a celebration. Memories. During the struggle we had a sighting of Elvis as he had dropped in on one game, auctioned the players on blind dates, Cherry Rock and an appearance by David Beckham long before he became a hate figure for his petulant kick during the

1998 World Cup. That 5,000 turned up, including my mum, who had never been to a game before, was in itself something. During the course of the game Mel left his seat to go to the bench, leaving Harry sitting behind my parents and me. Mum, who had become an ardent Cherries fan but did not appreciate the finer points of football, turned to me to say: 'I don't know what's going on. Our manager's down there on the sideline telling them what to do, yet theirs has disappeared. He can't be doing his job properly – I don't know what he's thinking about not being down there looking after his team!' Harry merely smiled . . .

Another Saturday, another long journey, this time to Preston, home to the new Museum of Football and with a marvellous stand depicting the face of Tom Finney. This was another club who had spent a fortune, picking up along the way two of the Manchester United players who had faced us in that pre-season encounter. The previous day I had had to go to our offices in Manchester and, driving across to Preston, bypassed the new Reebok stadium, home to Bolton Wanderers. It sat like a flying saucer in an uninhabited landscape and put to shame the old plans for our new ground based on the development at Yeovil Town, effectively a market village in the west of England – ironically now the target of Norman Hayward. I wanted AFC Bournemouth to become a centre of sporting excellence in a desirable tourist resort.

Despite investment and a flotation which brought a vast injection of capital into the club, Preston, like Millwall, still found themselves heavily in debt. They were unbeaten at home and battered us in the first half. When one of their forwards rounded the goalkeeper and fell over, rather like 'Stars on Ice', it was farcical. Christer Warren knew how to mark his debut. With his back to goal, the ball delivered to his feet, feinting one way, turning the next, he hit a shot crisply into the bottom corner to give us our first victory in seven games. We were back up to tenth place in the table. Yet small things can sour a victory: Preston were the only team we played that season who, when one of our players went down injured and we knocked the ball out, had not given it back to us from the throw-in. But, as the *Independent on Sunday* was to declare the next day, Bournemouth was very much enjoying its beach party of survival.

Another long journey home was enlivened by a break to watch England's success in Italy in qualifying for the World Cup. It may seem far-fetched, but this could provide a boost for us the following year in season ticket sales. The link between national success and enthusiasm for football on a local scale cannot be underestimated. Despite that prospect then and the World Cup the following year, we had much to keep an eye on within our own club. The wider picture of what was happening within the Football League was of secondary concern. In mid-October a meeting was called to discuss the League's future (a crucial meeting, yet seven clubs did not attend). Suddenly, the £138,000 we had been promised for youth funding without criteria had become £69,000. Given that everybody had been told it would be available back in August, this did nothing for cash flow planning nor any belief that we were part of an institution that knew where it was going or how it was to be run.

When a player signs for a club, he will often ask for a signing-on fee on top of his basic wages. This sum must be divided evenly over the length of contract – for example, a signing fee of £12,000 on a three-year deal would be payable in instalments of £4,000. If a player leaves a club without asking for a transfer, then the balance of any signing-on fee still has to be paid. In late October, three months after the event I suddenly received a call from the PFA stating Matty Holland would rather like the balance of his signing fee, £3,000, straight away. I was bloody annoyed. This was not a lot of money, but it all counted for us. I pointed out that we really had not wanted to sell him. It was only because he had asked to go once the bid from Ipswich had come in that we had agreed to release him. Don't doubt me: I think he is a tremendous bloke. Given that we were still heavily in debt, I was upset that he now sought to take advantage of the rule. Ipswich were probably paying him four times as much as we could afford. I had been as understanding as I thought I could be in finalising a deal which he had expressly stated he wanted – and we didn't. Anyway, we had no legal grounds for resisting payment, but this was a lesson to be learned.

So to the next Saturday. This, for us, was a huge game: Fulham, Keegan, Wilkins, Fayed and all. Another chance, as the papers put it, for those without to meet those with. Merely having access to large sums of money does not suddenly mean your team becomes an overnight success. You can lump any number of professionals together, but that in itself is no guarantee of success. One of the joys of my position as chairman is the variety of people I meet – such as the broadcaster Peter White, who never lets the disability of blindness overcome his cheery nature. I had often seen him on the train, an individual with a more enriched life, more perceptive, more appreciative, than those who complain week in, week out about their lot. It was good to go on his show on Radio Solent that morning, the first time I had been asked about myself and my life outside football . . . All that I remembered about Kevin Keegan as a player was when he came on as a substitute in a World Cup match in Spain in 1982, missing an excellent opportunity to give England victory over the host nation. Without being presumptuous, I guess people sometimes wonder now what the real Trevor Watkins is like, in that they only hear my voice on TV or the radio. I should like to think I was like Keegan, both on this visit and when we played at Craven Cottage later in the season. He was courteous and had time to spare for all those who wanted to talk to him, taking the trouble to say how pleased he was we had survived. He spent ages talking with Michael the vicar. After two fine headers from Ian Cox had brought us a 2–1 victory, Kevin was magnanimous in defeat, describing us as the best footballing side he had seen in the division. It was, I believed, not a sop but a compliment to use – and those three points brought us back up to fourth in the table.

Three days later Millwall visited us for what turned out to be another exciting game, albeit one that finished in a goalless draw. Only 4,700 people turned up, compared to more than 7,000 for the Fulham fixture, the upshot of European football on television that evening. So much for increased interest in the game. We did not see a penny of that European television revenue! A decade or more earlier, my dad had been taken aback to see a Millwall fan brandishing a crossbar 'borrowed' from some park pitch as he walked to the ground. Millwall's reputation had been built on a decade of intimidation, ripping up seats and 'in your face' support. The club was now run by Theo Paphitis, who had tried to buy Matty the day before Ipswich came in, but who, despite a new stadium, stock exchange listing and investment, still had financial problems. There was no intimidation on this October evening, an indication of how much football had changed.

By now there was something interesting about every game we played. We travelled next to Burnley, who had invested heavily in trying to achieve success. The season had started disastrously for them; they had not scored for six games and slumped to the foot of the table. It was an old-fashioned town and an old-fashioned club: the journey in took us past long steep rows of terraced houses with stone-cladding (virtually extinct in Bournemouth). As at Chesterfield, there were no women in the boardroom, probably in breach of some Euro law and decidedly antiquated. Instead, there was a group of perplexed gentlemen, bemused by the new structure at our club. As is the way of all northern clubs, they warmly welcomed us with a traditional carved joint to give sustenance against the extreme cold and snow on the hills outside. 'Do you want a drink?' they asked. 'No, I'm driving,' I said. 'We didn't ask how you bloody got here!' was the retort. Before the game, I laughed and joked with Eddie Howe during our inspection of the pitch that all we needed from him when a cross came in was a leaping, flying header into the top corner. Fifty-eight minutes gone and what happened? We had given away a ridiculous goal to their highly paid player-manager Chris Waddle – stubbed off his toe and bouncing over the line past a despairing Jimmy Glass. Another hash-up in the second half was rectified only by a lashed free-kick from Jamie Vincent that brought about a 2–2 draw. Yet Jimmy did his best to lose us the game when, in injury time, he decided to dribble across his own area before smashing the ball against an oncoming tram-sized player. It shot up and ballooned just over the bar. It was a game we should have won but brought us only a point. Afterwards, on live TV, the draw for the first round of the FA Cup pitted us at home to Heybridge Swifts, founded in 1880 and now of the Ryman League Premier Division. This was about as far below us in football's 'pyramid' as you could get in the FA Cup, the greatest of knock-out competitions. This first round would be their sixth match in the competition. We could always do with a home draw, but this sort of opposition never fails to strike the fear of God into League teams.

All of us went to church the following morning for what was to be the last service given by Michael Lowe, the club chaplain, at All Saints, Mudeford. He and the choir entered to strains of the theme to *Match of the Day* on the organ. He had been diagnosed as having an incurable muscle wasting disease, but his charismatic and enthusiastic zest for God and for football, which, as he put it, were one and the same thing, kept him going. Football and religion both required commitment and instilled qualities of good character. In the public eye Michael would never be seen to be down. We would often hear his voice echoing down the corridors, 'Up the Cherries' or, during a match, 'Why don't you go to bed, referee?' He was one of the few people I have met who can make the words of the Bible and repetition of the prayers offered each week come alive and have meaning. It is people like him that make all the effort involved in trying to save the club worthwhile. In many ways the club was to become Michael's source of inspiration and enthusiasm for the future. For all that he had given, without ever asking for anything in return, we decided to award him and his wife Pat two lifetime seats in the directors' box. Mick Cunningham, the club photographer, presented them both with a lovely animated shot of Michael sitting next to Kevin Keegan at the game against Fulham, the two men deep in conversation.

We gave him this picture and told him of the seats before our game against lowly Brentford at the start of November. They were ultimately to be relegated and made for dreadful opposition, yet we were unable to take them apart. All that I can remember from the game was that every time Jimmy Glass took a kick, the ball would sail into touch on the left or right wing. After twenty or thirty minutes of this, the opposing goalkeeper would put his arms aloft, as if signalling a conversion in rugby league, or maybe giving him something to aim at. Cold, rainy and a piss-poor game. At times like that you know you must be mad having paid to endure the experience. Funny to think now how, within a year, their chairman would be on our board!

It was lucky we had other news to break that day in the form of the launch of our own Internet site. Marginally more exciting, too! My sentimental rose-tinted view of life is that one should believe that it is generally good to trust people; if you show the way, others will follow. Having stood up to be counted, so others had followed and joined in the crusade. I knew about the Internet, but not the intricacy. When one of our supporters, Andy Smith, offered to create a website, we were delighted. He spent hours working on it and now the prototype was there, at www.afcb.co.uk. Many of our older supporters may not be aware of what it is, but in terms of reaching out to the community and a younger base, and allowing information to be passed around all over the world, this was to become a key way of gaining information. From thirty or so visitors a day, we now have more than 1,500.

Call it overwork or exhaustion, or just trying to do too much (my Achilles' heel – I never quite know how many hours there are in a day) but I have never felt as ill as I did in that first week of November. All energy seemed to disappear from my body. The human failing always to underestimate how long it will take to do something plagued me. I would count on doing everything at top speed and then wonder how the hours disappeared. What I reckoned to be a touch of flu was at least countered by the police's recognition of what improvements we had made in ground security and their decision to let us go 'police free', so saving a considerable amount of money. My mother always claimed that I tried to burn the candle at both ends and I guess I did on 4 November, when we were playing Wrexham. As usual, my idea was to get up at 5.30, go to London for a full day's work, take an afternoon train north (work on it), do a commentary for Radio Solent, get back home by 2 a.m. and return to London the next day. Illness intervened, however, and Michael Lowe, the now retired vicar, stepped in.

I hadn't listened to football on the radio for ages. It's an awful experience. The game itself was dire – we were 2–0 down after fifteen minutes and missed a load of chances before Warren pulled a goal back at the death. I must have been really ill as the result didn't bother me and I ended up taking the whole week off work, lying around feeling sorry for myself, achieving nothing at all. Not a good patient! By the weekend, I thought the perfect antidote would be a trip to Plymouth, not least for the chance to renew acquaintance with Dan McCauley, having been thrown out of the boardroom by him on my previous visit. There was a certain irony in his having to extend courtesy to us as officials of the visitors. With their club up for sale, discontent among the players, the local newspaper still resorting to covering games from a crane outside the ground (they had been banned) and with their star striker, Carlo Corazzin, away on international duty, all boded well for us. They had also had their main stand closed by the local Council for safety reasons. With the Dan dynasty seemingly at an end, it turned out he wasn't there.

Part of a chairman's role for away matches is to dictate how to allocate the twelve tickets the home team provides for visiting directors. Owing to the safety work, we were ushered into a temporary Portakabin erected high up overlooking a corner of the pitch. Normally we are put in a group of twelve seats, away from the home lot. Good thing too, given the amount of shouting we do! Not this time, though – home and away directors were all together in one room. The pained silence was broken by Michael the vicar leaning out and waving his arms at our supporters huddled below, behind the goal in the rain, gesturing to his flock. Whatever the Plymouth fans to the left must have thought of the sight of him laughing, proclaiming 'Up the Cherries', it certainly lightened the atmosphere. To be closeted in one room with the Plymouth directors was surreal. Not being the archetypal board, we still behaved like ordinary supporters. Suffice to say we did not actually have much to shout about. Within fifteen minutes we were two goals down again and well beaten. Plymouth had a young player, Lee Hodges, who had come on loan from West Ham and was making his debut. Harry Redknapp's embarrassment on the telephone, when he realized his debut would be against us, was well founded, as he tormented our defence. Just to disprove the theory that H. Redknapp did us nothing but good turns!

November was quickly becoming a month to forget. Mid-table boredom beckoned. Back to work the following week, I felt a lot better. Maybe the last ten months had caught up with me; if I hadn't noticed it, others had. That Friday evening, I went down to Chapelgate, our training ground, which hosts the school of excellence for players from nine to sixteen, run and coached by our staff. A youth set-up is not just for producing players, but to ingrain the club within the town. If a reputation is built for offering good coaching, more and more individuals will want to come. Even in adversity, Terry Wateridge had built up a school that now had over 120 kids coming each Friday, some on a 150-mile round trip. The sheer dedication and commitment of the parents in bringing their boys was amazing. They would then repeat this for games on a Sunday. There, in torrential rain and with the wind gusting, I knew it was occasions like this that made saving the club such a vital mission. Maybe I was growing old, but this was infinitely preferable to going down town and having a few beers. Terry said it was the first time anyone from the board had shown any interest for donkey's years, yet all of us felt committed – not because we were obliged to, but because we wanted to do so. From the parents' point of view, seeing the chairman take an interest meant a lot to them. For me it was their support that meant so much.

The next day Heybridge Swifts had their own cup final. They had already played five games and to have reached the first round of the FA Cup was a tremendous achievement. A League team in this situation is, of course, on a hiding to nothing as the expectation is an easy victory. Cup history reverberates with teams coming a cropper. We ourselves had caused a number of major upsets back in the fifties and early eighties. Beating the best in the land, or just a team from a higher division, carries enough meaning to sustain the hunger of fans for years to come. Moreover, FA Cup victories are a lucrative path to tread. Such results can carry a small club financially for years to come. For this particular non-League side, a mixture of youngsters, players with non-League experience and those at the end of their professional careers, this was a chance to prove themselves on a larger scale, to prove the doubters wrong and perhaps even to forge a career for themselves. Heybridge had a long Cup history, although it had a rather ignominious chapter. In 1893 they had been fined £2 and suspended for playing for six weeks. They had dragged a referee into a pond after he gave a goal when an opposing player had clearly caught the ball in the six-yard area before scoring!

For us, languishing in mid-table obscurity, the FA Cup meant we could forget about the League for a day. Despite reducing the prices, only 3,400 attended but were rewarded by a terrific goal from Russell Beardsmore from fully twenty-five yards, his first for three years. It earned him a national goal of the month award. Two second half goals from Steve Robinson, our talkative Irish international, sealed a victory marred only by the referee's decision to send off one of the youngest players on Heybridge's side. The Cup creates a lifetime of memories, so it was a shame his were ruined. Our crowd booed the decision.

The second-round draw brought the mouth-watering prospect of Bristol City visiting Dean Court in what we thought would be the tie of the round. I am never quite sure how these matters work, but all of a sudden we had the Football Association on the phone asking us to switch the date to Sunday, so that it could be the main, live game on Sky TV. If we were to consent, there would be the small matter of a cheque for £75,000 sent to us, plus £5,000 to secure radio coverage. I decided I would probably not need board approval and quietly said I would be more than happy to agree to this request. Compared to the profit of only £4,000 made when we played Heybridge, we were now looking at a twenty-five-fold increase in one game alone.

Back to League action and another lowly team, Southend, who had dropped out of the first division a year before and were having difficulty coping – not least in terms of the numerous contracts they had. Behind the scenes, Franck Rolling had been putting on weight, probably through eating too many of his 'galloping gourmet' creations, so the manager threatened to fine him. Not quick at the best of times, he was less than happy. The cascading rain meant an awful lot more work for the groundsman. I guess Steve was no different from any other groundsman – he didn't want us to play. The unsung heroes, for me, were his young assistant, Dave, and Duncan the kit man, eighteen, nineteen years old, who would work considerable unsocial hours for little public appreciation. I hardly gave a thought to how good the team looked in its kit each week. Duncan's responsibility is to ensure every kit whim and desire of the players is met. He had to clear up all the kit after the games, ensure all the balls were collected and that everything was ironed and pressed ready for the next fixture. Not the most glamorous job in a football club, but vital to the harmonious operation of any professional side. Pity he couldn't do something about that rain!

CHAPTER 14

And Now Live on Sky . . .

In spite of going behind to a fifth-minute goal we managed to grab the three points against Southend. It had to be admitted, here we were in mid-November, barely three months into the season, already looking for a kick-start, wondering where we would find the additional players to provide that cutting edge to our play. We had a great squad but were still suffering from the hangover of a close season spent dealing with the past. There had been no time to do the radical surgery needed to get an enhanced squad together on the field. It is only now that I get angry when I realise what the past cost us – not just money but a year of development on the field. The manager was delighted with his side's work rate but our resources were painfully thin. We still needed new blood, especially up front where Steve Fletcher was soldiering on with a succession of striking partners. We knew we could create the chances but we needed to put them away.

We chased Neil Heaney of Manchester City and Jonathan Macken of Preston. Preston had spent huge sums on their team, most of the money coming from being floated on the stock exchange. Yet there were plenty of stories doing the rounds about their directors having to stump up cash for survival and the club being in dire financial straits. We thought we might take advantage of that. While Mel dealt with Manchester City, I contacted Preston.

Their initial response was typical. 'The manager is not prepared to sell one of his best assets,' but 'it depends on the price you are offering'. Couldn't quite work that one out! Either they did want to sell or they didn't. Perhaps they were interested but weren't expressing themselves as well as they might.

I suggested they think about it and name the price they wanted. Like litigation I would always prefer not to name a figure first. At least if they told me I would know the ceiling and then try to bring them down from that. On the one hand Macken was irreplaceable but I received a call within forty-eight hours saying they would sell at £150,000. Quite a simple process in the end. It was high and beyond what we wanted to pay or even could afford. After some deliberation we decided there wasn't a player we could give them in return. I told them £100,000 would be nearer the mark. Does anyone (apart from us!) really name a price and then offer no flexibility on it?

Preston told the player and opened a dialogue. His terms were well within our structure but the message we got back was that he didn't want to move south. Unfortunate, given we thought he would give our strike force a much better opportunity to score goals. I'm sure our style suited him and indeed we were to be the more successful side that season. On top of that disappointment, Heaney also decided to stay put for the time being – although with £3,000 a week wages that was probably just as well!

Both of those potential deals had taken hours on the phone and all for nothing. The key is to avoid desperation. Our season was not going to pot, far from it. There was a need to hold our nerve rather than jump in with rash decisions that might cost more in the long run than perhaps the immediate benefit of a goal or two from a new signing at the outset. If we ever needed to sell we knew we could. Certain managers have favourite players and they all know who. A poor performance here or there never changes that. Every manager in the country is out there looking for that starlet. But we were looking for an immediate solution, not one that would take time to bring on. You would think each club would have a huge database of information, a precise scouting network and the ability to make rational decisions rather than the game of chance it actually is. There isn't. I am not even sure how you go about valuing a player when it is all so subjective. Take Burnley. They shelled out £750,000 for a thirty-year-old and paid him in excess of £4,000 a week on a five-year deal. They should have spoken to us first! There is no exact time for deciding when to buy or sell; you might as well get up in the morning, say which way the wind is blowing and then decide what to do. It is all chance.

The transfer market had been turned on its head that year by the introduction of a new system, similar to the American 'free agency' deal. Some average player in a foreign land had decided when his contract ended he should be able to do whatever he wanted to. His name, Marc Bosman, was to become famous not for his ability but the affect of his decision to go to court to assert his right to freedom of movement throughout Europe. So much for entering the Common Market to benefit this country – it has certainly cost us a fortune in footballing terms! The European court decided he was right. Any player coming to the end of his contract could have a free transfer to another club. For some arbitrary reason they said it only applied to players over twenty-four, a limit I believe will disappear soon. In the past, if a player did not stay with his existing club they would be entitled to compensation so long as they had offered him a new contract.

Given that most small clubs would count on selling to ensure their survival the old system protected them. The new does not. There was no lead-in time, the change being introduced suddenly and without time to prepare. Everyone had started this season knowing that anyone over twenty-four at the end of it and with their contract finishing could walk free. Players that might have cost hundreds of thousands of pounds normally could be signed by clubs for nothing. It has cost us a lot of money as the only way we are able to make sure that our assets are protected is to offer large increases to persuade them to sign new long-term contracts – then if a club really wants one of our players they will have to pay good money as there is now no opportunity for years to come for them to pick them up free under Bosman. Once a player comes within twelve months of finishing his existing contract it is extremely difficult to persuade him to sign a new one. Why would he? It would be much better financially for him to join a new club. Instead of their paying us a transfer fee they could pay nowt and, using the money saved on a transfer, offer the player a substantial wage increase.

We were lucky, all our players wanted to stay and eventually, after some lengthy negotiations, signed new deals. But we did try to take advantage ourselves. We offered £50,000 to Plymouth for their leading goalscorer, Canadian striker Carlo Corazzin, figuring that if they didn't accept it in January we would discuss terms with Carlo and get him to agree to join us in the summer – and Plymouth wouldn't get a penny. They laughed. We laughed too. By the following summer Carlo did leave his club but we didn't get him; there again, we were to sign three much better strikers for nothing. He would get almost £150,000 a year from a club that could ill afford it and Plymouth would have nothing. That is the madness of Bosman. We are lucky, on balance. I think we did well to restructure as we did. Others have not. They have ended up paying salaries they cannot afford. Clubs are getting further wrecked by the distortion of the market; affordability is so far off the wages that have to be paid, or so it seems, to meet not only the desire for success but merely to hold your own in one division. Time for a little control over the game, perhaps a bit of wage capping mixed with a limit on roster size? No, that is probably too much common sense for the leaders of our 'wonderful' game.

By now the leading goalscorer in the Football League was Jimmy Quinn, who at thirty-eight gave hope to me as I rapidly approached my thirty-second birthday! Way back in the summer we had met Jimmy but we could not afford his £60,000 package. Mel had been unsure whether he still had it in him to score goals at our level, markedly different from the third division where he was successful. Taking him in July would have meant losing one of the other staff, those who had been loyal throughout. So he had gone off to Peterborough where his goals took them to the top of the third division table. Mel now wanted to see if he would join us. My verbal agreement with Jimmy was that we could go back to him at any time – his assurance was that if we asked and paid £1,000 a week he would come at the drop of a hat.

Quite what his manager would think was another thing. I only knew what I had read or seen but without doubt was aware that Barry Fry is a character. Chubby, red-faced and extrovert, he would never be short of an opinion. Notorious for his amazing capacity to buy and sell players without any regard for the usual protracted rigmarole of the transfer market, he has brought a freshness to the game sadly lacking elsewhere. He has also, as seen on TV, developed a singular style that combines a cheery approach with the most colourful of language. 'Shrinking' and 'violet' are not words one would readily use in the same sentence when describing Barry.

Jimmy Quinn had scored nearly twenty goals in as many matches. Digging out his number early one Sunday evening I gave him a call. At last we appeared to be getting somewhere. Yes, he wanted to join us and as soon as possible. Jimmy would make the approach to get Barry's blessing; not that he needed to but felt honour bound to do it. Of course, Jimmy had played for us years ago in Harry's era.

Jimmy came down early the following week and played nine holes of golf with Mel. Everything seemed to be progressing smoothly: he said his contract made no provision for any transfer fee or compensation to be paid so long as he moved to a management position. Fine. We would make him a coach. Peterborough's owner controlled the Pizza Express chain, restaurants where Mandy and I always enjoyed eating. He was also a patron of the arts; indeed Peterborough United is probably the only football club to sponsor an art exhibition at the Royal Academy. Despite his wealth, he is an ordinary chairman who would still take the train to matches. I reasoned that losing Jimmy would be no problem, he would be easy enough to replace, with money no object.

Barry Fry was not best pleased – he was polite but not prepared to let Jimmy go until their injury crisis had cleared. I was not too concerned over a few days' delay. Our next game was in the FA

Cup and Jimmy would be cup-tied anyway. So long as he was with us by mid-December, all would be well. Having seen Barry in action in a 'fly on the wall' documentary, throwing tea over his players, I was not keen on making him angry. Anyway the deal appeared to be as good as done.

Part of being a community club is making sure with that we get involved in as many local projects as possible. *Children in Need* has long been part of the BBC autumn schedule, an evening dedicated to raising money for good causes. It was something I had grown up with. Now as chairman of a football club I offered our support to the evening. In the south they were taking over a local theatre for a whole evening. Although we had a game the next day, Mel was happy to allow those who wanted to take part in trying to break the world record for the fastest ever haircut. (Having no hair, Ian Cox was able to excuse himself.) I had made sure that my hair – such as I have left – had been cut. That left Ken Dando and Robbo to face their fate at the hands of these bizarrely attired hairdressers standing there shears in hand, looking like exiles from a Wild West movie set.

Robbo's concern was for his appearance on the pitch the next day. This was a man who when faced with an outbreak of acne, had asked the club if we would be prepared to pay the £300 his special treatment would cost to cure the problem. The justification he gave was that if we did so he would play better, not having to hide his face as he ran around! Perhaps it will come as no surprise to learn that he is Irish, a worthy representative of the Irish national side but with equal ability to blarney as to play soccer. Just for him, because he always claims I never say a nice, honest thing about him, I will record for posterity that he always has a smile on his face. An ambassador, someone who would never be shy of asking but the first to show concern, one who would always think of others first and typical of the type of character that Mel has brought to the club. (Now where's the fiver!)

178

Maybe it was the gel he had put on his hair but while Ken was finished off in record time, Robbo found himself looking worse than Worzel Gummidge. Amid frantic apologies from the poor woman who had inflicted this damage, the fact that loads of money had been raised gave little solace to a shocked Robbo. In front of a packed audience she tried to repair the carnage while reassuring him (as people often do in similar situations) that it was not as bad as it looked!

Back in the real world we faced our third home game in eight days. Not only is that not good for the pitch but it is also bad news for finances in the run-up to Christmas. At least the crowd picked up, once again approaching 4,000. Located almost on the border with Scotland, Carlisle is one hell of a place to get to but don't forget that for them every away game means a long journey. Ten hours driving through England is not much fun when you have to play football at the end of it. Years ago Michael Knighton had been on TV kicking a ball up in the air at Old Trafford as he came very close to buying Manchester United for what would now be a knock-down price of £10 million. Instead he bought Carlisle United and became chairman, dispensing with a manager and widely believed – despite his denials – to be the one who picks the team. His promise to his supporters that this team was going to be in the Premier League within a few years is going to take some fulfilling. He had used his money to invest in a new stand and bring players to an otherwise unattractive location. He may be shrewd, but during his tenure the team had yearly yoyoed between the second and third divisions; having been promoted they were now once again flirting with a rapid relegation. He left himself wide open to media-invented stories that would make fun of him. He once commented on the possibility of life on other planets and seeing UFOs – this led to strange tales in the press of his own alien abduction to the outer reaches of the universe. When the Football League suggested their schemes for revising the divisional structure in five ways, termed Venus, Earth, Neptune, Mars and Pluto, it was Michael who stood up and humorously suggested: 'I believe I should open this discussion as I do feel particularly well qualified to speak on these matters given my own extraterrestrial experience!'

We won the game 3–2 pushing us back up to ninth in the table. Going home in the dark, a sweet victory made the bad weather all the more bearable. (Pity Carlisle, flogging back up the motorway.) Even better news was that we were given a bye in the first round of the Auto Windscreens Shield, a competition exclusively for clubs in the second and third divisions that nobody paid any attention to until the later rounds. Why? Because the great prize is that the final is played at Wembley, the home of English football where every player dreams of playing. Now players who may have spent their entire careers in the lower reaches of the League have a realistic chance of fulfilling that dream.

Football has taken me to cities I would never normally visit. Carlisle's a good example. And Wycombe's another. A hundred interesting facts about Wycombe? Can't think of that many except I once had a girlfriend in Aylesbury and that's not too far away. Never went there, mind you. Such dynamic thoughts did not obscure a good 1–1 draw on a bitter afternoon. At least it was only an hour or so to drive home (normally, without taking into account Andrew's scenic diversion through the countryside). In daylight fine, pitch darkness no!

I have always hated birthdays since I was a kid. As at Christmas, I love to find a present for someone, spend time choosing something I believe they will like, but I always find it difficult to accept a present back. Maybe that's why I have also found it difficult to take in the many wonderful comments made by people in appreciation of what they thought I had done at the club. It is so important to tell people when they do something worthwhile and not just to criticise. Yet my inability to accept kind words has always confused me. Anyway I hate a fuss so it was convenient to find that on my birthday this year the Football League had kindly arranged for us to be at home playing York City. Something to deflect from my own personal occasion! It had been bad enough turning thirty and being constantly reminded by road signs with big numbers telling me the maximum speed I could do was now the same as my age. Yet thirty-two did not seem too bad and everyone was there and they did bake a lovely cake. Maybe I am learning with old age not to be such an insensitive, ungrateful bloke after all.

So 3,365 came to see us, the eighth team playing the seventh. Pretty poor in the round. Probably doesn't seem a lot to you reading this but it was still about 500 more than we might have got a year before. A year later we would be averaging double that. No goals to acclaim but a chance for me to sit, watching, thinking how much older I had grown in a year. Twelve months before I had been in America looking forward to Christmas, buying clothes on the cheap, eating good food, seeing the sights of Chicago – great city, with the Magnificent Mile and its Cheesecake Factory, Chicago pizza piled high with marinara sauce and melted cheese . . . A far cry from the catering at Dean Court but it took my mind off the numbing cold.

Four days later it was time for our first taste of being live on television. When I was a kid there was maybe one live game a week on TV, if you were lucky. Nowadays there might be as many as two or three in a day. That was all down to Rupert Murdoch's Sky TV deal with the Premiership and the Football League, pumping millions into soccer and broadcasting the game to homes across Europe. Some may say it is a bad thing; it certainly devalues the specialness of live football on television but it has increased crowds and made soccer a popular family sport again.

Sky have undertaken to show games from every round of the FA Cup, even the first and second where 'smaller' teams take part. When our home tie against Bristol City was chosen as their game for the second round of the FA cup no one realised how much preparation would be needed, beginning as soon as the game against York was over. The game was to be beamed all over

Europe and twenty-eight camera positions were erected, each signal sent up to a satellite and bounced back to earth, 50,000 miles in a quarter of a second. Forget about the endless debates over money in football, whether Sky should have an exclusive deal and the pedantic arguments over collective bargaining (where teams negotiate as a League rather than individually), the £75,000 TV bonus we got from this game would pay a month's salaries.

TV pays so TV dictates when we play. No Saturday afternoon or Friday evening – no, we were to kick off at one o'clock on a Sunday lunch-time to fit in with the assorted roast dinners, pub lunches and armchair drinkers of England. They wanted me to do a pre-match interview. Fine, I thought, not realising that meant going down to the pier in my suit two days earlier. Why? Something about images of Bournemouth for the punters watching at home, seagulls soaring, deckchairs stretched out, ice cream in hand . . . well, not quite but almost. It made for good TV, but standing in the sunshine it may have looked like the middle of summer but it was bloody cold in a thin suit! I wondered if anyone watching might think me mad for wandering the beach in my city clothes apparently on a Sunday lunch-time.

In my 'active chairman' role I found myself on Saturday morning sitting at Thomas Cook cutting through holiday brochures trying to find an affordable mid-season break for the lads. Meanwhile, back at Dean Court the shop was shut. The demands on the staff had meant that there had not been enough time to do everything that needed to be done. Heartless bastard that I am I reckoned we should have worked through and eased off once the game had gone. It was the third Saturday before Christmas. Yet, humanitarianism suggested they needed a break given they would all have to work on the Sunday. So, the shop was shut.

Mel had superstitiously insisted that unless the team trained on the pitch that day they would not win, much to the indignation of Steve the groundsman. It was no surprise when my mobile rang. Steve was about to resign, his beloved pitch allegedly in tatters while Mel in turn had found lots of people queuing at the shop with no one to serve them. It was a little like the Keystone Cops as every director descended on the ground. The customer is always right ... And as for Mel, the pitch and the groundsman, that was another thing. Steve was none too pleased with Mel's initial assessment that he would be no more than twenty minutes. After thirty he stormed off leaving his dedicated and eager junior, Dave, to prepare the ground. Good job too as the twenty minutes turned out to be two and a half hours! Steve eventually left the club a few months later.

With responsibility for the media, I had done my usual pre-match bits with the local stations. Jeff Barker on 2CR is typical of the thousands of DJs that keep us amused every morning. Terrific bloke, and a great supporter of the club. 2CR is not really a sports station but it had supported the club in the hard times and now by purchasing ground boards. On their FM side, the breakfast crew were led by 'shock jock' Graham Mack. Having listened at length to the wisdom of Rush Limbaugh, Howard Stern and Gordon Liddy, I knew that Mack was leagues adrift of even being mildly radical when entertaining. I had never met him but one of his assistants, a portly Canadian, asked if they could have six tickets for the game if they in return stood outside for the two hours leading up to kick-off distributing calendars and put out a lot of publicity on their show. I didn't have a particular problem with this, even when he called and asked if I could make it eight.

I was pretty annoyed getting to the ground the day of the game to find that they had been plaguing Di Edwards all week to put tickets by. In fact under Football Association Rules we would have to account for the face value of tickets given away and pay 40 per cent to our opponents. As they had helped to raise funds for the club I concluded they wouldn't mind if they stood rather than took seats that would cost the club money it could ill afford to pay.

I went into the supporters' club forty-five minutes before kick-off to take the microphone and tell everyone about what was going on, news about players and so on. Just as I was about to go in, my mobile rang. It was Mack's gang. They were huddled in the corner of the car park but I told them they would have to wait; anyway, they were not really doing anything but standing around.

I was extremely late for the supporters' club where, with a robust reception, everyone was up for the Cup. The last thing I wanted was any hassle. I gently explained to the giant Canadian why the ticket situation had changed. He pleaded ignorance. Richie, the travel chicken (yes, he dressed as a chicken while doing the travel news!), seemed happy enough with the situation. Some of their hangers-on began to drift away when I explained the problem.

The rain began to tip down. Perched up on one of our stands, the commentators were having a most untropical experience. Come to sunny Bournemouth and get absolutely soaked, frozen and numbed to the bone. Somehow this might be the last we see of Sky for a long time, I thought, even though we gave them the warmest welcome. Improvements are in hand, I promise. Then the floodlights failed and that said it all. The rain was by now lashing down like sleet, the wind blowing a gale. By now even the mysteries of Shipshape catering soup at half-time were beginning to seem attractive (only joking, Alan!).

The game was explicit, unadulterated passion ebbing and flowing. At least until the power failed. Bristol were second in the table, and had won nine games in a row. It just so happened that it fell to us to end that run. After thirteen minutes they found themselves a goal down when a devious free kick was hacked into his own net by one of their players. It is the number of goals scored that counts not the possession. We hardly touched the ball, had four shots on target against their thirty or so yet they got one goal and we scored three. City bombarded our goal and our keeper Jimmy Glass knew at the end of it what it was like to be in a blitz facing fifteen or twenty corners and twice as many shots. And it was our name that was going into the third round of the competition, the chance to pull out a plum tie against one of the top teams in the country.

Didn't that whisky taste good after I'd been out in the cold! By that time it was 4.30 and I was hoarse, exhausted and frozen. Then there was the third-round draw to sit through – that ridiculous rigmarole of waiting for the balls to be drawn one by one, numbers announced and teams listed. All we wanted was to come out first in a pairing so it would be a home tie. And we did: 'AFC Bournemouth,' the man said, 'will be at home to . . . Huddersfield Town.' Boring! A nondescript northern side with not much going for them save a nice new stadium. Certainly not the jackpot prize of drawing a top team; no, this was as good as winning a tenner in the National Lottery. Nice feeling, but it could have been so much more. Anyway, Mandy and I were going to be on a much-needed holiday then. I was glad that we were drawn at home but also mightily pleased to have a break to look forward to.

It was difficult to get excited about the draw. Yet that evening Mel, Ian Cox, his wife and I had been invited to the inaugural BBC South sports awards, a lavish dinner for 250 sports people at a posh hotel in Southampton. Why they had invited me, lard-bucket and literal heavyweight of the footballing world, I don't know. Maybe it was an act of charity. Mel and I sat at dinner, laughing at the months gone by. He reminded me how I had always joked that if he ever needed a player, I had my boots in the car. Now Andrew had begun to use that line too.

We were nominated as best team, Ian as the best player in the south. After all that had been done to save the club, I thought we might win this category on behalf of the town. It was the story of the year – it's not every day a community saves one of its main assets. We were in complete contrast to the other southern sides. There had been a corporate takeover at Southampton, asinine behaviour at Brighton and financial problems at Portsmouth. They had the pleasure of the former England coach Terry Venables donning his hat, bringing in Aussies, selling arguably their best player for £3 million and finding a safe home for a 10 per cent fee and a majority shareholding. We didn't get it anyway. Basingstoke did. A small town with its own hanging gardens and many roundabouts, best passed rather than visited, it has a football team which had beaten a professional side. I decided the best thing to do was to enjoy the evening, and the further exposure of our resurgence that this nomination signified.

Not one award came our way that night. I did not understand because I felt so much had happened and that the immense efforts of everyone involved deserved to be recognised. Then I noticed Mel had a big smile over his face. The last award was voted for by the people living within the southern region, the first-ever BBC South Sports Personality of the Year. Announced in reverse order: Kate Hallett, bronze medallist at the world cup in judo, was third; Roger Black, Olympic silver medallist at 400 metres, was second with one-fifth of the vote. And then, the surprise of the evening, no good at sport whatsoever but in first place . . . me! I knew that many supporters had placed votes by e-mail from all over the world but for once I was struck dumb. Those who know me will know how strange that condition is for me!

On the stage behind me there was a large video screen. All of a sudden, Mel's face came into view and there he was telling the world at large our secret joke about my boots in my car. I felt very humble. Mel had become a very good friend and his words touched me. It was a tremendous honour to achieve such recognition. Standing there feeling very small, I was acutely aware of the emotion inside me, thoughts of the hundreds if not thousands of people who had worked so hard to ensure the club survived. I really did not deserve the award, but for our fans, those who cared at the heart of the community, it was a tremendous accolade. As I spoke my thanks, my thoughts too were of Mandy, my mum and dad, my cats – the very things that had given me support through all of this. And not forgetting Michael at my London office without whom I would probably have been out of a job by then.

Getting into work the following morning I was really happy. That is until I received a telephone call. Graham Mack, a man determined to make a point, had launched into a ten-minute tirade on his morning radio show about my failure to let him into the ground for nothing. Apparently he had suggested the Queen Mum would be better off dead after her hip operation and blasted pupils at a local school for vandalising his car – only to name the wrong school! Now seeming to have decided that I was a man of depravity, broken promises and without integrity, he was on a mission to crucify me.

I tried to smooth the waters by taking a community-club

approach to the problem, offering him tickets to another game thinking he might then turn in our favour. Rather like a pit bull but with not too many teeth he prefered to hang on. He got a lot of mileage out of it. I was his Father Christmas promising to deliver a present only to take it away; we were a tinpot club (he was in good company there – David Mellor said the same thing). Yet why bother. Nothing really fazes me now after a few meetings with Roy Pack. These guys were, after all, only another bit-part player in life's grand adventure, more like a mosquito on a summer's evening that buzzes around the room when you're trying to sleep. The lesson I had learnt was to pick my battles carefully. Mack was warned by his boss but ignored it because he wanted a fight. I didn't. But I had to laugh when Richie 'the travel chicken' called to say a whole host of escaped mink were eating my Jaguar in the car park – although I then drove a Vauxhall. (I think he was mixing me up with the previous chairman whose car had succumbed to flames outside the supporters' club.) Anyway, to shut him up as he rambled on we threatened to issue a writ with any damages going to deserving community projects.

The problem was that people were beginning to be unable to distinguish between truth and fiction. The press has a lot to answer for. Like the time when a columnist likened me to Jesus Christ, suggesting that when I turned thirty-three I would be dead by April and for three days no longer chairman. Tongue in cheek? Yes – but quite a few seriously asked after my health or if I was getting ready to leave!

It must have been difficult for the owners of the radio station – here was a man who could attract high ratings by doing something provocative. I think they made the right decision when he vanished from the airwaves, here one moment and then gone the next early one spring morning.

Having heard Graham Mack, I didn't think my week could get any worse. I hadn't counted on Barry Fry. He was arguing that

Peterborough were now entitled to compensation. To be honest, if they were we would never have been trying to sign Jimmy Quinn. Barry did not mince his words. Sitting at my office a fax appeared. 'Here is the document you say doesn't exist. It does. Thank you for calling me a liar. Cheers. Barry.' There was also an indignant message on my home answerphone. Actually he sounded quite cheerful when he rang back that night.

'Your approach,' he said, 'I am attending to it, but Jimmy Quinn ain't about to become a Bournemouth player,' he went on. 'If you want to have him you have to pay f***in' compensation. He ain't going f***in' nowhere unless you do.' Charming. We had figured that if we paid up to £25,000 we would get most of the money back in gate receipts given the interest signing a good goalscorer would create but I was beginning to have my doubts. Something was not quite right. When I went back to Jimmy and told him we would do the deal he seemed to have lost interest. He had thought long and hard but no longer wanted to come because he felt he had to honour his commitment to Barry, who in the meantime had made him an offer he couldn't refuse. Another three weeks wasted, another opportunity gone. Just add it to our recent record. Hughes of Southampton: one week he was joining then he was staying. Heaney decided to come, Manchester City did a deal on his wages and then his wife decided she didn't want her man moving south over Christmas. Lund had Wimbledon after him, so we'd lost him too. This transfer business was getting ridiculous – and too time-consuming. I had another life to lead.

Another problem was our goalkeeper's increasingly errant displays. In training he preferred to play as a striker; often it seemed that way in a game. The team had lost confidence in him and his response was to criticise them. We knew we had to make a change. But how?

An agent flew in a goalkeeper from Malaysia but he was crap. At a hastily organised reserve game with West Ham United we did well to whip them 3–1. I got back early that evening and popped into the club where Mel Machin and Harry Redknapp were chatting. Arsène Wenger, the Arsenal manager, had recommended a couple of French players to Harry. You see, managers speak to each other all the time, which is the best way of checking out players. The season of good will was nearly upon us!

December is often the most demanding month. Not that Mandy and I got to share much. She had her dos and I had loads in London. With the number of office lunches and parties my campaign for fitness never got off the ground, a bit like me. Office Christmas parties. No wonder there are seminars on correct behaviour. Ours was amusing. That one evening of working out who else is working for your company, spotting the accounts girl with the mail-room lad as the riot police arrive at 1 a.m! Waiting boyfriends none too happy finding their girlfriends rolling out of the Langham Hilton entwined with others. At least it was an excuse to get away quickly; I always hated it if I had to stay up in town.

The team entered into the festive spirit by playing as if they had a hangover up at Walsall, the only good thing being we were close to our ritual post-match meal pickup, Andy's Fish and Chips opposite Morrisons. Chips and fish, chicken, curry sauce and mushy peas all round. We have moved on to pasta now we have a microwave on board but it was fun while it lasted. Not as much as Fletch's dubbed kung fu films or endless reruns of Travolta movies but welcome nevertheless. I wondered what the residents of the cul-de-sac thought every few weeks when our juggernaut of a coach turned up.

Managers are never much good when they have lost. Mel had done his best to smile when a family friend had met him after the game to hand over a large bag of presents carefully wrapped. We were just about to leave when the referee came into sight. Uh oh! Off Mel went. Good job it was pantomime season. Oh yes it was! Mel let out a roar and swung his bag up in the air, presents flying skywards as he demonstrated the finer tactical points of the official's game that day. Time for bed, said Zebedee.

We inherited many staff from the previous regime, and many ways of doing things that were archaic, from the dinosaur age. We wanted our own culture, our own way of doing things. But some traditions are more deep-rooted than others – like directors delivering a turkey to each member of staff. Turkey can be flavourless and inedible. We wanted to do something special; to fund a trip out for a meal and party for all the staff and their partners. Scrap the turkey! I didn't think we could lose – not that we wanted thanks, just the knowledge that it was appreciated. Did someone say you can't please all of the people all of the time? We issued an invitation but among the die-hards it started: 'What about the bird? Where's the turkey?' 'When are we having it?' Sometimes Christmas can bring out the worst in people.

By now, the 'boots in the car boot' thing was reaching mythical proportions, and the BBC were pressing me to put them on and run around in front of the cameras as a true demonstration of Christmas cheer. Firstly I did not think it was appropriate as it might look like I was glory hunting or abusing my position as chairman. Secondly (and more pertinently) I was unfit, overweight and crap compared to the lads and they would lose no opportunity to point that out. The telly people wouldn't take no for an answer, so I agreed to do it if the rest of the board did so. That fell on deaf ears. Only Andrew was foolish enough to agree to accompany me. And so, on a perfectly crisp Monday morning a few days before Christmas, we ran out on to the training field. I took heart that the team seemed to leave us alone, perhaps fearing our footballing ability might put them to shame. Maybe not. They were just laughing too much. Mel was conspicuous by his absence which I felt was a bit poor. We might have been the missing links to greater success. We wanted to prove we had a chance of selection!

It was bizarre to think that here I was actually taking part in a kick-around with professionals who played for the team I had watched from boyhood. The closest I had got was playing three-a-side with some kids one day alongside where the team was training back in the 1980s when Harry was manager and we were playing Everton in the Cup. One of those kids was Jamie, his son.

On this day it really was a privilege to be allowed to take part. I thought Willo had recognised our sublime skill when he said it would be one-touch football. It sounded very sophisticated. Especially as every time we lost the ball we had to change sides during the game! It was only later that Mel told me he had left specific instructions with Willo only to let us do that in the belief that it was the most likely method of stopping us kicking his players.

Well, we showed them. It was poetry in motion as Andrew lunged at a cross and looped the ball into the top corner; even funnier was when I managed to stab the ball over the line for the last goal of the session. They claim the cameras missed that one but of course I don't believe that. On Monday evening it looked good on TV, not us in isolation but among twenty-two professionals we even had some semblance of fitness – not that we touched the ball that much. If they hadn't passed us the ball I don't think we would have touched it at all. All those thoughts from the directors' box – what would I have done with the ball, how could they miskick so badly, why didn't they pass the other way? – were very much put into perspective when we were struggling to keep up over five yards let alone a full pitch. The most gratifying thing was the players admitting that we were at least better than they thought we would be. It is easy to criticise from the sidelines but playing out there these guys moved at three or four times our speed – and that's being charitable to me. I kept thinking, what if someone had told me a year ago this is what I would be doing the Monday before Christmas? You're mad, is what I would have said. It was a dream come true, just to have five minutes would have lasted me a lifetime.

I was quite oblivious of time, dates or place during December.

191

Running on empty, or on vapours alone, my energy had almost gone. All those days were beginning to take their toll. No room for emotion, nothing to spend on building personal relationships, bankrupting those that really were my bedrock, being eaten away by the time taken up by my job and by football. In the City it was was one long round of lunches, work, evenings out, work and then getting up again to start the whole process again. I am lucky that I can truthfully say that my closest clients are good friends, people who I would choose to meet for dinner. Seeing Cherryl and Laurence of Grant Thornton, Peter from Allied Dunbar, Doug and Richard of RE Stone, made me realise once more how lucky I was to have good friends in every part of my life, be it football, work or at home. Each lunch was a welcome break, a chance to relax. My favourite? Pont de la Tour, table by the window, overlooking the Thames, watching the boats go by. Business, romance or both if you prefer, one soda or a bottle of their best, the perfect place.

Life was chaotic. Not only in London but now in Bournemouth my diary was filled with Christmas events. We even got invited to Lloyds Bank's drinks evening. Given the problems the football club had had with the bank and vice versa it's surprising we were invited at all – but by now we were 'merrily' repaying £16,000 a month. In all this frenzied socialising my personal life went out of the window. Moments of reflection, peace and satisfaction came all too infrequently. But Mandy and I still managed our traditional break in France. Every year we had taken the ferry from Portsmouth, not a booze cruise as such but a voyage where twenty-four hours seemed like a full two-week trip! The food, the cabins are superb. Leaving late on a Thursday we were in Caen first thing Friday morning driving through the sleepy French villages, the morning mist hanging around the trees like the bunches of mistletoe. Twelve hours to wander the woods near majestic chateaux, the battlegrounds of Normandy, eat croissant and lunch while the market at Caen packed up before taking in the contrast of the hyper-marché. A few hours of peace and togetherness were small recompense for all the lost hours. No complaint but much hurt from my now long-suffering family.

The Saturday before Christmas – what a time to play Elton John's Watford. The advent of Sunday trading was a blessing for us otherwise the crowd would have been dire.

Elton was over doing concerts but rumours of his visit to Dean Court were much exaggerated. They had used his money and position as chairman to soar away at the top of the table, some players on over £6,000 a week. Guided by the ex-England manager Graham Taylor, they were a class outfit. I had to restrain myself somewhat as one of my clients, Mark, a gentle, kind man, had come down to watch, being a devoted Watford fan. One of his colleagues follows Gillingham, our next opponents – it's funny how easily football bridges boundaries and makes conversation. Taylor was the brunt of many 'turnip' jokes after a national newspaper depicted him as that humble root vegetable after dismal performances by his England side.

Our largest crowd since Fulham, over 6,000, saw a mudbath of a game; they started like a whirlwind in attack but gradually we clawed our way back. Only a perfectly executed but dubiously awarded free kick bent around the defensive wall gave them victory. Yet every day we were making progress and still the second half of the season looked exciting.

We had staff, friends and family at our house on the Sunday evening, drinking mulled wine, playing games and waiting for Henry the amazing goalkeeping cat to (fail to) perform his trick of catching a tennis ball. It was such a contrast to what they must have been going through a year before. Before the Watford game Mel had managed to persuade Alex Ferguson to let us take a midfielder, Paul Teather, on loan but we still needed a goalscorer. Paul had been on his way to his girlfriend's. One call and he had to be ready to get packed up and down to us, Christmas plans changed completely. Sitting around on the Monday, three days before Christmas, Mel thought maybe we could entice Steve Jones back. Formerly a soap-factory worker, he might not have any qualification but he knew how to

193

score goals. We had sold him for £215,000 two years before after he scored twenty goals in a season. A combination of the player's personal problems and the need of the old board for money, forced the manager to sell him to West Ham in part exchange for Mark Watson, now languishing in some non-League outfit.

Jones was playing for Charlton in the Premiership, sold on for £650,000 by Harry Redknapp, a good bit of business for West Ham. He was only on £1,000 a week. We were able to come to an agreement on wages with Charlton to take him on loan for a month. Steve wanted a permanent move. We reckoned his wages would be easily covered by the increased gate on Boxing Day; it made the perfect back-page headline to boost the support at Christmas. One signing a youngster, the other a cult hero; both glad to be playing football, one out of a soap factory, the other the product of a youth system now swallowed up by a multinational conglomerate that doesn't need to develop players but can pick and choose at random around the world. Both wanted and needed by us.

Christmas. My favourite time of the year. I went and chose our tree, a big one for all the decorations and a small tree for the garden where our first cat is buried. That probably sounds gruesome but we had been much happier to bring him home from the vet's the day he died than to not know where he was. At least he could sleep soundly in his garden among his trees with the birds flying above him, the ones that he used to chase but never catch.

It was a beautiful day. I will never forget how special it was, it was very important to me. For the first time Mandy and I decided we should do our own thing, to make sure we spent time enjoying the day rather than rushing everywhere. A walk by the sea, cooking beef, gammon and a vegetarian alternative, playing Scrabble, drinking wine and watching the fire burn, a house full of beautiful decorations, holly, cards and candles, the tree glistening majestically and the Christmas music playing. In those moments we could relax a world away from the rigours of that year. The clock ticked, night fell and each cat played contentedly with his present on either side of the room. The perfect end to a lovely day.

What a contrast to Boxing Day. There were scores to settle against Gillingham, with the ever-placid Tony Pulis and many ex-Bournemouth players back in town and riding high. A lunch-time kick-off meant an early arrival at the ground. Steve Jones had already eyed the litre of whisky for the man of the match sitting on Diane Edwards' desk. I had known him only for his goalscoring but here he was larger than life, smiling broadly like the Cheshire cat. Winking at Di he pointed at the bottle of Bells and reminded her to keep it safe so he could collect it later. Too right! Within fifteen minutes he had scored a tremendous goal. Three minutes later he went down just outside the penalty area pole-axed by Pennock, a former player of ours. If it were true I would rather have had the pile of bricks we had allegedly sold him for than the player himself. He was no use and here he was getting himself sent off and their afternoon was over. We would have trounced them anyway. They were lucky to get away with a 4–0 defeat. If the referee had been looking they would have lost another man who stamped on one of our lads. It was a celebration. Even Neil Young (nicknamed 'Horse') got in on the act with his first goal for the club in 161 games. Another score right at the death by Jones and everyone was happy apart from my mother who felt that as it was the festive season Gillingham should at least have gone home with one goal!

It was becoming a great Christmas – even though we had to make do without the the ever-lovely Lisa Marie, the Gillingham chairman's wife, singing her songs at half-time. A day later we were ready to go on holiday. While Mandy got ready to take the train to London, I had to head west for the away fixture against Bristol Rovers, before we could finally depart.

We were at the Gasheads, Bristol – Rovers play on a rugby pitch. Our fans were penned in one corner of the ground. Still we had plenty to cheer about when Jones again gave us the lead as early as the ninth minute. If David Coleman had been there he would have asked 'What happened next?' I can tell you. They scored four goals in twenty-nine minutes. At the final whistle it was Bristol 5

Bournemouth 3. I had good reason to be pleased to be leaving the country, if only to avoid hearing the manager's thoughts on that one. My last day in England that year saw us in mid-table but still in business and with every chance of getting promoted. And me on BBC Radio Solent's 'Desert Island Discs' – a bizarre end to a surreal year.

CHAPTER 15

Escape to America

Pouring rain, dark skies and a heavy defeat. Nothing quite like that for making two weeks away seem like bliss. At least the roads were clear, straight as an arrow to Heathrow. I can't believe how organised this whole adventure had made me. With only twenty-four hours in a day I had become this compartmentalised, calculating individual wringing every drop of life from the day but now it was vacation time. Thank goodness for American Airlines' wisdom in letting you check in the night before a flight. No queues, no noise and a quiet, relaxing check-in. After a leisurely breakfast there was time to wander round the duty free – the shopping nowadays is better than our town centre.

Taking off we were able to look down on the south coast, see the floodlights glistening, even pick out the house . . . and think how much we needed this trip. At 35,000 feet there's not much chance of spotting a polar bear on the ice below but it's fascinating to see a cold, barren icescape laid out, a fishing vessel frozen in an inlet miles from anywhere, the glaciation ravaging the bleak view. Descending across Lake Michigan, Chicago stood gleaming, upright in the winter sunlight. It's a great time of the year to visit when hotels are such good value. We had a huge room, quaint and antiquated, at the Intercontinental overlooking the magnificent mile, Michigan Avenue.

In this city the sunlight at times is only ever right above, blocked by the tallest towers, but the lake, the wedding-cake buildings, the snowman in his glass bubble over the Criterion, the police horse with a Santa hat, all make for a wonderful winterland. They call it, appropriately, the Windy City and a biting cold blew through the streets. We didn't care. Coffee of every flavour is available on each corner, while we could eat loads then look around at the locals and still feel thin. There's so much to do, what with the largest indoor pool in the world where the dolphins arc and dive against the backdrop of the lake, and then there's the Planetarium, art galleries, amazing bookshops ... I didn't think about football once. I didn't even have a single phone call.

It was a time to rebuild, to try to bring normality back to life. We spent New Year with our good friends in Milwaukee, Andy and Julie Smith. A Germanic city with a comfortable way of life, splendid bars and restaurants, a waterfront town with a brewing history. Andy had put in a few hundred pounds to Cherries International to help save the team. I only got to know him because I had sat next to one of his sisters on a flight to London and it turned out that her father was good friends with a friend of mine and taught at the same school in a small village in Eastern Ohio.

As strange and as disruptive as life had been the year closed with a feeling of satisfaction for all that had happened. I had been treading water in my own career. I had probably made up my mind that London was no longer the place for me to work. I was tired, not of my boss or my clients but the drag of the journey, the bureaucracy, the need to commit so many hours if I were to be a partner there. I had lost my sparkle too, the mission had drained that and I knew that if I were to rediscover it, 1998 must be a year of change.

We were with true friends that night but out there, thousands of miles across the sea, were Andrew, Sally, Mel, Joe, Andrew, Lisa, Rod, Peter, Margaret, Ken, Andy and Kathy, all of whom I had hardly known a year but were now good friends. True friends. Maybe we are each like a planet. Throughout our lives people come into our orbit and leave it. Some are like meteorites, bright

198

passionate lights, burning up in our atmosphere, never making a lasting mark. Others reflect light at a distance, passing acquaintances yet there in the background. And then there were friends like these stretched over both sides of an ocean, friends for a lifetime.

Everyone has a favourite place, a secret location that becomes a sanctuary. I wonder if sharing it now will in some way spoil the experience next time we visit way up in the mountains of New England not far from Mount Washington? Found by chance but remembered for ever, The Inn at Thorn Hill is a dream come true. Only two to three hours' beautiful drive from Boston, there was time to do lots of walking, skiing and hiking, ending each evening with excellent wine from a huge selection, sitting by candlelight, the snow on the mountains shining in the moonlight. And as for the shopping – we had to buy an extra bag to carry all the American designer-label goods we fell for. We were glad of all the shopping. Gone was any idea of enjoying the scenery when we had a storm the like of which I have never encountered. It began to rain on the second day but not rain as we know it. Each drop froze as soon as it made contact with anything, turning the landscape into a sheet of ice, making driving difficult and walking nigh on impossible. The ice storm would affect most of north-east America.

It was a comedy of errors as we groped our way across the lot into a brightly lit cyber café. At five o'clock local time it was past ten in England and I wanted to know the result. Huddling around a flickering screen in this small village, thousands of miles away, I was able to find that we had beaten Orient and were now through to the third round of the Auto Windscreens Shield. Even better, our Cup tie against Huddersfield had been postponed and wouldn't now be played until I returned. Brilliant! Two weeks' holiday and I would only miss one game.

Even with much to come home to, as I boarded the plane at Boston and realised that it was time to go back to work I longed to relive those two weeks. We were back in Bournemouth on a Saturday morning. There was no way I was going to make the board meeting. As I didn't quite know what time or place I was in, I would have talked more tosh than normal and sounded quite delirious.

We were playing at home. I just about made it in time to see us trounce Northampton 3–0, an emphatic victory over a top-five side. It was a special evening, too, for Andrew Kaye who was celebrating his fiftieth birthday. Mandy and I had scoured everywhere to come up with a present, eventually finding a bottle of cognac made in 1948, the year of his birth. Together we had dinner in an old mansion house in Poole. It was an evening of great company, eating, drinking and being very merry. As Mel led the waitress in a waltz around the restaurant, 1998 had begun wonderfully well.

I was brought back to reality when I got on the train at Southampton airport on Monday morning. What variety arriving in London and walking down the stairs to the underground, what a surprise (note the heavy sarcasm!), 'We regret to announce that the Waterloo and City line is suspended due to a defective train . . .' Another walk across London Bridge, another delay. Being a proponent of privatisation I had assumed that when the train companies were transferred to private investors we would have better services. Delays, cancellations and misinformation offset marginal improvements like brightly coloured trains. I had become used to leaves on the line, the wrong type of snow, engineering works overrunning and the driver's tea not being hot enough as explanations for why I would be late in or home.

It was a shock being back in London. Living, working in London all seems so exciting. Really, I loved it. Yet now when I meet friends and they say, 'Gosh, you look so much better,' I wonder what damage my day-to-day travels will have in the long term. Coming back after a break to the daily grind of commuting, at first you feel fresh and alive. That first phone call begins to erode the well-being built up on holiday, then after a day or two you are ensnared again, blind to the fraught, frantic lifestyle of those around you in the city. There's no time for values, courtesy or good humour. Everyone is rushing somewhere. Looking for a moment with clear eyes, I knew I had to give up my place in this mass of humanity fighting their way to work, glaring at you as you ask: 'Is that seat taken?' I needed the salary but at what price life?

For a cold January evening it was amazing that 7,385 turned up to see us give away a sloppy goal but then bombard Huddersfield in much the same way as Bristol City had done to us previously. Neil Young equalised with a fantastic goal only for the linesman to disallow it. I could see why it might be a good idea to have decisions reviewed on instant replay. Referees in England get their expenses paid and a fee but precious little else, no video replay, no real help in making decisions. The sheer frustration at their attitude can affect managers at pitch level who can at least release it by talking to the referee. In the stands it can breed resentment, anger and create a simmering cauldron. One more bad decision and a serious situation becomes a potential riot. We once had Barry Knight who has a reputation for send-ing people off. That time he sent two off in the first twenty minutes – a performance that provoked even our older patrons to get off their seats and subject him to a barrage of comfy cushions!

This evening other officials in our view cost us £50,000 as they ignored what seemed clear to us and everyone else, disallowing a goal that only they thought was offside. No redress, no ability to challenge. We were stuck with the decision. No wonder the Football League Managers Association issues guidelines that referees should be left alone for at least half an hour after a match and that managers should never approach direct.

I thought I had overcome my tendency to feel either ecstasy or deep depression after a result. That week it hit me hard, sent me into absolute depths of despair at our defeat. Morose, plodding round the house, feeling wretched. It is only a game but somehow it is much more than that.

I was becoming increasingly frustrated by the long drawn-out effort to get all our players to sign new contracts both to protect us and give them more income. You would think it simple. Sign up, get more money and know that at our level if a big offer came in we would be unlikely to turn it down. A player couldn't lose. We are a small club with limited resources, we want to offer the best incentivised terms we can afford but without any overdraft or loan facilities to support wage exuberance (or irresponsibility depending on how you see it). We needed to renegotiate our top players' contracts before Bosman kicked us below the belt. I just decided we should start with the back four and move through one at a time sorting them out. With a settled side and seven or eight excellent players there was a lot to do; each new contract means a pay rise not budgeted for. Thanks, Europe!

Ian Cox, the club captain, was rescued by the manager from obscurity in London and transformed into one of the best defenders outside the Premiership. Nicely spoken, with a charming family, he was offered an awfully good deal by us in October. Now it was January. I could have read *War and Peace* four times over in the four months that it took to get a deal agreed. Why? One six-letter word – 'agents', the scourge of the modern game. Ian had one of the better ones. The amount of media-generated stories linking him with other clubs threw him. There are many who can pay far more than us. We rely on our footballing reputation and sandy beaches to get lads to sign.

A player's career is limited. If you or I had a chance to double or treble our income we would take it. But that option wasn't there for Ian, even if others told him there were teams sniffing after him. Kevin Keegan commented on how good he was but no more than that. We are known as a good footballing side so as many as twenty scouts might watch us each week. You knew they were serious when they bothered to track us to away games, leaving en masse before the end of the game in their knee-length padded coats.

Negotiations took four months to conclude – four months with the uncertainty hanging over both Ian and the club, four months with not one single inquiry even though the delay had been well publicised. Ultimately he signed virtually the same deal he was offered four months earlier, missed the extra money and had to give his agent a healthy percentage. Why the delay? Agents again. Ian behaved impeccably throughout; the agent did too but kept on holding out for more money, money we just did not have. The players have their own union, the PFA, which gives free advice. At our level, agents really make no difference.

Mel still wanted to take the players away for a mid-season break. Thomas Cook had not yielded anything definite. I could see the sense of it as a morale-building exercise but how could we afford spending £20,000 that had not been budgeted for? Would it make so much difference now we were out of the FA Cup? We couldn't do it, we had too much debt to service and fixture congestion too. I reckoned it would be cheaper to go to the USA. Our trip at New Year had cost only £200 or so for the flights. So, it was agreed, an end-of-season trip to the USA if the season went well. I had made lots of contacts with teams while I was out there and we arranged to play sides in the Chicago and Milwaukee area. Oh, for the Internet, Sabre systems and my travel planning!

We had begun to balance the business. Barely a year on but many soon forgot the difficult circumstances of the takeover. That initial period of euphoria in which everything seemed possible was now overtaken by a 'realism' among some supporters. Rather than the gratitude for having a team the demand for success was now perceptible. 'Where are our new signings . . . the board have no ambition . . . they have not signed Jones and Charlton must be desperate to sell . . . we want success on the pitch . . . now!' Still, there hadn't been any chants of 'Sack the Board!'

Many just ignored the financial difficulties we still faced. Seven months into the project, the board was still gelling. In assembling the team I had gone for the six with the most diverse abilities, skills and opinions, figures to represent the differing groups whose support carries the club. It would be easy to have a group of yes-men but that would achieve nothing. Instead we had six individuals who could be team players yet not be afraid to disagree. Board meetings were lengthy, invaluable, progressive and great fun.

That desire for success, those dreams of playing in Europe, had to be balanced with the need for prudent handling of finance. To be honest it was a company that could quite easily employ perhaps seven more members of staff to make it function properly. With the hours we were putting in we were effectively those extra members. My day was still full, maybe not with meetings, but certainly, as my family will bear testament, with football. Each evening I would find myself alone, sitting at my desk working on e-mails, draft papers or correspondence.

The board included strong personalities, each used to running his own area of business. There were bound to be tensions but we never fell out in a big way. To start with I oversaw every area but if my health, life and business were to survive I knew I had to delegate more effectively. Every ounce of energy had to be maximised and its potential fulfilled. The supporters' club was a dead loss – not the good people running it but as they themselves admitted they were not businessmen and had not run it to make a profit. There were two fundamental pillars of our income plan that were making no money. That and the lottery. Those holes had been covered in the first year by the Matty Holland sale, but they needed to be addressed. Imposing direct management control was something that the staff had never experienced before.

When budgets are not met it was not as if we could magic a rabbit out of a hat and say 'hey presto'. I knew then that at some point before we could consider building a new stadium we would need one more big player sale. The first opportunity to dispose of a player for at least £1 million and we could clear debts, build for the future and trade profitably.

There are agents and *agents*. Once Ian Cox had signed his contract, others followed, led by Neil Young. Sensibly he did not use an agent – if he'd had one he would have secured no better deal. A new face in the agency world was an average ex-player with no real business pedigree, Gary O'Reilly. His company had picked up Jamie Vincent, Jimmy Glass and Eddie Howe and would represent them in negotiations. At nineteen, Eddie had signed a six-year deal with the club without an agent only months earlier. As with any other player, if he did well we would unilaterally improve his terms to ensure he felt rewarded. Word of O'Reilly had spread along the south coast.

I met him by chance in the corridor. With hands clasped in front of him and with a strained, constipated Blairesque delivery, he sounded like a cross between a used-car salesman and an American evangelical minister. Rumour alone had it that he had been touting Vincent, our young left back, to other clubs. Mel believed it and had blown a fuse, turfing O'Reilly out of the training ground.

The Reading boss Terry Bullivant kept phoning to discuss something with Mel. On the third occasion, I figured it was time to speak to him. He wanted to find out whether the rumour that Vincent was leaving Bournemouth was true. Sitting at Wembley a few weeks later, representatives of Millwall and other teams would ask me the same thing. We didn't want Jamie going anywhere. Months later he too would sign up on a new deal.

Jimmy Glass, our goalkeeper, wanted a new contract. We didn't want to keep Jimmy but until we found an alternative we couldn't say so. Could we be certain if we told Jimmy we were seeking a replacement that he would still give every effort for the club?

Much is taken on trust with agents. We were told about a 'fantastic' player in Holland, the brother of Leeds United's top goalscorer Jimmy Floyd Hasselbaink. Come to Holland and see him play, was the invitation by his agent. So we sent assistant manager John Williams on a plane, costing us £400. The agent stopped outside Amsterdam to buy petrol and a newspaper. Looking down the fixture list, he turned to John and said, 'I think the game was yesterday.' John thought he was joking! The money might not seem much but when you are counting every penny it does not help.

Charlton would not let Steve Jones stay after his first month on loan. We wondered whether they were trying to force us to make a bid. Rumour suggested they only wanted £150,000 but in reality they were talking a minimum £400,000. It was frustrating. All credit to Steve. He had even offered to take a pay cut if that would help. He spoke his mind, did not understand why his team were insisting he return only to play in their reserve side. We would never have £400,000. Our record purchase was only just above £200,000. We tried everything. Mysteriously Gillingham found out about our plans and started to try to outbid us. Then Charlton pulled down the shutters and decided to keep him. We would have to make do and let him go.

The flip side of looking to buy players is understanding and disposing of those who are not good enough. The manager knew who they were but you cannot just let players go, they are fully protected. It would be the end of the season before we could move them on. Everyone has a fixed-term contract and when it ends we have to pay an additional month. We were not yet high enough up the ladder to be sure that our cast-offs would be picked up lower down the food chain. Certainly not at a price. We would have to make do.

CHAPTER 16

Tuesday – Must Be Walsall

Following a defeat up at Blackpool and a goalless encounter with Oldham at Dean Court, we looked to improve our fortunes with a good performance in the Shield quarter-final against Bristol City. City were talking about settling old scores after what they saw as our lucky win in the FA Cup. This time, however, we played a lot better and the game was balanced. We won 1–0, and were one of only eight teams left in the competition.

It was just a year since we had gone into receivership. As I drove up to Luton, a town famous only for its airport, I thought how happy I was that we were still in existence, let alone holding our own. The enormity of what we have done has never properly sunk in. Luton's wage bill was four times as high as ours; the club's directors sit a few rows back in their box to escape the hostility and abuse of the crowd. David Kohler, filling his boardroom with family, friends and animals, made it a welcome place to visit. Within a year he would have a petrol bomb pushed through his door. He and the others had sunk vast personal fortunes into keeping afloat, standing mounting losses from purchases made. Who else would support a business that leaked £2 million a year? Maybe they had agreed deals that with hindsight should never have been done. Yet in that desire for success how many make rational decisions?

Luton is a new town, a multicultural community among rows

of terraced houses, a marked contrast to the uncosmopolitan residential side of Bournemouth. It was a freezing day as we entered the bunker-like club car park behind barbed wire and an underground tunnel up into the stadium. And true to form, I had managed to lose my ticket. They were adamant that was that and I was not coming in. I am particularly good at losing things, especially at airports – I am the guy with all my pockets emptied swearing blindly that I had 'it' somewhere. Plane tickets, house keys, car keys, credit cards – I've lost them all . . . Enough humiliation. We beat the high-salary Hatters team 2–1 (in a valuable dress-rehearsal for our clash in the next round of the Shield) and suddenly the drift in our season was changing – now it was onwards and upwards and we were ninth in the table.

John Bailey had been a key figure in the side all season. He had come to us late, at twenty-four, after playing non-League, amateur football. Our ex-Marks and Spencer chief scout had spotted him. John is a man who speaks his mind and for whom his son was more important than his income as a professional footballer. He was one of the few remaining players to travel up and down each day to his home in London, because he did not want to disrupt his son's schooling. I can appreciate the importance of family relations. It had all become a bit too much for him. He wanted to leave, go back to amateur football and to painting and decorating, which would make him far less than we were paying. We didn't want to lose him. Luckily Mel was able to talk him out of it.

In the space of a week, Mel traversed the country to see games in Manchester, Basingstoke, Sheffield, and even Ayr on a dismal Tuesday evening standing in freezing rain among a crowd of barely a thousand. Who would want that job? The luxury of a manager's life? I wouldn't be one.

Games began to come thick and fast as February arrived. We had to play Bristol City again in the League. It was our fourth meeting this season. Although they had only lost three games in thirty matches, all bar one to us, they could not stop the rot. We beat them yet again and inched up to eighth place. Valentine's Day arrived and my die-hard romantic nature was put on hold as two goals by Christer Warren were enough to beat Chesterfield for our fourth win in a row. The only star-gazing I did that night was standing in the car park after midnight looking up and contemplating another week in London.

Gates were edging up (a fan had suggested a clever slogan – 'bring a mate, double the gate') and, although they averaged stubbornly below 5,000 over the season, we were making a small profit. Quite amazing when you consider that the same business had been losing £80,000 a month and all we had done was to change the management. We were not complacent – we knew the wage bill would rise dramatically next season, the necessary consequence of having to re-sign our players and compete. At least our progress in the cup competitions – something you cannot budget for – made for good income. It was also exciting. Over 5,000 turned up to see our Auto Windscreens Shield southern area semi-final against Luton. Franck Rolling, our French player, scored late in the game and we were through to the southern final, to play Walsall over two legs, the winner going to Wembley. The Luton directors were in tears in our boardroom. Goodness knows what difference this would make to cash flow. Sad to think that whatever the result my thoughts would turn to the net effect on our financial performance. Always conflicting with my emotion as a lifelong fan!

Fulham were by now reaping the benefits from all the money they had received. We went there on a Tuesday night in late February, the most wonderful setting for a football ground down on the banks of the River Thames. Spend, spend, spend had been their approach and we faced a much-changed side. Forty or so of my colleagues and clients met on the opposite side of the river for a beer or two. Mohammed Fayed, the owner, was not there. He missed a great game. Our football was complete in its domination, probably our most impressive performance of the season as we beat them by the only goal, the have-nots pummelling the haves. With fixtures against lower-placed clubs to come, I really thought we were ready for a great push towards promotion with only two months left to go. Mel asked me to consider spending £20,000 or £25,000 to push through a transfer before the deadline of the third Thursday in March after which you cannot buy players and use them during the season. It is designed to stop unfair competition. Maybe the authorities ought to consider how to apply that and make a more level playing field for the season as a whole.

Flicking through the books, Mel had noticed that Mark Stein was still at Chelsea. He hadn't played in their first team since 1996 but had an excellent record. This man was an icon – he had a record run of nine goals in seven consecutive matches. Unlike our other attempts at signings, this was over within hours. Mel was straight on to Chelsea, they agreed and he was going to be a Bournemouth player for the rest the season. It was great news and spread like wildfire, electrifying our supporters with eager anticipation for what would surely now be a top six finish.

Unfortunately, he could not play in our game the following evening against a Plymouth side that had been struggling near the foot of the table. It was a horrible rain-soaked evening with a greasy pitch, the ball running fast but not true. We took the lead with an excellent goal from Steve Fletcher but then fell to two sucker punches. It looked like Jimmy Glass was at fault but if you ever suggested his professionalism might be in question woe betide you! At half-time one of the lads asked him why he had let the first goal in. He went ballistic – then he ran off. With the referee knocking on the door to call the teams to the pitch for the second half Jimmy was nowhere to be seen. This was no park game, it was the Nationwide Football League and there were 4,000 people watching.

We were thinking we might have to make sudden preparations to put young Eddie Howe in goal. In an attempt to buy time the team delayed coming out. Eventually we found him in the boot room. At least he came out for the second half but thankfully he didn't have much to do. Maybe it inspired the defence to keep the ball well away from him.

It wasn't until ten minutes before the end that we scored our equaliser, a fantastic thirty-yard shot from Vincent. Then once again we conceded a sloppy goal a minute from time but amazingly straight from the kick-off we propelled the ball downfield and Fletcher made the final score 3–3. Plymouth was, of course, run by Dan McCauley, my 'old mate' who had thrown me and Andrew out of his boardroom! Dan celebrated the draw in some style in our boardroom until almost midnight. I don't think he would have left unless I had asked him to be on his way, politely, of course.

The only pain of playing on a Tuesday night is that I would get home at midnight and still have to get up little more than five hours later for work. I don't mind having five hours' sleep once in a while – it's difficult only when it comes on top of all that travelling. I was even more depressed the next morning as I totted up how few points we had taken in six games against teams of poor quality. We knew we needed to be ruthless but were just not finding our feet in the bad weather.

With the potential of a trip to Wembley, having to play in London at Brentford was an unwanted distraction. We lost 3–2 (Franck Rolling continuing his new 'super-striker' role with both our goals) and it all seemed rather inconsequential compared to the upcoming game against Walsall. The only point of note was the welcome extended to us by their chairman.

Tuesday came soon enough. Another of those early mornings. Hitting the pillow the night before seemed an uncomfortably short time ago. Driving to work, the dawn spread over the horizon, staining it a rich vivid crimson. While Lloyd Cole did his best to enliven me, the clock approaching 6.15 a.m., it was the usual auto-pilot drive to the station, thirty minutes through the New Forest. I wondered whether this meteorological display should be taken as a sign that the red and black of Bournemouth would prevail or, more ominously, 'red sky in morning, Bournemouth fan's warning'. Today, Tuesday 10 March, was the first leg of our own cup final, a lengthy trip to Walsall where we had failed to make any impression in recent years. I was happy to be playing the away leg first in what was probably the biggest game in the club's history. The team had gone up the day before so that they would have a chance to stretch their limbs after the inevitable slow crawl on the M6.

There were masses of things to get done at the office. My new case was building a head of steam and that meant a trip down to the Serious Fraud Office. This case and others over the years showed how within human nature there exists the potential to exploit one's fellow men ruthlessly and without contrition. I had never really come in contact with it prior to the football – then the threats, the abuse, the constant need to keep on my toes were all alien to me.

I dashed over to Euston. As the train sped north through the lush green countryside under leaden sky and teeming rain, I tried to contemplate the enormity of the evening that lay ahead. I got off at Birmingham International, a stop just off the M6 and within easy reach of the Kaye/Dawson ensemble driving up from Bournemouth. They had treated themselves to the delights of a Little Chef meal – a childhood favourite of mine (oh! those cherry pancakes with vanilla ice cream melting on top!) – then somehow got themselves hopelessly lost. At last they picked me up and we eventually found our hotel.

I had not fancied driving back to Bournemouth that night but didn't relish the prospect of an overnight stay up here on my own after the game. With an 8.30 a.m. meeting the next day I had ruled out getting home at 1 a.m. only to get up at 5.45. Staying at the hotel meant the most sleep but suddenly it struck me as an awfully lonely prospect. We grabbed a sandwich in the leisure club surrounded by Danny Wilson, the Barnsley manager, Nigel Spink and Marcus Gayle. Eating with little appetite, the time seemed to pass painfully slowly.

We set off in good time but then hit heavy traffic. With the noise of the windscreen wipers, the windows steaming up and the incessant beat of rain on car it was not a pleasant journey. Bescott Stadium was about seven miles away but it seemed to take forever.

Seeing a cab I leaned out and asked the driver if he could give us directions to avoid the snarled up roadway. Turned out he was on his way to the ground, a fact we realised when the occupants suddenly started waving and cheering. It was great to be part of the travelling army, approaching the venue in all sorts of vehicles but all feeling the same thrilling anticipation of a big game.

The Bescott gleamed against the darkness. There is nothing quite like a football stadium, floodlights blazing against the night sky, to create an atmosphere. Not that this game needed one. The prize was a first-ever trip to Wembley for either side, dreamland for anyone in the game. And the financial rewards could be massive. While our early rounds had earned us little money, this tie offered the prospect of about £60,000 to each team and for the winner maybe as much as £500,000 of which 20 per cent would be shared in bonuses.

The players had been uncharacteristically subdued. The executive rooms were being redecorated so when we opened the boardroom door there was a crowd of people sitting down eating dinner. We declined their warm invitation to join them. Actually I much preferred to go out into the night air and watch the build-up to the game. Far from being a sell-out there were plenty of empty seats. At our end, however, was a sea of a thousand fans stretched out with flags and scarves aloft already singing mightily.

After thirteen weeks' absence Russell Beardsmore returned to the side. Unbeknown to me three key players, Fletcher, Bailey and Young were all carrying injuries that would have kept them out had it not been this game. Considering our miserable record against Walsall both the Andrews and I agreed that we would be satisfied with a one-goal defeat to take back to Dean Court the following week. With the rain having stopped, the pitch was still slippery and would play at a lively pace. As kick-off approached I had a sense of trepidation given our recent inconsistent performances.

We need not have worried. From start to finish the team was superb, first to every ball, first into every challenge. It was as good as I had seen all season. Top drawer! In the thirteenth minute there was a beautiful move with O'Neill crossing to Fletcher who headed it on for Franck to meet with a perfectly placed header – Walsall silent, AFC Bournemouth jubilant. Never shy of celebrating a goal the thirty or so of us sitting in the directors' box leapt up. I rang Mandy but she knew, listening to it on Radio Solent back home with Sidney the rabbit, Henry and Thomas. Within another fifteen minutes it was 2–0: the ball was floated across once more to Fletcher in the area, he cushioned it with precision to Beardsmore standing with the centre of the goal in his sights just outside the area. He let fly and a slight deflection took the ball into the right-hand corner. Unbelievable.

With the adrenalin pumping all the way to the final whistle, Walsall never got a look in. Then, shouts of 'Wem-ber-leee!' and a healthy lead to take back to the second leg in a week's time. But we strove to play down the achievement. With another ninety minutes to go there was still all to play for. Jan Sorensen, the Walsall manager, said so himself when talking on television, his public face after the defeat. With the cameras stopped he took the mike and turned away: 'We were crap!' I had my own broadcast to do, a prearranged piece with my old friend Richard Williams on Radio Solent. It was Richard who had done my very first interview when the whole takeover had begun a year or so earlier. We chatted about the game and about how life had changed over the year, and how the football and my legal work were now dominating my life.

Driving back down the M6 I really wished I was going home that night. It was a night to share a wonderful achievement with those who had borne all the pressure of the last few months. Instead, in the driving rain Andrew dropped me off at the hotel. I booked my alarm call for 5.15 a.m., a cab for 5.45 and hoped I would drop off to sleep. Having discovered the healing and energy-giving powers of ginseng I took a capsule and did find myself falling straight off to sleep, despite my aversion to kipping in a strange room. One night in a hotel is my limit!

Although I consider myself a morning person, I only meet this description if I have managed to locate a strong cup of coffee. Waking at 5 a.m. I surprised myself by feeling so alive – maybe it was the result the night before. A cab on time, a train on time, a nice empty carriage, a cafetière of delicious coffee and papers containing glowing reports of our victory made for a perfect start to the day. Arriving at my meeting in our main offices I was greeted with such warmth and cries of 'Here we go' by my colleagues. It gave me great pride. All this and Hammond Suddards bacon sandwiches too!

The phone didn't stop ringing all day with enquiries from journalists eager to talk to the chairman of a football club on its way to Wembley for the first time in its history. The media as a whole have been amazingly supportive to us throughout this great adventure of creating the community club out of the ruins of past mismanagement. Only that delightful character Graham Mack could not quite bring himself to offer us his good wishes. Nothing new there then . . .

How to keep your feet on the ground when you know you're ninety minutes away from Wembley? Two goals to the good and no one could stop us? Not quite. Even if we were two up with two minutes to go, I would still bite my nails, wonder if we might scrape a draw. Having been caught on camera during a game I know I am capable of a surprising range of facial contortions!

Wrexham stopped us. Yes, just because we were in the middle of our two-legged cup final we still had to play League games. Three days before Walsall came to us, we lost by a single banana skin of a goal to the Welsh side. The game itself just happened. There was no real atmosphere or depth of meaning to it, just a field of expectation, a waiting for the main event.

Tuesday 17 March could not come soon enough. Sleep was fitful. Knowing this was a big day, under the layer of unconsciousness I twisted and turned waiting for the light of dawn. Surely we would brush them out of the way and make our first trip to the home of football? Remembering our main stand had come from the Wembley Exhibition of 1924 I thought it was about time we went there ourselves to say 'thanks'!

Even their fans appeared to have given up on their team. With so few coming down we had sold the away standing area to home supporters. Putting it in context this was a game that would rival beating Manchester United in the FA Cup, securing promotion or survival itself. Of course I felt sure we would win. The problem was that without tempting fate to make us lose or looking over-confident we had to plan ahead. If we did win, every man and his dog would want to know what happened next. We would want to celebrate too. I decided not to tell anybody but discreetly went off and bought eighteen bottles of champagne. As kick-off time approached the excitement was palpable but uneasy, heavy with expectation. This was the last act, the last ninety minutes in a journey whose prize of £500,000 would dwarf the £50,000 grossed so far.

In the first half the plot unfolded like a drama, a script every fan could have written. Within minutes Stein was harshly adjudged offside, a goal that would have put us three to the good. Goalless at half-time, we were still leading 2–0 on aggregate. There was a sense of looking on as history was being made, of remembering the windswept days of my youth when my dad had taken me as I now take him. Feeling every moment as real as the day each game had happened, the 4–0 beating of Crystal Palace when we stood among their fans and could still cheer for our team, our goalkeeper hitting the post against York in front of only 2,000, the rain storm in 1977 against Hereford . . . all meaningless to you unless you were there. The spirits of ninety-nine years echoing around the ground waiting for the success that must now surely come.

Eight minutes later the dream was a nightmare. I never want that feeling again, the anguish that overtook us all. In those first eight minutes of the second half they scored two goals out of nothing. Howls of disbelief as Jimmy played his part in gifting them their ticket back into this tie where they should be dead, and giving them the momentum. Horror and confusion were etched on the faces around me. How could it be? This was our destiny, our fate, there should be no room for heartache.

And then maybe an angel passed by. Many prayers were being offered – I prayed that divine intervention would not take this from us. If you saw it you would believe that there were angels in our penalty area. After fifty-five minutes Youngy made a surging run and delivered the ball harmlessly across the edge of the penalty area; there was no danger whatsoever eighteen yards out, with none of our guys near it. A defender stuck out a foot, the ball spun off his boot along the ground and swung tantalisingly around the outstretched fingers of the goalkeeper, drifting slowly into the net. We were still losing 1–2 on the night but were back in front 3–2 on aggregate. It was the most unusual own goal I've ever seen.

Suddenly Dean Court erupted with life and impetus. Bloody lucky too as Walsall had only been denied a third by Youngy's outstretched leg a minute before. With only thirty minutes to play, it was a good test of the condition of my heart as I lived every kick, every tackle, every moment, my emotions soaring then plummeting. Now we were almost there. Walsall threw on their last substitute, a wimpish figure wearing gloves but we knew Tholot was dangerous – the French Peter Beardsley, his agent had told us when we were offered him. Unbelievably with his first touch he slipped the ball past Glass to make it 1–3 on the night and level at 3–3 on aggregate, with ten minutes to go. I could not watch as the ball went up and down.

If no one else scored it would go to sudden death. The first team to score in an extra half-hour would win in a 'golden goal' competition. We were beginning to wonder whether Walsall might be content to run the clock down. Yet no one had counted on Franck Rolling. I do not know why he did it. He had been jogging back to his position in defence while we had the ball upfield on the right. Suddenly he turned and began to run back up the pitch. It was unsafe, unplanned and if they got the ball it would be up and over him leaving him short and exposed. Mark Stein had taken the ball with his adhesive feet towards the corner, no one would get it off him. He turned and gently pushed it across the penalty area. It took a slight deflection and rolled straight into the path of Franck who caught it on the full, low and hard. The keeper didn't see it until late, dived despairingly, got a hand to it but it squirmed underneath him. Suddenly we were ahead again. Even if we lost the game on the night, who cared? Those final few minutes lasted a lifetime. Waiting, waiting, waiting until finally the silence, the tension was broken with that last blow on the whistle. We were there! Hundreds, thousands of fans ran on the pitch. I just jumped and jumped and jumped! Mandy, Andrew, Andrew, Peter were all around me, hugging, shouting, bouncing. Unbelievable! I just wanted to hug as many people as possible! I will never forget that moment, how that one thing could wash away the pain, frustration of all we had been through, how for those anonymous faces filling the pitch this would be their party, their joy in saving their club.

Mel took the team into the dressing-room for ten minutes where he could speak to them, so they could reflect, take in what they had achieved. Then it was time to celebrate. I got the champagne and ran down the corridor past all the media, everyone smiling, into the dressing room making sure everybody had a bottle. Franck, the hero of the moment, took his and sprayed it all over me. Figuring attack is the best form of defence (even though he is much bigger than I am) I ran off down the corridor trying to open my last bottle as he chased me before I turned and started spraying back. Back on the pitch thousands were singing Mel's name over and over again. After all that had happened it was our chance to celebrate. I had lost my voice but still carried on singing. One by one the lads came up into the main stand. No one wanted to go home. It was probably midnight before the last fans departed. In 1997 we were going under, now in 1998 we were going to Wembley. Superb! Not England at Wembley, not even Michael Jackson, but *my* team – AFC Bournemouth.

CHAPTER 17

Wembley

Waking on the typical morning after the night before, memories of the evening were hazy to say the least. With the precaution of a later start at the office it was all systems go with a planning meeting with the staff. First question – tickets. It would be the one thing on everyone's lips. We had done some top-secret planning before we even knew we were going to Wembley. I did not want to tempt fate but we would have fallen flat on our face if we hadn't. It had been very difficult to hide the excitement but it was bizarre planning for an event that might never come off.

Instead of dealing with the usual game sales of 5,000 our primary allocation from Wembley was 26,000 tickets. Without a modern, automated telephone system – we only had four lines and one telephonist – and no information facility, every call had to be taken. Improving it was £3,000 we did not then have. We would have to cope with thousands of enquiries. Andrew, Diane and I had decided on a limited range of merchandise – the infamous fun hands, T-shirts, flags, pennants, musical footballs and even red coloured wigs. I had spoken to hotels, coach companies, film and media outlets. Our kit manufacturers, Patrick, agreed to bring forward the launch of the new shirt. Subject to deciding the exact colours they could have 3,000 and a limited edition of 500 ready by Easter, the week before the final. (Ultimately it wasn't until the

Friday before the final that the shirts were ready in large quantities; we had to disappoint thousands of fans.)

Luckily, Wembley would not have the tickets with us for five days, the following Monday afternoon. It gave us time to announce the arrangements. Already the ground was something of an attraction even with nothing going on, supporters milling about outside. They just wanted to be part of what had been achieved. The chants of 'Wemberlee, Wemberlee, we are the mighty AFC Bournemouth and we are going to Wemberlee!' hung in the air, as if lingering from the night before.

My only concern was whether a final between Bournemouth and Grimsby Town would inspire the armchair fan and local resident to put on a good show. The last final had drawn 40,000 odd and only when a big city had taken part had it got above 60,000. Here with two small-town sides it was anybody's guess but the first question was whether we would sell our 26,000. The staff were already worked to the bone and the prospect of coping with that many applications was clearly beyond their physical capabilities.

Plan A went into effect. Wembley had by 10 a.m. sent us a helpful guide to our big day and lots of information on the blocks of seats allocated to us in our half of the ground. We decided to buy a dedicated phone line and contract out telephone sales to Ticketmaster. At a hefty cost, of course, but we had no choice.

The immediate financial implication was that we could expect a cash boost of at least £200,000 of the £500,000 receipts once we had paid bonuses of up to £3,000 a man to the manager and players. Not bad going when you owe £2 million or thereabouts! The sponsors' enthusiasm and dedication were clear, lovely people, not least when they awarded us 'the performance of the round' and a cheque for £1,000 to go towards footballs for the youth team.

We were still playing League football but you might not have thought it. Given our recent form we did not relish a trek across to Southend, a pig of a journey. After the usual accidents and incidents on the M25 we arrived at two minutes past kick-off. Our entrance was across a bridge, like entering a medieval castle but with stone cladding. Into a darkened bar, stale beer and fags in the air, we were led through this Alice in Wonderland adventure and suddenly were in the main stand. The most interesting thing in the first half was identifying how many flats overlooking the ground were occupied by voyeurs of the action.

The second was altogether more interesting. We took the lead but our defence had a mental aberration, conceding four goals in seven minutes. I took it that Mel was upset as he immediately brought on three substitutes. He would have liked to replace the whole back four if he could. Franck, our French hero, was now the villain as his poor defending led to two goals.

The others didn't give up and we eventually lost 5–3. We had known all along the problem was our goalkeeper. We decided that if we didn't make a huge effort to get a new one before the deadline the following Thursday, Jimmy Glass would be in goal for the rest of the season. Even after losing games we still had a good chance of promotion.

Getting a decent keeper had been a blessed lottery. We'd had ten or fifteen players on trial and hadn't signed one of them. Steve Jones had recommend Sasa Ilic at Charlton. He had come to the ground in January; we had offered him a three-year contract and the wages he had demanded. He was on a month-to-month deal there. As soon as his club found out, they offered him a better contract and from being the third reserve he was in their first team and within months playing at the highest level and for his country.

It is all very well being able to spot players but it is another thing trying to secure their services. Next choice was either of the Wrexham goalkeepers. We let them choose and Cartwright came to us on trial. We agreed a fee and they changed their mind. Who else? Reports suggested that Mike Pollitt, the second-string goalkeeper at Notts County, might well be a good purchase. Mel asked if I would speak to their chairman, Derek Pavis. An honest and dignified man, Derek said that Gillingham were pestering him to sell Pollitt, but he would be happy to let the boy come to us for the same fee (£40,000) just to get Paul Scally off his back.

When I next spoke to Derek, his secretary was having great problems with Scally. He was demanding she send transfer forms to the Football League. The lad had told Scally of our interest to which he had supposedly uttered words to the effect that we were a shit club, with terrible finances and no future. The player, however, had other ideas and decided to join neither of us. Within days Sunderland signed him for a small fee. Weirdly, within two months they released him, signed the other Wrexham goalkeeper and Pollitt ended up signing for Rotherham, a division below either of us. By the time he came back and asked if we would reconsider we had found two excellent goalkeepers who had not been available at that time.

Jimmy was no fool. He knew we did not want him. Imagine working for a company where you know you are not wanted, where your colleagues have little faith in your ability. Time was short. Only three days remained before transfer deadline day. Mel and Willo called every club in the higher divisions. We got close, first with West Ham and then Tottenham but both fell through. So, it was Jimmy for the last eight games and I prayed that his professionalism would overcome his understandable sense of rejection.

What a nightmare! The Wembley tickets did not arrive until 4 p.m. on the Monday afternoon. We had designated Tuesday until Friday as a priority booking, for loyal fans, season-ticket holders and other affiliated groups. Before we could sell anything we had to hand-count all 26,000 tickets to make sure they were there. More expense but to cope with the flood we again contracted out and brought in three more staff from Ticketmaster.

The tickets were most unimpressive. Having produced a plan showing what we were allocated half the tickets seemed to be missing. Mysteriously Wembley had held back some of the 26,000. With a capacity of 80,000 there were another 28,000 floating around somewhere if Grimsby had the same as us. And it was the best sections that were not there.

By 6 a.m., queues were beginning to form even though by our estimation only 13,000 of the tickets might be bought by priority holders. After four hours' waiting there was considerable hostility when the best tickets were not available. People smelt a rat. Even though we explained to them it got nasty. It was worse as others tried to sell on above face value. We then broke out food and drink – by 11 a.m. it would take three hours to get to the front of the line.

The town was beginning to take on the carnival atmosphere, with shops dressed up in our colours. Not so in Grimsby. Instead of the four days and four-ticket limit we had allocated, they decided to offer season-ticket holders one day to buy theirs, with no limit. Unfounded rumours abounded that one person bought 900. Our tickets were selling extremely well, so much so that we got a further 8,000 sent out making it 34,000 in all. It was going to be a huge gathering. We had waited ninety-nine years to get there but the town was responding magnificiently. There would be 30,000 supporters who might not otherwise watch their local team play. It was these that we wanted to attract back to games in the future but, of course, there was some resentment among existing supporters that now we had some success others jumped on the bandwagon. Balancing these sensitivities was one of the most difficult things I had to do. A game like this provides an opportunity to have long-lasting effects on a club, town and its community. Whatever the result it would shape our future.

I enjoyed working with the media and they constantly came up with new ideas to mark this wonderful occasion. Meridian asked if I would carry a hand-held video camera for a month for a TV documentary that would reveal the highs and lows. That was easy to agree to. Reporters came down from Grimsby, two young ladies who, at our fixture on 4 April against Wycombe, had Andrew and I stand on the pitch holding an inflatable haddock, called Harry, stabbing it and behaving aggressively. This was their mascot, their hero! The only problem was the very strong wind. Harry took to it quite literally and at one point lifted over our shoulders and gathered pace towards the goal-mouth. It was the only thing to go in the net that day.

I had arrived, camera in hand, to spot people at the entrance to the ground selling unlicensed flags and scarves. They were clearly nothing to do with us. A number of supporters were shouting abuse at them. I suggested they should move on before we got the police involved. I felt like Roger Cook. As I moved towards them, filming as I went, they buried their heads in their jackets, to little effect. Deciding to copy what I had seen on TV, I started shouting, 'Come on, show your faces, face up to the truth', and then asking them to explain how they were making money out of innocent victims. I must have touched a raw nerve. One turned to me and started having a go back. We were the criminals, ripping people off by charging them high prices in the club shop! It was a strange afternoon. That was more exciting than the boring 0–0 draw that followed.

The prospect of Wembley gave me energy but couldn't hide the rigour of my day job and the travelling. By now, four or five firms had come looking to see if I would move south; my own 'transfer' negotiations were under way. What had kept me there that long was only my loyalty to my boss Michael. The rest of the team were wonderful people save for one eccentric and I would miss them. But it wasn't a good life. Reality was having a happy home, Mandy, the animals, coming home in daylight most of the year. I needed that. I knew I could work on the coast, build my client base and bring in more with my skills and ambition. I could do the work and do it well, pragmatically and cost-effectively. I believed in myself but was unhappy with my present performance. There was no way I would be able to carry on functioning at any reasonable level if I remained in football and travelled so far every day.

Some wanted me to give up on Bournemouth, to put it behind me and concentrate on law. It was an ultimatum not from Michael but from above. They wanted me but I had to be wholly theirs. What would it get me to choose that? Perhaps a salary of £200,000 after a few more years' work. Would it be worth it? No. As long as I could pay the mortgage, have a life we enjoyed and do work that I was completely committed to then I would be happy. Now would be as good a time as any to say I was leaving, just a question of choosing the right time to speak up. And all along I had Mandy's total support, hers the one voice I would always listen to.

Getting to Wembley was a chance to have some fun. Every cup final team deserves to make a record. On our away travels, Fletch, our tall centre forward, would constantly remind us he was the new John Travolta. It was a good job I hadn't seen *Saturday Night Fever* – on our coach we couldn't escape watching it time and again. As we had almost gone out of the League, fifteen minutes from extinction, what better song to use than 'Staying Alive'? A local recording studio offered help. Surprisingly it almost sounded decent. We may not have made *Top of the Pops* but it was an experience. The BBC made a video at the Opera House, a local nightclub, and airplay was confined to the team bus. The *Echo* gave us a realistic insight into Fletch's other life, superimposing his head on Travolta's body – a real page three stunner!

We still didn't know what clothes the team would wear walking the pitch at Wembley. To get support the lads all posed in the 'Full Monty' in the dressing-room, each strategically holding a football to protect his own assets. Whatever happened to the negatives and photos when each ball was thrown in the air is anybody's guess. Probably banned on grounds of public decency! It did not make the newspaper but the one that did brought a swift response from Debenhams and a set of blazers, ties, shirts and trousers for every player.

League life continued with the long haul to Carlisle. By coach we would not return home until the early hours of Sunday morning. Bournemouth boasts an international airport; we even have scheduled services. For £10,000 we hired a jet to fly the team and supporters north. With hindsight the £99 fare for the flight, transfer, lunch and match ticket was too low, which is probably why they sold out quickly. It cost us £3,000 but we would have spent that money on hotels and dinner anyway. To be able to roll out of bed and be at the airport within ten minutes was heaven, and similarly to return home at a civilised hour that night.

We had just an hour's flight to Newcastle; the runway was too short in Carlisle. During the flight Mel and I were introduced to Adam, then sixteen, a leukaemia sufferer. A bright, lively lad, he was more excited than anyone on the plane. He had lost his hair and his dad had shaved his own head so he did not feel out of place. His only request was that the team sign his autograph book. We asked if he would come with us on the team coach. His spirit was amazing, shining through. It was difficult to comprehend that within three months he would be dead. All the minor grumbling, criticisms and frustrations of life fell away to insignificance.

Carlisle had been to the final of the Auto Windscreens Shield twice before and were the current holders. They saw it as 'their' competition. We took a first-half lead and luck was with us when four minutes into injury time they missed a spot kick.

The next day, Andrew Kaye and I took up an invitation to the Coca-Cola Cup final between Chelsea and Middlesbrough. Neither of us really had much interest in other teams but only went to get a flavour of what Wembley was like behind the scenes on a big match day.

In the last twenty years big business has had an enormous impact on the divide between big and small clubs. Large successful teams invest in grassroots football so they get the pick of young players as they come through. Resources are concentrated with the largest clubs, leaving us to rely on cast-offs. We are determined to change all that and will develop our own schemes to grow our own players. Yet here the game was awash with money, bypassing us minnows and the concerns of the ordinary fan.

In the Grand Hall overlooking Wembley Way, a couple of hundred dignitaries supped wine while the fans had their cans of beer. A four-course lunch eaten off bone china, rounded off by coffee and mints – all far removed from my experiences as an ordinary fan, when there was only a metal trough to pee into in the open air at Dorchester Town, rickety old seats at Oldham, and standing for hours in the cold just waiting for a gate to open.

The room was full of football representatives and corporate sponsors. It was the same when we took our seats. Great view, right next to the Royal Box. Yet the best seats were all reserved for guests of football, not the followers of the teams. Maybe that's why they called the AWS the 'people's final'. At least supporters had a fair chance of getting a ticket. As I said to Andrew, the FA should be supporting our community philosophy; it would do a lot of good to have us as ambassadors. Were we really the poor cousins who should be hidden away? Looking down at the sea of fans rolling up towards the stadium, it was amazing to think that in three weeks it would be our turn.

The seating plan for our final fell to me. I had tough decisions to make. I couldn't please everyone. Wembley provides varying degrees of entertainment on a match day. Thirty tickets in the Royal Box with lunch and afternoon tea, thirty tickets with tea alone and another twenty invitations for tea. Complicated? You bet. Who should be allocated the seats? There is a protocol set out by Wembley and the Football League – club main sponsor, long-standing officials, directors, club president and chaplain. As for the rest what was I to do? I knew I was on a hiding to nothing. When the other members of the board suggested that my parents, now in their seventies, should be invited, and Andrew's too, I was touched. I did my best and for the most part it was fine – a good mix of business people who had helped us, supporters, investors and friends of the club.

I was still trying to organise our trip to the USA – Wembley had slightly disrupted that. Easter was the perfect time for me to go out there to plan it but then there was really no good time to leave, a million things to do with only a week to the final. Bournemouth was like a pressure cooker. I figured going to the States, getting knackered, running around was too much. Instead I spent most of Good Friday travelling to York with the team. We stayed right on the river in the centre of this ancient city. What we had not bargained for was the horrendous journey, roadworks everywhere and major flooding too. With Roger, our usual coach driver, missing we had a real jobsworth in his finest glory. It was embarrassing enough for me as I made the mistake of letting them see the first part of my Meridian home video, revealing the finer points of my home life.

York's chairman is fairly enigmatic. Good job, too, as he did not reveal much as his side slumped to a defeat against us. I had only dealt with him once, when we tried to buy Rodney Rowe from him months earlier for £70,000. He refused to deal unless we offered more than twice that amount. Happy with the win, we made ready for a quick exit. Our driver had other ideas. Ignoring the ring road he chose a pleasant route through the centre of town with all the Saturday shopping traffic. We held Fletch off for a while but then were subjected to hell as he recited every single word of *Grease* three seconds before it was spoken, and sang every song aloud. I'm sure there is an acting career for him once he stops playing soccer.

One more game before our big weekend and as fate would have it we were to play Walsall. They had been magnificent in defeat. On that Tuesday, we won again but still they were prepared to enjoy our good fortune. First question was where had we hidden the champagne from their last visit?

Suddenly it was Friday morning. Two days to go, the month of waiting almost over. The team was due to leave on Friday lunch-time to give them time to settle, visit Wembley the day before and then play the match on Sunday afternoon. Separate hotel accommodation for staff was half an hour from the team hotel. After the match we would go there and have a party whatever the result. Everything was planned meticulously. What we could not control was whether we would have our new kit!

With a one o'clock departure it was still not ready. The fans had taken all the replica stuff so we packed an old outfit just in case. Mel put back his departure time by two hours. Coming back to the ground from my morning in London, the crowds were huge, waiting for more shirts to arrive, just like the team. A riot mentality was developing on and off the team coach. John Bailey, our tigerish midfielder, was in the shop, bare-topped, serving customers and drumming up a roaring trade, no matter that he would be out at Wembley playing in two days' time. Looking at the problem of 600 people queuing, we decided to make a populist move. Andrew agreed an immediate £5 discount on shirts and we resolved to charge it to Patrick. For three hours the delivery had been 'ten minutes' from the ground. We did get a roar of approval but even by providing drinks, people's patience was amazing. But not much good for the players facing the biggest weekend of their careers, sitting bored on an overheating coach.

We had announced our new one-year sponsorship deal with Sewards, the main local Rover dealership, the night before as they had opened their new showroom. It had been a good way to start the weekend. Now far from being relaxed we were getting too tense. All the major TV networks had programmes set up to go live with interviews at the team hotel.

At 3.30 a rusty old van trundled around the corner. Brown and with bits falling off the side, it looked like the new age traveller's vehicle of choice. Perhaps the deception was deliberate. In fact it was a courier company van. Had the fans recognised it the driver would probably have been set upon. Never mind the appearance, there were three boxes, one of which contained the team shirts. It had gone four o'clock and we had to leave. There was no time to check it. God knows what we would have done had it been wrong – borrowed spare shirts off the backs of our fans!

Everything worked like a dream at our comfortable hotel in Bracknell. The staff were impeccable and managed the check-in procedure very efficiently. I was so glad to reach the sanctuary of my room. Mandy was not joining me here until the next day. It was beautiful there. Inside, placed on a table were six long-stemmed white lilies, alongside six bottles of champagne sent by the Stakis at Bournemouth with a fax saying 'Good luck at Wembley' from Southampton football club. My balcony overlooked the courtyard, grass stretching into the distance with woods beyond. In the stillness of that late Friday afternoon, rabbits were munching and birds flitting between the trees. Five minutes of that and it was back to chaos.

Downstairs Mel, Ian, Russell and I switched between ITV and BBC, running from sofa to sofa doing live interviews. Andy Steggles of Meridian had become a good friend of the club and we invited him to join us for dinner. The procedure was nothing different, all the team together eating early and then the management later. Over breakfast the next day I lapped up all the newspaper features on Bournemouth, and even one on Sky TV.

At the third time of asking we had managed to persuade Wembley to let us walk around the stadium the Saturday morning before the final. We had to promise that we would not take shirts or balls in with us. It was a good way to kill some time, a chance to get accustomed, to take some of the fear away from the next day. Often what is worse is the unknown. That morning was our time to get rid of that.

As we caught sight of the famous twin towers of Wembley, you could feel the excitement building. I didn't need to tell anyone that Wembley was coming into sight. John Bailey saw it the moment we got the briefest glimpse and let out a shout. In the distance the stadium glistened. As we had sung 'Staying Alive' in various a cappella forms on the way to York, we now all joined together to chant 'Wemb-er-lee, Wemb-er-lee', just as we had on that famous night when we beat Walsall. I wondered if people realised the emotional intensity released in grown men by the sight of Wembley in the sunshine.

Swinging around, suddenly the whole stadium was there in front of us. Built to resemble the Coliseum in Rome and to be as intimidating, only a solitary traffic cone barred our way. A hundred yards away was the stadium; Roger manoeuvred around the cone before driving up beyond the perimeter fence to the huge portcullis gates hiding the entry to the stadium. This was where on cup final days team coaches arrive to drop their passengers, who walk through and up towards the pitch itself past the dressing-rooms lining the tunnel. In the distance, a square of light shone at the furthest end of the tunnel beyond the gates.

As we headed up, the sky grew bigger until we were there standing on the very edge of the great arena as it opened out around us. No one said a word. Between us and the oasis of green there was a ring of sand. The place was silent save for a small group of school kids high up in the stands on an official tour. I wanted to shout out that tomorrow we, the team I had supported since a kid, were playing here on this hallowed turf. This, the spiritual home of football, was to be our field for ninety minutes, a place of destiny, our field of dreams.

In silence we walked slowly across the plastic that lay over the sand. At that first step on the turf you could almost imagine the shouts, the noise echoing around the ground. Then John broke into a run. And we followed, each taking in every part, drinking the elixir that just being there meant. All around the field there were smiling faces, laughing and joking. I went right into the middle, looking up at the sky, seeing the great space above and visualising how it might be tomorrow. Then the mobile phones came out, everyone ringing their loved ones, friends, asking: 'Guess where I am?' I did just that too. It was like being a kid again. We all looked for where our families would be sitting, players remembering so they knew where to wave.

After the phones, it was time for the cameras. We took a wonderful picture of Steve, our physio, Mel, John and me, arms across each other, that I will always treasure. Mel had played at Wembley in 1975. Laughing, he re-enacted how at one end he had dived to his right and turned the ball around a post. A great save except he was a full back, not a goalkeeper. Today he would have been sent off. Not then. The neon sign flashed up 'Welcome to Wembley'. It said it all.

For a national stadium I can see why they want to rebuild it. The facilities are not much better than at Dean Court. A few bent coat hangers, twisted metal sink, basic wooden benches were just about everything within our dressing-room. The most striking aspect was the size of the bath. I feared for the likes of Mark Stein, John Bailey and others under six foot six – you wouldn't want to get into it if you couldn't swim! Even when you stood up the water would still be a good two or three feet above you. It was all tiled in a garish Art Deco crimson, possibly to hide the blood after some of the tackles in the '66 World Cup. And then we went off to train that afternoon at Bracknell Leisure Centre on a rutted, puddle-covered pitch, which certainly showed us the other side of football.

If we did it all again I would not have had a celebration dinner the night before at another hotel. Mel and I trekked the twenty miles over, me driving John Bailey's car so it would be there for the party the next evening. The evening was too much, too anxious and it would have been nice to be on our own with friends and partners. It was all too much hassle and the only major stumbling block to a perfect weekend. When I got back to my bed and hit the pillow that night, I was glad the planning was over, our day had arrived.

Our supporters had bought 34,000 tickets. Ten times the average crowd before we took over. I wish I could have seen every bridge between Bournemouth and London decked with our flags and scarves, a sea of red and black travelling northwards on the motorway. As we headed in with our police escort from the west we saw more and more fans making the same journey. Unlike any travel to a game before, all sat silent. With the sun streaming down and just less than two hours to kick off we turned towards the stadium. Where yesterday there was emptiness it was now filled with our supporters. From all sides hands were held high, stretching up, cheering, 'We love you Bournemouth, we do, we love you Bournemouth, we do'.

I felt sick and excited, nauseous with adrenalin pumping and I was not even playing! Eventually we pulled through the portcullis gates into the sanctuary of the tunnel. It was the real thing. The day had taken so long to come. The night had seemed so long but now the morning was running away with itself. I wanted it to slow right down, to move at half speed and savour every breath.

The players, resplendent in their new suits, grouped together and walked steadily up the path towards the light with dignity and pride. With courage and conviction we had fought through long darkness but survived. Now, instead of silence, noise greeted us, a crescendo of sound as suddenly we were in the stadium.

The 'problem' of being a director is sometimes the formality that comes with it. We knew we would have to make an appearance at the sponsors' lounge. I was delighted to do so with the wonderful people involved in organising what is the most community-oriented of the cup competitions. The responses were amazing, realising what a special day it was for us, the only club truly run by its fans. Then we found our seats, directly overlooking the halfway line, the most perfect view. I wanted to mix, to mingle with all our supporters. A celebrity game was taking place, the likes of Chris Evans and Tim Lovejoy taking part. 'Our' team won 3–1, a great sight on the scoreboard.

I went down on the pitch side. Sixty-four thousand people in the stadium was an amazing sight. I felt very humble as our fans called my name, wanted to shrink and hide before I was overcome by emotion. Many clients and friends had come to see the game. I walked around the concourse past all the food stands, chatting, meeting, greeting as I went through all sections to find them. Painted faces, huge banners, Wembley shirts, and an atmosphere like taking in the finest champagne, the most wonderful view and the greatest love all in one.

By the time I got back to my seat my voice had almost gone. Conversations with hundreds of people who just wanted to give their best wishes, send us luck, had taken their toll. This day in itself was our time to put the past behind us, to stop living by comparison with others, to strike out on our own. Seeing Brian Willis with huge foam feet, waving hands and looking like Coco the Clown it was both ironic and heart-warming that he cared enough to want to be there and make such effort. Today was not the time to remember the past and all the bad things that had happened.

Looking out over Wembley Way earlier, I'd seen a samba band strike up a rhythm in support of our team. Now in the stadium the sound system played out 'Football's Coming Home'. It had come home to Bournemouth and been reinvented. There in the distance, Ian Cox was walking slowly up the tunnel, leading the team behind him. The announcer asked us to stand to welcome the teams. Even writing this now, as I recall that moment the most tremendous sensation comes over me, my whole body tingling. We all stood together, as one. We were not ashamed to cry. I was so proud, so so proud as I looked at the team, the supporters. Then and only then did I see what had been achieved and what it meant, a venture begun in seemingly vain hope but a year ago.

Sitting on our padded, gilded chairs I wondered why the Queen did not use her box that often. No royal guest for us, instead it was Lawrie McMenemy, the Northern Ireland manager and former director of Grimsby Town. You even got a blanket each, which given the age of most people running the FA was a good thing. Mandy and I agreed (and unless you have animals you will think us mad!) that Henry, Thomas and Sidney would have enjoyed it. But it was Andrew who came up with the cunning plot for the FA Cup to be stolen and then found by my rabbit . . . but that is another story for another book.

Grimsby had to be favourites – they had won both our previous encounters. Mel had agonised over team selection. Football logic suggested Franck should not play. His performances were not up to those of Eddie and Ian and he could not really fit in elsewhere. We had experimented with him at full back but he was easily exposed and Grimsby used the flanks well. Sentimentality said he should play. It was his goals as substitute that had got us here. Franck had been to Wembley three times and never played. Now his family, girlfriend and baby were here to watch him. Mel went for the footballing decision, a brave move and one that could not be easily reasoned. Our team had been assembled for barely £200,000. Grimsby had one man worth five times as much, Kingsley Black, and he was only a substitute.

And then it began. Everybody said the time would fly but instead it passed painfully slowly. It was almost impossible to enjoy the match. Both sides cancelled each other out, until on thirty-one minutes Vincent hit a long ball. It fell to Fletcher who with a nonchalant flick lifted it up and over his shoulder to Stein. He dropped his shoulder one way and twisted the other, slipping the ball back across the area. The keeper reacted late. Rushing off his line he collided with his defender just as John Bailey arrived. With a deft touch of his left foot he took the ball to one side, strode forwards and brushed it into the net. Whether the Royal Box has any protocol for these occasions I neither know nor care.

We did not give the most dignified response to taking the lead. Andrew Kaye piled through from a row behind, hugging me as we jumped up and down screaming. To our right there was a little more decorum among the Grimsby supporters, stunned into silence. Goodness, surely we deserved to win, wasn't it the only result, the one that every neutral wanted? And how wonderful that it was John who put us ahead, who a few months earlier had spoken of never playing again.

Half-time, a cup of tea, biscuits and a trip to the loo. We had controlled the play, scored a good goal and now had only forty-five minutes to survive. Ten minutes into the second half Grimsby put on Kingsley Black to shove balls high and long from the wing into the area. We withstood that well to begin with. I tried everything superstitious to protect our lead, crossing my fingers, praying, repeating that it must be our game after all we had been through. Someone had other ideas.

Our defence was coping comfortably enough until the seventy-seventh minute, when a long right cross was hit towards the left-hand side of the goal. A striker just got up above the defence but only managed to nod the ball softly downward and back across the goal. For some reason Glass had been preoccupied with defending his other post. Running back across the area he managed to collide with the ball, it hit his shin and ricocheted sideways into the net. Time and again I would watch that on video and ask 'why?'

Glass did redeem himself with two terrific saves, one in the last minute of normal time. The match was tied and neither team had disgraced themselves. Now we would be subjected to the 'golden goal' decider. Thirty more minutes but the first to score would win the game. No comeback, no continuation, the match would be decided in a split second. No one has ever come up with a solution everyone is happy with, to decide such games.

Fifteen minutes and no score, time for the teams to change ends. Suddenly we drove the ball right into the middle of their area. It bounced, Stein headed the ball and the keeper somehow got down to save. A minute later it was back down our end. There was no communication between keeper and captain, Jimmy was all at sea and kicked the ball away. They crossed it back towards the goal and Eddie launched a flying header away for a corner. As the ball was delivered it seemed to cross many players, the faintest touch taking it into the trailing leg of a player running in on the goal. It ballooned up and off with spin back past Vincent and the lunging keeper into the net. The scorer continued running, jumping the hoarding towards his fans, team-mates following on behind. We had lost.

For a moment we were silent. Each player collapsed on the turf. That was it. I could not believe it. This was not the way it was supposed to end. I could make no sense around me, things were happening but I was in my own world not wanting to believe. The lads had to come past to get their loser's medal. Automatic shaking hands, 'well done' to the opposition, accepting their condolences underneath an immediate feeling of anger, bitterness, the feeling that we had been cheated, wronged, deprived of our inheritance. The people of Grimsby had their success, they had been winning, but we had nearly died. We deserved that victory. Not for me but for every single person. Looking around at Michael the vicar, Geoffrey, Mel, and my dad I so much wanted it to be different. How many more years before we got there again? What about those who might never get another chance to be there again? It was all right for Grimsby. In a month, not that they knew it then, they would be back in the play-off final. Yet as John Bailey said to the vicar, 'Even God gets it wrong sometimes, Michael.'

Wembley Stadium was silent. What could I say to lift souls when my heart was heavy? For once I could not find the words. No positive spin about a bright future, come back and win next year or let's just look to promotion. Nothing could hide the bitter disappointment. The great ground that had seemed so warm and friendly was now desolate, overcast beneath a leaden sky. With that the rain began to fall.

We would wake to be called the gallant losers. The disappointment has spurred us on in search of much larger prizes. This town, this club has achieved a lifetime of memories in barely eighteen months. We are a shining light, a beacon to follow and be guided safely by. And life has gone on to new adventures, achievements and success. I began that mission on a wet January evening. Then there were six of us and by that day at Wembley in April 1998 we had 34,000 following on what we had started.

Nearly 7,000 turned up for our last game and 3,000 lined the streets for a celebration tour of the town. We did miss the promotion play-off but only by four points. A team that was predicted to finish bottom had beaten the odds in so many ways. We were written off but had our most successful season, run by a bunch of fans who many gave no chance to. Within weeks we were on a groundbreaking trip to the USA, I left London, six players went and as many joined, work began towards the most exciting new community stadium project and I wrote this book. Don't ever underestimate the power of people.

Would I do it all again? Oh yes! It has turned my life topsy turvy but enriched it beyond compare. The adventure continues, day by day. One person can make a difference. Stand up; state your business and others will follow if you care passionately. Never lose that faith even when all those around you may be inclined to do so. I have met wonderful people, yet seen traits in human nature I would prefer to believe never existed, and witnessed the corruption that even those with money suffer.

I regret only how this whole new world has at times found me letting down those who have cared the most. Their faith worn down while I built it in others. And that is what I would most want back. Yet there is time. It is not a story to span one year or eighteen months, it is never ending. In reality this story has only just begun.

Epilogue

And that is it. Our first season. A year crowned by Wembley left us with no cup, no promotion but still in business when many had claimed we would fail. At season end it was the chance for me to start looking at my own life and putting things straight.

The travel, the toil and the inability to take anything more out of the day eventually caught up with me. I knew that I could not pay the price asked to become a partner in London. I did not want to let Michael down, for all the support he had given me, but the time had come to leave London. It was a sad parting. I took the offer to join the lawyers that helped us at Lester Aldridge, to bridge the gap between City and coast. It's ironic that I spend less time on football business now that I am only working five minutes' drive from the ground.

The move came at the right time. I am lucky. The clients have followed me, all good friends and confidants. Coming home to work has opened many doors, a new range of cases, and given me stimulation to carry forward a project that has such potential. I needed a break between jobs but spent it writing this book. The team went to America, using some of the Wembley proceeds. Fletch and the lads took Chicago and Milwaukee by storm!

I am still just an ordinary fan. I put my boots on when I can and cheer as loudly as any other. I do not have the hide of a rhino but listen to every word spoken. When 99 per cent are positive, it is much easier but then the other one per cent still hurts deeply. The further we get from the start of this story the easier criticism will flow. A first season with success gave us a long honeymoon period. A second has just made the expectation all the greater. In adversity much was done that everyone applauded. Now as time has gone on those without responsibility begin to pick holes. It is natural, I suppose. Change is demanded without ever thinking through the rationale.

As we corralled the supporters to save their club we also had to talk to those with money who could provide the financial backbone of our future. We may have made a profit of £200,000 in our first year but in just keeping up with the other teams we will make a loss in year two despite our success. Our club is worth twice over what it owes. No overdraft facility means a rained-off game, a late payment or a fallen sale can easily cause problems only remedied by new injections of capital, money well beyond what the town ever raised, without which the short-term prognosis might be dire.

As chairman I will always take the brunt of criticism. Heckled when the transfer of a lad from Portugal went horribly wrong, sometimes I wonder if it might just be easier to give up and hide away. Then there are the hundreds who come up and urge me on. And I realise how valuable the work we are doing is. We are in many ways no different from other clubs but are singled out by the government as an example to follow.

The system, the board, the way things are run is all my doing. That does not sit comfortably with me. I would like change. We have a group of six good and true men on the board. We must become ever more representative of all the fans. We must ensure the liaison is ever closer. It is not enough just to have me writing e-mails, for Ken and I to be in the supporters' club before games – there must be forums, representatives elected to address the board, to make certain that the strength we found in dark times never diminishes.

We approach our centenary year with much done but so much more to do. We have embraced the Euro in a disappointing experiment signing French players. With £1,700,000 of debt left, I know that I will not sleep peacefully at night until we have sold one player, made one big deal to give us financial protection and stability. At last we could then begin to move away from being known as a selling club. If we do not sell we cannot afford the squad we have. We would have to go back to youngsters on £300 or £400 a week and do away with the top players that have given us the jump up in quality we have achieved.

With Mark Stein on a permanent free transfer and six others signed for a total transfer outlay of £40,000 we were still predicted to finish bottom in 1998-99. How wrong they were. The team has grown and developed, Steino leading the league in goalscoring and the club producing a home record unequalled by any team other than Arsenal and Chelsea. With every prospect of a top six finish it is a season even more successful than our first. Fortress Dean Court it may be, but soon we want to move to a new twenty-first century community stadium, our project for the millenium.

The move back to Bournemouth has done me good, my stresses and strains all the easier for the sea air. Mandy and I benefited too; the second half of 1998 was probably our happiest six months together. We found the time to do the simple things, saw our friends for Thanksgiving and enjoyed a wonderful Christmas. The years have been hard, my character, behaviour never the most understanding. Now it is her turn to do what she has always wanted to do, to find her happiness again on the other side of the world in New Zealand where she is working in a hospital. Without her, I am unsure whether this would all have come to pass or whether we would have taken the path that now sees us half a world away. Separate lives, separate days and the real human costs of what has happened.

I wonder how long I will go on balancing all the interests in running the club, the competing views, the problems of being a lower division team in the hierarchy of professional soccer. I do question what the next step is for me but I will not lose my faith in what we have begun. When a fellow chairman has a petrol bomb put through his door, I ask is it all worth it? When a supporter will not listen to any reason should I ever begin to explain? Can a club like ours ever make a difference? Yes is the answer to all three.

We must go on trying to bring openness into football. I am only one voice yet there are many who echo my words. All it takes is one smile on a face to know how worthwhile it is.